RINGSIDE

RINGSIDE

A History of Professional Wrestling in America

SCOTT M. BEEKMAN

PRAEGER

Westport, Connecticut
London

Library of Congress Cataloging-in-Publication Data

Beekman, Scott.
   Ringside : a history of professional wrestling in America / by Scott M.
Beekman.
     p. cm.
   Includes bibliographical references and index.
   ISBN 0-275-98401-X (alk. paper)
   1. Wrestling—History. I. Title.
   GV1195.B44 2006
   796.81209—dc22   2006008230

British Library Cataloguing in Publication Data is available.

Library of Congress Catalog Card Number: 2006008230
ISBN: 0-275-98401-X

First published in 2006

Praeger Publishers, 88 Post Road West, Westport, CT 06881
An imprint of Greenwood Publishing Group, Inc.
www.praeger.com

Printed in the United States of America

∞™

The paper used in this book complies with the
Permanent Paper Standard issued by the National
Information Standards Organization (Z39.48-1984).

10 9 8 7 6 5 4 3

CONTENTS

Photo essay appears following page 72

INTRODUCTION

Like Rodney Dangerfield, professional wrestling receives little respect. Often decried as ignorant or juvenile, pro wrestling is frequently lumped with other forms of "trash" culture, such as television soap operas and NASCAR. The situation for wrestling is, if anything, even worse than its fellow cultural bottom-feeders. Although NASCAR receives a measure of support as a legitimate sport and soaps are viewed as an aspect of escapist entertainment, wrestling resides somewhere beyond the pale. Only the heartiest academics embrace this maligned stepchild of sport and even then, they only approach it with caution. Those scholars who have studied wrestling invariably examine it like a science or sociology experiment. They pick wrestling apart and examine slivers of it to determine how pro wrestling relates to blue-collar catharsis, masculinity, sexuality, and gender relations. I suspect this standoffish approach reflects the general view of wrestling as lower class and primitive. Even in an academic world where the studies of popular culture and sport find increasing respectability and status, studying professional wrestling seems somehow suspect. I have grown accustomed to the double takes when I am asked about my current research. What is curious is that every colleague I have discussed this project with related to me his or her own personal contact with professional wrestling. If even the denizens of the ivory tower spent parts of their formative years watching Saturday morning wrestling, then surely wrestling deserves some measure of attention from historians. I intend, therefore, to attempt to rescue wrestling from this sad fate, one no 150-year-old entertainment form deserves, by providing it with the basic cloak of respectability granted through possessing a written history.[1]

Although I do not expect this work, the first nonpictorial history of wrestling, to result in the elevation of wrestling to the cultural stature of, say, the films of Orson Welles, I contend that wrestling's scholarly marginalization stems in part from a general ignorance concerning its history. If one thinks of history as those past events transcribed for posterity, wrestling, to a significant degree, has no history. Not only are the achievements of past wrestlers ignored by current fans, but those in control of the business willfully distort wrestling's past in order to market current product. In wrestling, ballyhoo is king. Promoters market their current product as bigger, faster, and better than ever. The admission that early wrestlers possessed great ring or microphone skills would only serve to undercut such claims. Because past wrestlers cannot be used to draw crowds, they are ignored. Further, in a world dominated by egos and personal grudges and bereft of statistics and quantifiers, wrestling promoters frequently rewrite history to serve their own ends. For example, the National Wrestling Alliance (NWA) claimed a title lineage dating to the nineteenth century, even though the organization only began in 1948. For those who control wrestling, history becomes nothing more than another marketing tool, twisted and distorted at will. The abominable condition of wrestling history made my task more difficult but also more important. I have sought to untangle the myths and legends of wrestling to present an accurate portrayal of the development of the entertainment form in this country.

While cultural critics ignore or criticize wrestling, perhaps accurately, as a frequently lowbrow form of entertainment, at least they have offered it some measure of attention. American sports historians offer an almost solid front of silence. Professional wrestling developed in this country in the wake of the Civil War as a real sport. Although shady and scandal-rocked, wrestling continued to be a legitimate sport until World War I. Along with baseball, boxing, and pedestrianism, wrestling became one of the most popular sports of the late nineteenth century. However, general American sports histories completely ignore wrestling. I suspect the absence of wrestling from sports histories reflects not only the difficulty in obtaining accurate information on the sport but also an anachronistic approach toward wrestling that assumes pro wrestling always resembled the modern "sports entertainment" version. I hope that this study will help return pro wrestling to its rightful place in discussions of the development of sporting culture in the United States.[2]

Wrestling also serves as an important instrument for examining the effect of media forms on entertainment. After a decade-long decline, wrestling exploded in popularity during the early 1950s. This altered circumstance reflected the increased importance of television in American culture. Wrestling, along with boxing, served as the chief sporting forms on early television. During the 1980s, wrestling became a staple of cable television and helped cable networks thrive in a marketplace dominated by the "Big 3" networks for decades. Wrestling promoters such as Vince K. McMahon and Jim Crockett Jr. also helped pioneer pay-per-view television. To this day, World Wrestling Entertainment (WWE) remains the leading pay-per-view provider in the United States. Wrestling, then, should be viewed as an entertainment form central to the growth of new media technologies over the last half century.

The effects of television on wrestling are vast and dramatic. While sports historians continue to argue about the degree to which television alters sporting forms, there can be no doubt that it shaped pro wrestling. Television made wrestling livelier and more colorful. The demands of the medium forced wrestling promoters to develop elaborate story lines to hold viewer interest. For wrestlers, television compelled them to adopt elaborate characters and to develop successful microphone skills. Further, television became a tool of domination for wrestling promoters. Those who produced slick or widely distributed television programs stood to expand their empires at the expense of those who did not. During the 1980s, McMahon used cable television as the means for his ascendancy to the top of the wrestling business. In the 1990s, Ted Turner's cable networks served as the basis for a legitimate challenge to McMahon's preeminence.[3]

These late twentieth-century efforts to use television to control the business of wrestling signify only the most recent manifestations of a long-lived power struggle in the industry. This struggle, and this book, can be divided into two broad periods. Until World

War I, individual wrestlers, particularly national or world champions, maintained a level autonomy that gave them substantial power over both their careers and the sport. After World War I, wrestling promoters began to exert their control over the business of wrestling. The most significant aspect of this control became the adoption of fake (or "worked") matches at the expense of legitimate contests. The promoters recognized that predetermined finishes kept fans interested in their product and left wrestlers at their mercy. From this point on, the real power in wrestling resided with the promoters. The battle between various promoters over wrestling profits propelled much of wrestling's history. While I examine the work of individual wrestlers, the way the in-ring aspect of professional wrestling changed and how wrestling relates to larger cultural issues, the struggle for control of the business of professional wrestling lays at the heart of this study. Chicago promoter Bob Luce once noted that "wrestling is what America is all about." While I believe Luce may have overstated his point, I can say that wrestling is what this book is all about.[4]

As with all book projects, the name on the cover only tells part of the story. In this case, I have benefited from the assistance of a number of independent wrestling researchers. J Michael Kenyon graciously opened up his vast collection of newspaper clippings, which proved to be an invaluable tool. The "Old Fall Guy" also deserves credit for coining the phrase I co-opted for the title of Chapter 5. Mike Chapman of the International Wrestling Institute and Museum gave me unfettered access to his vast library and archive. Karl Stern, Mark Hewitt, Steve Yohe, Vance Nevada, and Joseph Svinth all provided assistance by answering my often inane questions on a variety of wrestling history forums. Dr. Mike Lano and Brian Bukantis provided excellent illustrations for this work. At Praeger, Eric Levy championed this project at its inception, and Dan Harmon provided patient guidance through its completion. Thanks guys. My wife, Kimberly K. Little, proofread the manuscript, cajoled me to keep working, and patiently sat through hours of Ric Flair videotapes. The importance of her help cannot be calculated. And, as always, this work is for Miller.

1

ORIGINS

The hot lights of the television studio brought beads of sweat to the forehead of the puffy, fast-talking, middle-aged announcer. After brief comments he foisted the spit-guarded microphone under the chin of a hulking man whose muscles roiled under a silky robe. The larger man then began a lengthy diatribe concerning his undefeated wrestling career, his victories over cheating opponents, and his status as a champion. He ended by noting that the jealousies of other wrestlers, who were often afraid to face him, forced his early retirement, but he has returned to the sport to once again prove his abilities. The wrestler's soliloquy completed, the announcer shook his head in consternation and announced a short commercial break before the next match.

This pattern of interview to build excitement, advertisements, and then in-ring resolution of conflict is familiar to anyone who has watched professional wrestling programming on television. The example above, however, while archetypal, is fictional; only the summarized contents of the wrestler's speech are factual. And while his comments are also familiar to modern fans, they were first carved into stone, not transmitted through an electronic medium. The wrestler in question was named Hermodorus, and he was active in the second century; by this point, professional wrestlers had plied their trade in the eastern Mediterranean for more than half a millennia.[1]

Wrestling is generally acknowledged as one of the two oldest sports known to man (running races is the other). Accounts of grappling are found in almost all ancient civilizations around the globe. The function of wrestling, however, varied widely, dependent on the culture examined. For some peoples, wrestling represented an autotelic means of celebrating the human form; for others, it was a functional activity for military or religious purposes.

For the western tradition, grappling arts were commonly practiced in the ancient Near East. References to wrestling matches are found, for example, in the Babylonian epic *Gilgamesh* and appear with regularity in Hebrew and early Christian writings. Near Eastern accounts generally document the victory of a hero over an evil force that serves as a right of passage toward a position of leadership. As with many aspects of the Bible, the references to athletics continue to be debated. Even if matches involving Job, Jacob, and Judah were meant to be allegorical, the fact that their stories involve wrestling terminology helps demonstrate that early Judeo-Christian writers expected readers to be familiar with the sport and its language.[2]

For the ancient Egyptians, wrestling bouts demonstrated to the nobility the physical and military prowess of soldiers. Surviving artifacts frequently included visual representations of wrestling (dating back to c. 2500 B.C.), but beyond the fact that the Egyptians engaged in a form of belt wrestling, no substantial written records exist and the rules are unclear. Wolfgang Decker, the preeminent scholar of ancient Egyptian sports, has argued persuasively that, in keeping with other Egyptian sports, wrestling was primarily used as part of the training regimen for soldiers and as a public activity only during festive occasions presided over by the pharaoh.[3]

Although sports were important in Egypt, the ancient Greeks first made organized athletic contests an integral aspect of their culture. Regardless of ongoing debates concerning whether Hellenic sports were primarily religious in orientation or simply a means demonstrating physical prowess and beauty, the Greeks elevated sports to a level of importance like no previous culture. And wrestling, along with running races and the pentathlon, was among the most celebrated of all Greek sporting contests.[4]

While it was at the great athletic festivals, the Olympics being the most celebrated, that Greek wrestlers gained the most renown, grappling arts were practiced throughout the Hellenic world, and boys were expected to learn the rudiments of the sport even if they harbored no desire to compete in the festivals. Every Greek city of note housed a *palaestra*, or school of wrestling. In these schools, boys learned the simple, but rigidly enforced, rules of Greek wrestling. The Greeks wrestled in a sandpit called the *skamma*, and contestants were covered in oil and then a layer of dust before entering the pit. Greek matches began with a lockup from an upright position, and the object was to score three falls by causing your opponent's hip, back, or shoulder to touch the ground. Holds below the waist, as countermoves, and tripping were probably allowed. Those inclined to violate the rules faced the wrath of a referee armed with a forked stick.

Because of its popularity, wrestling references to the sport permeated all aspects of Greek culture. Vases depicting figures from Greek mythology, particularly Heracles and Theseus (the reputed discoverer of scientific wrestling), often showed them defeating fantastic monsters using standard wrestling holds. Images of wrestlers appeared on the coins of Aspendos, Syracuse, and Alexandria, and accounts of matches can be found in the writings of Homer, Statius, and Quintus of Smyrna. Even Plato oiled up for competition in games held at Delphi and Nemea.[5]

This popularity also led to the development of professional wrestlers in Greece. These men competed as paid representatives of their cities at the increasing number of festivals. The most famous Greek professional wrestler was Milo of Croton. Milo first gained acclaim by winning the boys' wrestling Olympic title in 540 B.C. He then won the men's title in six successive Olympiads and a number of titles in other festivals. On four occasions, he was *Periodonikes*, or winner of the title in all four "crown" festivals in the same cycle. Allegedly this legendary strongman met his demise at the hands of a pack of wolves.[6]

Despite his strength and skills, even Milo avoided participation in a more brutal form of wrestling known as *pankration*. Much more like modern professional wrestling or mixed martial arts matches than classic "upright" wrestling, catch-as-catch-can *pankration* first appeared at the thirty-third Olympiad. *Pankration* eliminated most of traditional wrestling's restrictions on holds (only biting and gouging were prohibited), and victory was achieved by forcing your opponent to concede. Not surprisingly, *pankration* matches often ended in serious injuries and fatalities were common. It is also not surprising that the dangerous *pankration* matches were the most popular Greek sport among the Romans.[7]

The Romans took the Greek notion of athletics as a participatory, religiously flavored celebration of the body and converted it into something very modern—the spectacle. For the Romans, the *ludi* were a celebration of pleasure and entertainment, a time to view (mostly) slaves competing with each other for the benefit of the assembled crowd. And while the Romans enjoyed *pankration*, it (and other Greek athletic contests, including wrestling) faced systematic marginalization due to the popularity of chariot racing and gladiatorial contests. The rise of "Roman" games and the subsequent fall of Rome ended the first era of professional wrestling in Europe. Although local forms of the sport in Asia and the Pacific, which quickly developed professional forms, were established at the same time that the Roman Empire crumbled, the sport of professional wrestling was entering a long period of silence in the West.[8]

Professional sports of all types suffered as a result of the collapse of Rome, and wrestling was no exception. During the Middle Ages, wrestling, reflecting the parochial lifestyles of most Europeans, became a local pursuit. Town champions were frequently crowned according to local rules on market or festival days, but there was no longer an opportunity for successful grapplers to compete in Greek-style athletic festivals. Instead wrestling became a popular pastime that required no special equipment and facilitated wagering. Throughout Europe, local nobility and eventually the Catholic Church approved of wrestling as a recreational activity that served as a training for warfare.[9]

On the cusp of the Renaissance, wrestling became a more organized activity and was probably the most popular spectator sport in northern Europe. Not only were special matches between local champions organized as entertainment for the nobility, but meetings between well-regarded competitors became frequently held activities in taverns catering to the lower classes. These matches, fueled by alcohol and heavy wagering, often became bloody affairs that precipitated violent confrontations. Loosely regulated or controlled tavern-organized matches, like those rural bouts involving peasants, occasionally resulted in the death of competitors; riots frequently occurred in the aftermath of London matches during the thirteenth and fourteenth centuries.[10]

In England local variants of wrestling had developed and codified by the Renaissance period. The required opening hold differentiated the various styles. For example, in the Cumberland and Westmoreland style, combatants began the match with their chins resting on their opponents shoulder; and a fall was gained by simply dropping your opponent to the ground. In Cornwall, a type of "jacket" wrestling became the preferred form, with holds below the waist disallowed. The brutal Lancashire "catch-as-catch-can" style, which corresponded to an equally vicious style of boxing practiced in the region, was frequently decried as barbaric by contemporaries, but it eventually became the foundation for the most popular American professional style of the late nineteenth century.[11]

The frequent references to sport in early European publications reflected the popularity and diffusion of the sport. German illustrator Albrecht Dürer created more than one hundred drawings of wrestling holds, and Fabian von Auerwald's *Ringerkunst* (1539), one of the earliest illustrated books, detailed wrestling techniques. Given wrestling's popularity throughout the kingdom, it is not surprising that the sport also appears frequently in English works of the period. Mallory's *Morte D'Arthur*, for example, includes an account of a match between Gawain and Lancelot, and references to rural bouts appear in *Piers Plowman* and *The Canterbury Tales*.

English authors also promoted wrestling as part of a regimen for physical and martial training. Thomas Elyot's *The Governour* (1531), the first prominent English work on physical education, promoted wrestling as healthy exercise. A century later, Cambridge-trained mathematician Sir Thomas Parkyns published *The Inn-Play or Cornish-Hugg Wrestler*, a work that not only advocated the sport but also laid down rules for avoiding "ungentlemanly" behavior during matches. Parkyns's book was geared toward a gentry audience and demonstrated how different social classes adopted wrestling for different purposes. For the upper classes, wrestling was a means of staying physically fit in preparation for military activities; for the peasantry, it was a means of gaining local status and a form of entertainment. The rigidness of English social structure also prevented members of different classes from facing each other, but the peasantry undoubtedly were aware of the nobility's participation in the sport (Henry VIII's love of wrestling, for example, was widely known).[12]

By the seventeenth century, a semiformalized sporting culture had developed in England. The English Puritans viewed horse racing, boxing, and, to a lesser extent, wrestling as destructive and dangerous behavior, but sport was rejuvenated after the Restoration. Wealthy patrons supported and promoted working-class athletes, and professionalism and wagering flourished by the early eighteenth century. Sports critics continued to excoriate both athletes and their patrons (the "fancy") but found themselves fighting a rearguard action against professional sports before the eighteenth century closed. This English sporting society eventually served as a model for the development of a sports culture in the United States.[13]

The American sporting culture, however, developed more slowly than that in England. New England Puritans decried the pernicious aspects of many sports, including wrestling, and prevented them from taking hold during the seventeenth century. Their animosity reflected concerns about the gambling, arguments, and inflamed passions that often accompanied sports and games. Sports such as wrestling could be engaged in, but only in moderation, and only if those involved adhered to Puritan restrictions on "idle amusements." The legacy of Puritanism would affect the growth of New England sports until the nineteenth century. Only after waves of Irish immigrants and changing attitudes concerning physical activity served as counters to this tradition did a true sporting culture take hold in New England.[14]

In the southern and middle colonies, a sporting culture did begin to develop during the seventeenth century, but it was not until late in the century that anything approximating the English model emerged. By the end of the seventeenth century, wrestling was both a common occurrence on festival days and a frequently used method of settling disagreements between laborers and wagoneers. As in England, taverns became the centers of sporting culture. Tavern owners, recognizing the profits to be made off spectators, encouraged sporting endeavors on their property. For example, Benjamin Berry of modern-day Berrytown, Virginia, retained local strongmen to engage in fistfights and wrestling matches with teamsters who stopped by for refreshments.[15]

Wrestling also developed as a popular pastime for the southern gentry, and by the late seventeenth century, they also competed in matches at festivals. However, like in England, rigid rules concerning social hierarchy prevailed, and the elite only competed against their social equals. Horse racing eventually became the preferred sporting activity for the southern gentry, but wrestling maintained a position of importance. Participation in the "sport of kings," however, was restricted to exclude the lower classes. This restriction may have helped increase the popularity of sports such as wrestling among the nongentry because it was one of the few athletic avenues left open to them.[16]

George Washington was an avid wrestler, as were most southern youths, and the first in a long line of grappling presidents. Washington's concern over physical fitness led him to promote "games of exercise for amusement" during the American Revolution. Wrestling was part of militia training in the south, and the future president believed that athletic activities made his men better soldiers. However, his promotion of sports also reflected his view that games relieved the tedium and temptations of camp life. As a result, Revolutionary soldiers engaged in a variety of physical activities, including wrestling. Many northern officers viewed wrestling and other rough sports as rowdy and low class and promoted ball games and foot or marching races in their stead. The popularity of these more rugged sports, however, prevented officers' from eradicating them in the camps. In at least one instance, champions from rival military encampments wrestled for local bragging rights.[17]

By the early nineteenth century, wrestling had become a popular pastime for manual laborers and the youth of all classes but was distinctly out of favor among adult members of the "better sort" across the country, who increasingly turned to dueling as the means for resolving honor-related disputes. Most of the elite viewed violent and physical pastimes such as wrestling as primitive practices reserved for the unlettered and rambunctious children. This view emerged in the south and in the frontier, in part from the degeneration of traditional wrestling matches in these areas into a bloody style known as "rough-and-tumble" or "gouging." Rough-and-tumble matches were "no-holds-barred" events fought until one combatant gave up or was incapacitated. Typically, only the use of weapons was outlawed in a rough-and-tumble match. What made these matches especially brutal was that gouging out an opponent's eye became the most important aspect of a contest.[18]

The hyperviolent rough-and-tumble style dominated along the frontier during the late eighteenth and early nineteenth centuries, but its popularity quickly waned as an area became more densely settled. Westerners bent on civilizing their new settlements found the style too barbaric to be maintained by people striving for respectability, and many states and territories passed laws against "maiming." Midwesterners and Mississippi Valley dwellers adopted a more restrained style of wrestling in the antebellum period. Although upright wrestling, in which the object was to throw your opponent to the ground, was practiced, a modified version of rough-and-tumble predominated. This less bloody version of rough and tumble typically banned gouging, biting, and punching but still maintained the excitement of the earlier style by allowing holds of all types and requiring pinfalls or submissions for victory. This exciting style served as the foundation for the catch-as-catch-can form that came to dominate professional wrestling at the end of the nineteenth century.[19]

Stripped of rough-and-tumble's most dangerous aspects, the new free-for-all style was a popular and generally acceptable form of amusement for children and entertainment for adults. Success in these matches was often a way to establish one's local reputation and earn money from wagers. Kentucky-born presidents Zachary Taylor and Abraham Lincoln both found wrestling to be an entertaining, and potentially profitable, diversion as young men, and their experiences were hardly unique.[20]

Lincoln, however, pursued the sport with far more dedication than Taylor. By some accounts, the Great Emancipator engaged in approximately three hundred matches, most in the Cornish "side-hold" style, when he was a young man living in the Ohio and Mississippi river areas. Lincoln's most famous match, an 1831 New Salem, Illinois, encounter against local tough Jack Armstrong, established his reputation in Illinois and put him on the road to local leadership and politics. The physical prowess demonstrated by the New Salem match became part of the Lincoln mythology while he was president and certainly helped contribute to the popularity of the sport in the post–Civil War period.[21]

The first half of the nineteenth century also marks the period in which athletics along the Atlantic seaboard emerged from the long shadow of Puritan concerns over "idle amusements." As the century unfolded, American writers, educators, and physicians became increasingly aware that mental health was dependent on physical health. This developing notion led to the publication of a spate of treatises on exercise, increased press attention on the subject of physical fitness, and, in 1824, the importation of Friedrich Jahn's gymnastic training techniques. Physical toughness and health also became an increasingly central aspect of the definition of masculinity during the Jacksonian era. Reflective of the increasing American interest in sporting activities, William Porter began publishing *Spirit of the Times* in 1831, the first American magazine solely devoted to sports. In this new climate, organized professional sports also began to emerge.[22]

Antebellum professional sports, however, faced serious challenges. Horse racing was by far the most popular spectator sport, but it faced continual allegations of fixed races and suspicions of "hippodroming" (allegedly real horse races held so that the competitors could split the gate receipts). Prizefights, which were still governed by the brutal London rules, were technically illegal, often viewed as little more civilized that rough-and-tumble wrestling, and frequently crooked. Baseball and pedestrianism possessed less unsavory reputations, but their popularity rested primarily in the mid-Atlantic region and New England. Important roots of professional sports are clearly evident in the antebellum period, but their full flowering awaited the altered circumstances of post–Civil War America.[23]

The antecedents of modern professional wrestling can also be discerned during this period. For example, the early sporting journal *Spirit of the Times* favorably noted a wrestling exhibition in New York City in 1832. And while wrestling continued to be practiced by native-born Americans, various immigrant groups helped popularize unique styles of the sport. Cornish immigrants came to the United States with a willingness to work in the mines and a desire to continue to practice their traditional form of jacket wrestling. Scottish and Scotch-Irish immigrants introduced American versions of the ancient Caledonian Games—which included wrestling—in the 1830s, and the Games blossomed into popular spectator events in eastern cities by the 1850s.[24]

The Irish, however, deserve the most credit for establishing American professional wrestling. The Irish were renowned (and frequently belittled) for their love of rough play and sports, and most of the prominent early American pugilists were of Irish descent. But it was wrestling, not boxing, that had been the most popular sport in Ireland since the Middle Ages, and Irish immigrants brought the sport to America with them. The favored style among the Irish was a mix of stand-up and ground wrestling known as collar-and-elbow (colloquially referred to as "scuffling") because of its required opening stance. Because of this specific upright beginning position, collar-and-elbow avoided the violent rushes and punches of rough-and-tumble but maintained the excitement of catch-as-catch-can by allowing ground holds once one participant fell. Further, the opening stance, which promoted speed and dexterity, helped offset size differences, making the style attractive to smaller competitors.

While Irish immigrants practiced collar-and-elbow wherever they established themselves, it was to be the farming region of southwest Vermont that became the birthplace of nineteenth-century professional wrestling. The area witnessed a massive influx of Irish immigrants during the 1830s and 1840s, many of whom spent their leisure hours by wrestling in their traditional style. The Vermont Irish, in particular, were ministered to by a cadre of Irish Catholic priests who had also wrestled as youths. Chief among these was Father Thomas McQuade, who recognized that scuffling was not only a healthy pastime to keep his flock occupied but also a means of peacefully diffusing the disputes that frequently emerged among Irish immigrants from different counties.[25]

This special combination of official encouragement, opportunity, and temperament led to a thriving community of wrestlers in the decades leading up to the Civil War. Vermonters made collar-and-elbow matches an integral part of their weekly relaxations, held matches as part of festivals, and recognized local champions. As with prior generations in England and the Tidewater, local innkeepers happily organized matches between local experts and strangers passing through the area, recognizing that the assembled crowd would provide a ready source of customers. Local champions could also establish larger reputations by competing in regional tournaments that might attract hundreds of scufflers. The sport became so popular in the Green Mountain state that, on the cusp of the Civil War, particularly adept collar-and-elbow stylists were supporting themselves as itinerant professionals. However, professional wrestling in the antebellum period, as Elliott Gorn has noted about the related sport of prizefighting, "remained a local phenomenon, largely ethnic, decidedly working-class and traditional in origins."[26]

The collar-and-elbow style might have remained a regional and ethnic phenomenon had it not been for the Civil War. The heady excitement of the war's early days quickly soured when the bloody realities of combat were realized; soldiers who enlisted with romantic notions of war were quickly disillusioned by the long periods of stagnant camp life, with only infrequent fighting. Union officers, concerned about both the spread of vices among bored soldiers and declining morale, latched onto sports as a wholesome recreational activity that would also keep the men in proper physical condition. Wrestling, along with baseball, was one of the primary sports to gain popularity because of these wartime expediencies.[27]

In the Union camps, thanks to Vermont soldiers, collar-and-elbow rapidly became the preferred style for wrestling matches. Northern companies frequently declared their own champions, who competed against each other for divisional bragging rights. Larger tournaments also occurred, with Vermont scufflers often emerging as the victors. Jacob S. Bailey gained a certain amount of status for winning a large tournament in April 1863, but his success paled in comparison to the acclaim of fellow Vermonter George William Flagg. A six-feet-four-inch, 220-pound behemoth, Flagg scratched out a living during the 1850s as a strongman and wrestler, then enlisted in the Second Vermont Infantry at the beginning of the war. Flagg achieved recognition as the finest wrestler in the Union army after winning the "grand championship of the Army of the Potomac."[28]

The Civil War transformed the United States in a number of profound ways, including how athletics were viewed and practiced. As Lawrence Fielding has noted, the war was a "melting pot for sport traditions." The collar-and-elbow style of wrestling, so recently marginal, became dispersed throughout the country as veterans took the newly learned style back to their hometowns. Collar-and-elbow was poised to become the preeminent wrestling form in the country. Spurred by postwar developments in transportation, communications, and demographics, collar-and-elbow wrestling built on this wartime popularity to become one of the first sports to benefit from America's burgeoning professional sporting culture.[29]

2

BARNSTORMERS

Sports became a major element of American popular culture during the last third of the nineteenth century. Although stirrings of the emergent sporting culture can be discerned in the immediate pre–Civil War period (particularly with regards to baseball), the full flush of what John Betts dubbed the "athletic impulse" emerged only after the guns of the Confederacy fell silent. While prewar trends helped create this new sporting culture, fundamental alterations to American society hastened the rise of sports in the postbellum period. The related phenomenon of industrialization, immigration, and urbanization created a ripe environment for developing a larger sports presence; the nurturing of athletics by enthusiastic promoters, journalists, and returning veterans ensured that professional sports blossomed into an integral aspect of the burgeoning national culture. These factors not only propelled baseball into its status as the "national game" but also allowed professional wrestling to expand beyond its rural base.[1]

Between 1820 and 1870, the percentage of the American population living in cities quadrupled. The growth of eastern cities developed to respond to the needs of an increasingly industrialized American economy. Factory owners needed a large, ready pool of workers, and cities provided them; poor immigrants landed on these shores, often lacking the funds to move west, and found industrial jobs available in ports of entry. After the Civil War, the "industrialized radial city" became the dominant American urban pattern. The radial city and the concomitant rise of industrial capitalism, as Steven Riess noted, "enriched a small number of people, improved the standard of living for the nonmanual middle class, weakened the position of the artisan class, and gave rise to a huge pool of poorly paid, semiskilled and unskilled industrial workers who worked long hours at a backbreaking pace."[2]

These economic and demographic shifts provided the funds and interested individuals for the American sporting culture. The urban middle class had sufficient discretionary income and free time to participate in sports and to patronize sporting events. Middle-class sports fans helped legitimize sports as a respectable pastime and pushed promoters to create safe, clean venues acceptable to "gentlemen." Involvement in physically strenuous sports such as boxing and wrestling also helped these urban dwellers maintain their notions of gender roles. For many middle-class residents of American cities, sporting culture participation helped them assert the masculinity that seemed threatened by the "female" softness of urban middle-class life. Middle-class magazines of the period frequently linked sports and manliness, which soon became defined as the opposite of feminine, rather than (as it was previously) the opposite of childlike.[3]

The working classes, the base of sports supporters before the war, also continued to follow the exploits of their sporting heroes during the Gilded Age. However, the new industrial order of the period wreaked havoc on traditional patterns of work. The mass production of consumer goods drove many craft guilds out of the market, introduced regimented work schedules, and reduced wages for manual laborers to near poverty levels. This declining status for industrial workers hampered their ability to focus on sports, but also created a reservoir of young men willing, if not required, to attempt a career in professional sports. For the economically circumscribed urban youth of the period, sports represented not only an avenue to wealth but also a surrogate workplace where they retained "their autonomy and traditions, their sense of craftsmanship."[4]

Those who followed sports during the period, particularly the labor aristocracy and municipal service workers, kept abreast of sports information primarily through visiting local taverns, which continued to be centers of the sporting culture. Becoming a "regular" at a particular tavern helped urban residents establish themselves as part of a community in the increasingly faceless and transient American cities; this search for community also led individuals to band together to support teams and athletes. However, taverns did far more than create an environment for the sports-minded to meet, they also fostered the growth of professional sports. As products of the bachelor subculture, athletes frequented the taverns and often negotiated terms for matches in them. By the Gilded Age, New York City had established itself as the center of American sports not only because of its population and status as the hub of American publishing but also because it became the home of numerous large taverns devoted to hosting boxing and wrestling matches. Middle-class sports fans viewed many of these establishments as disreputable and dangerous, but the brave and fatalistic helped make Owney Geoghegan's Broadway Bastile, "The" Allen's Bal Mabille, and, especially, Harry Hill's Houston Street entertainment hall popular locations for wrestling and boxing matches.[5]

For sports to spread beyond the oral culture of neighborhood taverns, however, a network of journals and newspapers committed to publishing athletically related material had to develop. William T. Porter pioneered the American sporting journal as publisher of *Spirit of the Times* in 1831, but other enterprising journalists began to devote increasing attention to sports. During the 1850s, for example, the editors, particularly Frank Queen, of the New York *Clipper* promoted their newspaper (and its offices) as the nation's central clearinghouse for sports information. Other newspapers, however, quickly recognized the potential increase in readership that sports coverage provided. By 1870 many metropolitan newspapers included box scores and other sports information. The ultracompetitive New York newspaper market provoked Gotham editors to explore new ways of attracting sports fans to their respective publications. Joseph Pulitzer's *World* set up the first separate sports department in the early 1880s and William Randolph Hearst's *Journal* provided readers with the nation's first sports section in the 1890s. While the expansion of newspaper sports coverage during the Gilded Age helped fuel the explosion in newspaper readership during the period, it also created an environment in which wrestlers and other sports figures developed name recognition in areas they had never personally appeared. This building of national reputations helped wrestlers engage in profitable tours beyond their home regions and also established the validity of claimants to championship titles.[6]

The preeminent source for sports information during the Gilded Age was not a daily newspaper but the weekly *National Police Gazette*. Founded in 1845, the *Police Gazette* initially focused on reprinting accounts of criminal activities from newspapers. The journal flourished until the mid-1850s but then declined. In the mid-1870s, Richard Kyle Fox, an Irish immigrant who arrived in America in 1874 with five dollars in his pocket, purchased the struggling *Police Gazette* and systematically rebuilt its subscription base by altering the journal's content. Fox recognized that to succeed as a journal for the masses, the *Police Gazette* "needed to shock and titillate as much as inform." Fox began including sexually charged articles and images of scantily clad showgirls to match the lurid red paper on which the *Police Gazette* was printed. He also recognized the explosive potential of sports articles and began to add limited sports coverage in March 1879. This attention to sports paid immediate dividends, and Fox dramatically increased the amount of space devoted to sports in 1880. During the late nineteenth century, the *Police Gazette*'s weekly circulation averaged one hundred fifty thousand. Fox's aggressive efforts to sell subscriptions to barbershops, taverns, and workingmen's halls (the bastions of the male bachelor subculture) undoubtedly resulted in a weekly readership closer to 1 million.[7]

Fox usurped the New York *Clipper* as the journal boxers, wrestlers, and other athletes used to issue challenges (known as "cards" or "defi") to potential opponents to establish the *Police Gazette*'s prominence in sporting circles. Boxers looking for battles by posting public challenges can be traced to English pugilism. American boxers began the practice early in the nineteenth century and were probably influenced by both the English sporting culture and duelists, who also issued public challenges; professional wrestlers of the postbellum period readily adopted the technique. Until the rise of sports coverage in periodicals, the practice revolved around declarations made in taverns, but Fox made public challenges a staple of the *Police Gazette*. The posts occasionally included open challenges to all but usually the issuer directed the notice at a specific opponent. A typical post resembled Peter McCoy's 1880 challenge to John T. Grady to wrestle for $100 a side "at any place the latter names." Fox's willingness to devote seemingly endless space to both these notices and accounts of actual sporting events helped propel the *Police Gazette* into a prominent position in sporting circles. Further, the national readership of his journal, as opposed to the geographical limitations of the New York newspapers, made the *Police Gazette* the most attractive location for the issuance of challenges.[8]

The wrestling that early sporting journals reported emerged from the wartime camp experiences. Returning veterans dispersed knowledge of the collar-and-elbow style across the country, thereby generating new fans and participants. By promoting the adoption of collar-and-elbow, these Civil War soldiers inadvertently helped foster the growth of professional wrestling. With collar-and-elbow rules now familiar to members of the sporting culture across the country, the style positioned itself as both the preeminent form of wrestling and as the style capable of having recognized national champions. When coupled with the larger transformations in American society regarding sports, this expansion of collar-and-elbow converted professional wrestling into a truly modern sport.[9]

Despite the increasingly national nature of collar-and-elbow, many of the prominent early postwar American champions continued to hail from the Green Mountain state. The Vermont wrestlers' dominance reflected the long tradition of the style in their state. Vermont communities continued to host large tournaments in the postwar period, which encouraged many area youth to participate in the sport. The large number of active wrestlers in Vermont also ensured that eager novices and experienced professionals could readily find matches to help improve their grappling skills. Finally, the success of Vermont wrestlers in Union army tournaments during the war encouraged the notion in the Green Mountain state that their wrestlers represented the pinnacle of the sport in this country. At the conclusion of the war, these confident Vermont wrestlers ventured out of their New England base to earn so-called easy victories against inferior grapplers from other states.[10]

Vermont pride, however, proved sorely tested by the feats of a New York wrestler named James Hiram McLaughlin. He learned to grapple at a young age, and the large population of Irish and Scotch immigrants in Oriskany, his hometown, ensured that the young McLaughlin learned the collar-and-elbow style. McLaughlin began wrestling locally for side bets at age 15 and then, like most of the early collar-and-elbow stars, joined the Union army when the Civil

War began. In the military, he competed not only in wrestling competitions but also earned a number of battlefield promotions for bravery. When the war ended, the now Colonel James McLaughlin once again began to wrestle professionally.

McLaughlin's postwar wrestling career illustrates two important issues of postbellum professional wrestling. First, the sport's new-found popularity created a national environment for highly profitable matches. McLaughlin traveled across the country (and possibly to Europe as well) competing with other professionals for purses exceeding the annual salary of industrial workers. By the 1870s, McLaughlin regularly competed in matches with winner's shares of $1,000 or more. Although McLaughlin earned more than most grapplers as a championship-caliber wrestler, his purses were close to the range champion prizefighters were paid. Pugilism may have been the more popular sport in the immediate postwar period, but professional wrestling did not lag far behind.[11]

McLaughlin's career also illuminated the sport's darker side. The potential to earn large sums of money wrestling corresponded with an equally large potential of serious injury. McLaughlin allegedly killed two of his opponents and maimed several more. Wrestlers of the period locked up in matches they personally arranged, without any legal or regulatory oversight, without attending physicians, and generally on grassy clearings or wooden floors. To make a living wrestling, an individual regularly put his life and physical well-being on the line. Nineteenth-century wrestlers certainly knew of these dangers, and the threat of serious injury tempered the ambitions of some young men who contemplated a career as a professional scuffler. Like pugilists, then, those who became professional wrestlers in the postbellum era were generally men who found themselves with limited career opportunities and decided to risk death or maiming as a means of escaping the economic vicissitudes of the labor market.[12]

McLaughlin's wrestling success during the Civil War positioned him as one of the leading professionals at the end of the war. He parlayed this fame into a claim to be the collar-and-elbow champion of the United States in 1867, the first recognized American champion. Despite losing to Homer Lane in 1868, McLaughlin continued to claim the title after winning a March 1870 tournament in Detroit. Illustrative of the growing national interest in collar-and-elbow, the tournament featured wrestlers from seven states and Canada. However, the premier Vermont wrestlers did not compete, and, of the nation's leading collar-and-elbow stylists, only McLaughlin and Lane appeared. For winning the tournament McLaughlin received a diamond belt financed by Richard K. Fox; this marked the beginning of wrestling's continual maintenance of a "championship" belt. He spent the next six years defending his title throughout the northeast. McLaughlin faced stiff challenges during this golden period of collar-and-elbow, and he repeatedly traded the title with Vermonters James Owens, John McMahon, and Henry Moses Dufur. McLaughlin last relinquished the collar-and-elbow title in 1884.[13]

The redoubtable McLaughlin, however, continued to lockup long after his championship years. He worked intermittently as a railroad engineer and relocated often. Throughout most of his peak, McLaughlin was based in Detroit, but, throughout the 1880s, he moved westward. After periods living in St. Louis and Butte, Montana, McLaughlin established himself as proprietor of the Weed House saloon in Seattle, Washington. He continued to wrestle throughout the period and attempted to organize an 1894 tournament restricted to competitors who had previously wrestled for the collar-and-elbow title. McLaughlin's vagabond nature eventually led him to the Alaska Territory, where the aged colonel competed in matches as late as 1901.[14]

McLaughlin's wrestling style faced serious challenges by the 1880s. During this period, professional wrestling made great strides in Europe as well. The traditional styles of England continued to be practiced in that country, but on the continent, a Mediterranean folk style became the dominant form. First codified in the 1840s, the *la luttes á mains platte* style gained popularity in France during the middle of the century. By the 1870s it had spread across the continent and, while occasionally still referred to as "French" wrestling, was erroneously called Greco-Roman, thanks to the perception that this was the ancient Hellenic style of the sport. The Greco-Roman style prohibited all holds below the waist, making it a more deliberate form of wrestling that favored large, strong competitors. During McLaughlin's tenure as American collar-and-elbow champion, this style became increasingly popular in the United States. For many collar-and-elbow practitioners, who tended to be small and agile, this development hastened the demise of both their careers and the collar-and-elbow style.[15]

Although a middle-aged Henry Moses Dufur claimed to be the American collar-and-elbow champion into the mid-1890s (with John McMahon as his only significant challenger), the straight collar-and-elbow title was irrelevant by the end of the previous decade. The style retreated to its traditional bastions, the Irish enclaves of New England, where it slowly withered away. When Canadian collar-and-elbow "champion" John H. Quinn came to the United States in 1892 he found it difficult to locate an opponent for a $500 a side match. *National Police Gazette* sports editor William Harding noted that Quinn encountered difficulties because "there are but few 'trippers' outside of Vermont and not much interest taken in this style of wrestling except in the New England States."[16]

However, Greco-Roman did not represent the only new style to gain recognition during the period. In both England and this country a fast-paced, individualistic style known as catch-as-catch-can also developed. The origins of the catch style are somewhat more difficult to trace than Greco-Roman. It developed out of the violent Lancashire style. To this foundation, wrestlers added aspects of frontier rough-and-tumble, holds from collar-and-elbow, and elements of Japanese jiujitsu. The catch style did not require specific opening stances, nor did it bar any holds (matches fought under the *Police Gazette* rules, however, disallowed chokeholds). Catch matches also diverged from other styles of wrestling in that victory could be obtained by pinfall or submission. This style grew in popularity alongside Greco-Roman and emerged as the dominant form of professional wrestling by the end of the nineteenth century.

The increasing popularity of these new styles forced many wrestlers who formerly specialized in collar-and-elbow to learn Greco-Roman and catch techniques. With newer styles gaining ground, the "Vermont trippers," who devoted themselves solely to collar-and-elbow slid, like the style they promoted, into the backwater of professional wrestling. Wrestlers who continued to make a career out of the sport often competed in matches of mixed styles. Typically, the mixed-styles matches involved three falls, one each in collar-and-elbow, Greco-Roman, and catch-as-catch-can. By the fin de siècle, this practice became so common that a mixed-styles championship was established. Reflecting collar-and-elbow's waning influence, these mixed-styles matches increasingly included only falls in catch and Greco-Roman.[17]

Before catch came to dominate the sport, however, the Greco-Roman style experienced a brief period as the country's most popular form of wrestling, partly due to the style's relative safety when compared with catch (or even collar-and-elbow). To be sure, Greco-Roman stylists often emerged from matches battered, but, typically, their injuries did not match the severity of wrestlers in collar-and-elbow battles. With its reliance on upper-body strength and power, Greco-Roman heavily favored larger wrestlers, which also contributed to the style's popularity; wrestling fans, as with boxing fans, have always preferred to see heavyweight competitors. Many of the Greco-Roman wrestlers of the period also performed as professional strongmen, an occupation that first rose to prominence during the 1880s.

That both feats of strength and well-muscled Greco-Roman stylists became popular at the same time reflects the growing concern for physical fitness that flourished during the late nineteenth century. An increasingly large number of social commentators decried the ill effects of sedentary modern life on American men and encouraged an adoption of the "strenuous life." Finely chiseled strongmen not only demonstrated the potential of the human body but also served as exemplars of health to be emulated. The Greco-Roman style, with its emphasis on sheer strength, perfectly served the needs of hardy young men seeking to prove their fortitude. Its alleged links to classical culture gave the style an air of respectability the rough catch form of wrestling lacked. As a result, it became an acceptable activity for young men trying to protect their health. The notion that Greco-Roman represented the "proper" style of wrestling gained further credence when it became the chosen style for the newly established Amateur Athletic Union and the resuscitated Olympic Games.[18]

Perhaps the most significant single force in popularizing physical fitness during the period was the muscular Christianity movement. Muscular Christianity developed out of the combination of the British sporting tradition that imparted a yearning for competition and contact, the scientific quest for physical perfection embedded in the German gymnastics movement, and a Christian notion of fair play and ethical behavior. The movement's origins can be traced to early-nineteenth-century England, where it was popularized in general fiction, such as *Tom Brown's School Days*, but it was clearly discernible in the United States after the

Civil War. Supporters of muscular Christianity in this country included such respected public figures as Josiah Strong, G. Stanley Hall, Oliver Wendell Holmes, and Theodore Roosevelt. They advocated physical exercise as an antidote to the sedentary aspects of urban life, as a way of making leisure time wholesome, and out of a belief that a physically strong Christian denoted a spiritually strong Christian.[19]

Many of those who advocated muscular Christianity felt that professional sports, because of the gambling and drinking that typically accompanied them, needed to be approached with caution. However, by the late 1880s the muscular Christianity movement embraced professional athletes as examples of good health who could popularize the notion of physical fitness. The movement's supporters never wavered in their belief that the trappings of professional sports tempted the nation's youth, but the dangerous softness of urbanized Americans presented an even larger threat. Therefore, they provided a measure of respectability to Gilded Age sports. The movement coincided with the rise of sports heroes in this country; athletes who benefited most from the public support offered by muscular Christianity advocates were those who could be promoted as clean-living role models, such proper sports heroes as coach Walter Camp, fictional hero Frank Merriwell, and wrestler William Muldoon.[20]

Often hailed as the "father of American wrestling," Muldoon gave professional wrestling a recognizable champion to popularize and legitimize the sport (at the same time, John L. Sullivan did the same for boxing). Muldoon's skills in the ring were matched by an outsized personality, a devotion to health and hygiene that made him acceptable to respectable Americans, and a keen understanding of the business of sports. He reigned as Greco-Roman world champion for more than a decade and contributed greatly to the rise of that style as the dominant form in this country. So great was the force of his popularity and personality that he managed to sustain the appeal of Greco-Roman against the rising tide of catch-as-catch-can. Muldoon's retirement in 1891 not only signaled the end of his tenure as champion but also the end of Greco-Roman's period of dominance in this country. The style briefly reemerged as an important element of American professional wrestling at the end of the 1890s, but even then Greco-Roman could not challenge the ascendant catch style for preeminence in this country.

Muldoon's public acceptance stemmed in part from his avoidance of the seamier aspects of the sporting culture. He neither drank nor used tobacco and he carefully cultivated his image as a proper, well-to-do gentleman. Perhaps most importantly, he represented a shining example of how dedication to health, exercise, and clean living might allow urban dwellers to maintain their strength and vigor into middle age. To health reformers, Muldoon served as a bright star in a constellation of troubling (and troubled) famous sports personalities. Dubbed the "solid man of sport" after a popular song of the period entitled "Muldoon, the Solid Man," he embodied the intertwining of muscle and morality stressed by physical culturists. For muscular Christianity advocates, no better proof of their righteousness could have occurred than the bloated and besotted John L. Sullivan's request to the upright Muldoon for assistance in returning the heavyweight boxing champion to fighting trim for his 1889 match with Jake Kilrain.[21]

Muldoon's usefulness to health reformers would have been negligible had he not supplemented his respectable persona with remarkable wrestling skills. He first wrestled as a member of the Sixth New York Regiment during the Civil War. After the war, Muldoon drifted to New York City and worked a variety of manual labor jobs. By the early 1870s, he learned the Greco-Roman style and scratched out a living by working as a bouncer at Harry Hill's. Muldoon also began his wrestling career at Hill's Houston Street hall, earning $7 for each victory. He joined the New York Police Department in 1876, quickly became the department's champion, and then retired from the force in 1881 to devote himself to professional wrestling full time. Muldoon's work for the police department contributed to his reputation as an exemplar of the proper sort of sporting hero for American youth.[22]

Muldoon's muscular 250-pound physique was perfect for the Greco-Roman style of wrestling. After defeating Thiebaud Bauer at Madison Square Garden in January 1880, Muldoon claimed the American Greco-Roman championship. In 1883 Muldoon defeated Edwin Bibby of England in San Francisco and claimed the world Greco-Roman championship. He reigned as the undisputed Greco-Roman champion until his retirement in late 1891. While Muldoon proved unbeatable at Greco-Roman, he proved less adept at the increasingly popular catch style. Despite his difficulties at catch, Muldoon engaged in mixed matches to maintain his prominence in the sport. Recognizing his limitations in the catch style, Muldoon mostly stuck to mixed bouts in Greco-Roman and collar-and-elbow. Muldoon and McLaughlin engaged in a profitable series of mixed bouts of this type during the winter of 1884–1885.[23]

The growth of disparate styles of wrestling during the 1880s created a dizzying array of mixed-style variations. Matches occurred in seemingly endless combinations of catch, Greco-Roman, collar-and-elbow, side hold, back hold, and sumo. Typically, mixed-styles matches involved three falls, the odd number facilitating the declaration of a winner, but stretched occasionally to five-fall marathons. In one all-day affair at Salem, Massachusetts, in 1889, H. M. Dufur, Duncan C. Ross, and Pierre Delmar used the mixed-styles format as the basis of a three-man tournament. Ross also frequently engaged in a variety of "mixed" sports competitions. Anointed by Richard K. Fox as the *National Police Gazette's* champion all-around athlete, Ross competed in multiple sport competitions that included wrestling against single opponents. While Ross posted open challenges to engage in horseback-mounted broadsword competitions, he did not appear to engage in horseback-mounted Greco-Roman bouts as did the active "Greek George" of Peoria.[24]

Greco-Roman remained, however, the most popular style of wrestling in Europe during the 1880s and coupled with the increasing number of American wrestlers specializing in catch resulted in Muldoon's increasing reliance on foreign opponents in straight Greco-Roman battles. Throughout the decade a steady stream of hulking European wrestlers came to the United States to challenge Muldoon. His tenure as champion included victories over Old World invaders such as Carl Abs of Germany, Matsada Sorakichi of Japan, and Spaniard Carlos Martino. These bouts not only demonstrated the international popularity of the Greco-Roman style but also denote the origins of wrestling's obsession with maintaining a large stable of "champions." Most of Muldoon's European opponents styled themselves national champions, and, in instances where their homeland's title already possessed a claimant, some promoted themselves as regional Greco-Roman kings. For example, August Schmidt came to the United States in October 1883 claiming the title of "champion wrestler of North Germany."[25]

The lumbering nature of many Greco-Roman wrestlers, who focused on developing upper-body strength at the expense of speed and agility, helped contribute to the decline of the style. Two muscular heavyweights locked up and pushing on each other, without any recourse to holds below the waist, often devolved into matches, as Joe Jares noted, "as exciting as watching two sleepy elephants lean against each other." Muldoon and his great rival Clarence "Kansas Demon" Whistler engaged in a series of matches that demonstrated both Muldoon's status as America's finest Greco-Roman wrestler and the numbing dullness of these encounters. Each of these shoving matches went several hours; one particularly extended encounter was mercifully called a draw after eight hours. The increasingly common fast and lively catch matches steadily pushed the Greco-Roman style out of the professional mainstream in this country, leaving Muldoon and his ilk to ply the form on exhibition tours.[26]

Muldoon, like many wrestlers and boxers of the period, toured the country as part of a traveling athletic troupe. These groups used the extensive new rail lines of the era to move from town to town to provide masculine entertainment to those living outside of major urban areas. Muldoon's troupe, like most, included strongmen, wrestlers, and boxers. These troupes often provided titillating entertainment for the ladies in attendance by having the scantily clad, muscular athletes pose as "living statuary." By promoting these performances as both displays of physical fitness and artistic reflections of then-current notions on classical ideals of human perfection, the touring groups neatly skirted potential indecency charges while attracting larger audiences. Boxers and wrestlers on the tours exhibited important holds and often challenged the townspeople. Typically, these matches operated under a variety of handicap rules. Local competitors often received an advertised amount of money for lasting to an established time limit, avoiding being thrown within a time limit, or avoiding being thrown a certain number of times before time expired. For a wrestler of Muldoon's stature, these national tours proved highly profitable, and he spent much of the 1880s touring with his own group and with John L. Sullivan's troupe.[27]

The matches between two wrestlers traveling with the tour often amounted to pre-rehearsed exhibitions. For example, on the 1881–1882 tour of Muldoon's troupe, the American Greco-Roman champion wrestled almost nightly in fifteen-minute "contests" with Whistler. Further, Muldoon regularly sent troupe employees ahead to scheduled tour stops to wrestle locals and establish a reputation in the town, generating excitement over a match with Muldoon when the athletic company arrived. It seems highly unlikely that the locals received notification that these men worked for Muldoon or that any wrestler in his employ would risk his employment by defeating their boss. Edward Van Every, Muldoon's sympathetic biographer, claimed the practice "was merely by way of setting the stage for the appearance of the champion, and also, in event of no local champion being able to screw up sufficient courage to go against the great Muldoon, that there would then be some sort of an opponent." Given the number of troupes profitably crisscrossing the nation during the 1880s, a dearth of challengers does not appear to have been a significant problem. Rather, the methods used by Muldoon's group reflected the universally decried practice of "hippodroming" (supposedly authentic athletic contests engaged in solely as a means of making money by drawing a large gate).[28]

Hippodroming was a significant problem for nineteenth-century sports in general. The practice reflected what many social critics viewed as the general dishonesty of professional sports. Baseball and boxing underwent periodic scandals throughout the century over fixed contests, and harness racing became notoriously rife with hippodromed match races. Wrestling, although viewed as somewhat more respectable than pugilism, was also criticized for staging matches under the pretexts of legitimacy. Muldoon himself engaged in some highly questionable matches that undoubtedly contributed to these criticisms. For example, in January 1890, the *National Police Gazette* reported that he and Evan "Strangler" Lewis "have been giving wrestling exhibitions in Philadelphia." At the end of that month, the two then engaged in an allegedly competitive Greco-Roman match in the City of Brotherly Love. Hippodroming and the "carrying" of lesser opponents to generate excitement certainly occurred regularly in the first two decades after the Civil War, especially on the athletic tours; however, the practice was not as common as it came to be at the turn of the century. And compared with the massive number of fixed contests in boxing, wrestling appeared almost angelic. Professional wrestling's (immediate) future lay in showmanship and "sports entertainment," but for the immediate postwar practitioners of collar-and-elbow and Greco-Roman, it clearly represented an authentic sport.[29]

The publicity surrounding the athletic tour exhibitions and reportage of repeated matches between the stars of the era in some ways skewed the true nature of the sport. Most of the legitimate matches engaged in by men such as Muldoon and McLaughlin occurred while they toured, squaring off against local champions for side bets in bouts unacknowledged by the national sporting press. These matches served as the lifeblood of the sport during the late nineteenth century and allowed many men to support themselves as professional wrestlers. For a touring professional to have recklessly "carried" a legitimate opponent or continually agreed to willingly lose in matches where the winner received all the money would have resulted in their economic disaster. Men seeking careers in professional wrestling during the postbellum period wrestled to win in the majority of their matches.

Nor should the hippodromed matches of the period be viewed as part of an inexorable march toward the show wrestling of the twentieth century. Although laws against professional boxing were only selectively enforced, prizefights were illegal in every state for periods during the late nineteenth century. To earn a living, professional boxers engaged in the same sort of exhibitions and athletic tours as wrestlers. As Elliott Gorn noted, John L. Sullivan "made far more money from his 'knocking-out tours' than from championship fights; in fact, bare-knuckle matches had become virtually a means to promote exhibitions rather than the other way around." However, boxing emerged from this period as a legitimate, albeit often shady, sport. That wrestling did not follow a similar course toward respectability and honest competition derived from the unique circumstances that developed in the decades bookending the turn of the twentieth century. During this period (1890–1910), wrestling became increasingly dominated by theatrically minded promoters and hucksters concerned with profit more than honest competition. And in a sport bereft of even the marginal centralization of professional boxing, these forces faced little opposition in their perversion of professional wrestling.[30]

Questions about the legitimacy of some of his matches did not, however, affect the public's opinion of Muldoon. He later carried both his reputation and his health ideals into a successful postwrestling career. He opened the Olympia Hygienic Institute of Purchase, New York, in the early twentieth century as a clinic for imparting information on fitness to the well-heeled. Novelist Theodore Dreiser spent time at the institute in 1919 and came away from the experience awed by the vigor of the sexagenarian who he described as a "tiger in collar and boots." The former wrestling champion also continued his lifelong association with boxing. Muldoon remained friends with many pugilists of his era and assisted many who skittered into ill health and poverty after their careers ended. Muldoon served as a freelance newspaper reporter for high-profile boxing matches during the early twentieth century and then became a respected member of the New York Athletic Commission after World War I. In 1921, he became chairman of the commission, a position he maintained, along with the operation of his institute, until his death in 1933.[31]

Muldoon's association with boxing reflected the connections of that sport to professional wrestling during the nineteenth century. Boxing and wrestling maintained a status among the bachelor sporting culture as the two most "manly" of sports and therefore appealed to many of the same fans. Their rise during the 1880s rested on the broad backs of famous heavyweight champions—John L. Sullivan and William Muldoon. These two champions also shared similar racial views that affected the development of their respective sports. Sullivan and Muldoon both viewed the heavyweight championship, as did most American sportsmen of the time, as the sole preserve of Caucasians. Given the hypermasculinity of boxing and wrestling, and the subcultures from which they emerged, the reluctance on the part of supporters of these two sports to provide equal opportunities for the participation of women is also not surprising.

During the nineteenth century, African-American fighters regularly competed with white fighters, including world championship bouts in the lighter weight classes. However, a sharp color line was established in the heavyweight division. Fears of swelling African-American pride or potential uprisings resulting from a person of color winning the heavyweight championship, and the recognition as the best fighter on the planet that accompanied the title, led John L. Sullivan and other nineteenth-century heavyweight champions to bar legitimate African-American contenders from competing for the title. Wrestling followed suit, and no African-Americans contended for significant titles during the century. Further, this racial attitude prevailed in wrestling far longer than it did in boxing. Jack Johnson won boxing's heavyweight championship early in the twentieth century, but no African-American wrestler received the necessary support of wrestling's promoters to even achieve the status of contender for the sport's top crown until the 1930s.[32]

Viro Small was the chief victim of wrestling's nineteenth-century color line. Born into slavery in South Carolina in 1854, Small moved to New York after the Civil War, and, in 1874, began wrestling professionally in that state. He later fell under the influence of Vermont collar-and-elbow stylist Mike Horrigan, who relocated Small to the Green Mountain state. Small, who often wrestled under the name "Black Sam," proved to be an adept pupil and eventually won the Vermont collar-and-elbow championship. However, it appears that the racial attitudes of the time prevented him from ever competing for the American championship in that style or for the world title in Greco-Roman or mixed styles. No direct comments by Muldoon concerning Small are extant, but his views concerning the color line can be deduced easily from Edward Van Every's 1929 statement that, with regards to boxing matches, "it happens to be Mr. Muldoon's opinion that contests between white and Negro boxers for the title do not turn out for the best interests of the game."[33]

Curiously, Muldoon appears to have held no similar racial views with regards to wrestlers from the Pacific rim, at a time when Asians in this country faced open hostility so severe that Chinese immigration ended in the 1880s, and Japanese immigration dwindled to a trickle early in the twentieth century. Muldoon's more enlightened views concerning Japanese wrestlers may have stemmed from his admiration of the martial arts and wrestling traditions of their homeland. Whatever the reasons, Muldoon willingly engaged in bouts with Japanese sumo who competed in the United States. In 1884, he published a defi offering to wrestle Hamada Kirokichi and Matsada Sorakichi on the same night, at both Greco-Roman and sumo styles. In one 1889 encounter, Muldoon and Sorakichi engaged in a match under "go-as-you please" rules, which permitted punching and butting, that ended when the frenzied crowd swarmed the combatants. Muldoon eventually befriended Sorakichi and served as his second in several matches. Even the rabidly racist Richard K. Fox admired Sorakichi's grappling skills enough to overcome his personal views (although he continually referred to Sorakichi as "the Jap") and anoint the Japanese wrestler as the *Police Gazette's* mixed-styles champion. However, Sorakichi frequently fell afoul of the racial attitudes of the period, with several of his matches ending with him unfairly declared the loser against white opponents. Sorakichi's wrestling tactics also contributed to his difficulties with crowds. He often performed public exhibitions of his remarkable capacity to head-butt solid objects without sustaining injury, and many of his opponents claimed the sumo cheated by resorting to illegal butting during matches.[34]

The male-dominated sporting culture also overwhelmingly prevented women from competing in "masculine" sports. This exclusion reflected larger trends in American society regarding women and physical exertion. As the nineteenth century unfolded, a concern with the well-being of white middle-class women arose alongside similar concerns over the detrimental effects of urban life on white men of the educated classes. However, the prevailing view maintained that these women needed to be physically fit only so that they might be prepared for childbirth and motherhood. Overly strenuous sports, such as wrestling and baseball, could potentially damage women's reproductive capabilities, and exercise enthusiasts strongly denounced female participation in these athletic forms. And while more progressive reformers lobbied for women's participation in sports such as tennis and swimming, the association of boxing and wrestling with brutality and disreputable characters kept these sports outside the spectrum of activities engaged in by respectable women.[35]

A few women, however, engaged in professional wrestling bouts during the nineteenth century. Their effect on the sport proved negligible, and the women's matches seem to have been undertaken primarily as lurid entertainment for male crowds. For example, an 1884 *National Police Gazette* illustration of a St. Paul, Minnesota, bout between two women shows the combatants in the skimpy attire associated with burlesque shows. Some female wrestlers of the period, though, clearly viewed themselves as legitimate athletes, rather than as sexualized objects operating in the male sporting culture. For example, Alice Williams emerged as Richard K. Fox's women's champion in 1891 and promoted herself as the women's world champion during the last decade of the nineteenth century. The pioneering female athlete Hattie Leslie, best remembered as a boxer, also competed as a Greco-Roman wrestler. In 1890, she gave up pugilism to devote full time to the "more refined calling of wrestling." As with men of the period, professional strongwomen such as "Minerva," the leading female weightlifter of the late nineteenth century, often adopted Greco-Roman wrestling as a sideline to earn extra income. The attempts of these women to carve out a niche in the wrestling world, how ever, proved to be premature. Female wrestlers only emerged as an integral part of professional wrestling in the 1930s and even then, continued to be viewed only as a comedic or sexualized interlude on wrestling cards.[36]

The course of professional boxing's development as a sport also aided the perception of wrestling as a distinct athletic endeavor. From the 1830s on, most prizefighters agreed to compete under the London Prize Ring rules. London rules matches were fought without gloves and rounds ended when one competitor fell to the ground. These fights had no set number of rounds and ended only when one competitor could no longer rise ("come to scratch") for the next round. Because pugilists fought without gloves, they could not risk damaging their knuckles with repeated punches to the solid mass of their opponent's skull. Rather, successful prizefighters focused on wearing down opponents with less stamina (or, in nineteenth-century sporting terminology "bottom") through body punching and the variety of wrestling holds allowed under the London rules. A successful nineteenth-century prizefighter wielded an arsenal of grappling techniques to gain an advantage over opponents. They used chanceries and head locks to hold an opponent's head steady for accurate punching to the soft, fleshy areas of the face and often resorted to tosses to bring rounds to conclusion. The most popular toss for pugilists was the cross-buttock, which provided ready opportunities for "accidentally" landing on top of a downed opponent. These techniques proved so essential to nineteenth-century prizefighters that sportswriters often based their fight predictions on a fighter's grappling skills, rather than his punching power.[37]

To improve the widespread perception that prizefighting was a brutal and barbaric struggle, the Marquis of Queensbury developed a new set of boxing rules in the late 1860s. The Queensbury rules required that gloves be worn and that bouts be scheduled for a set number of rounds. Further, the rounds lasted exactly three minutes, with a one-minute rest period between them. Queensbury intended to make prizefighting more respectable and gentlemanly, and, as part of this endeavor, his rules disallowed the wrestling holds that had been an integral part of the sport but which he felt brought an unnecessary crudity to the "manly art." The general acceptance of the

Queensbury rules developed slowly in this country, but by the early 1890s, they held sway in almost all prizefights. With wrestling eliminated from boxing, professional wrestling became a completely independent sport.[38]

One factor that hindered the acceptance of the Queensbury rules was their reflection of larger societal trends unacceptable to the working class. With time limitations and set rest periods between rounds, the clock regulated prizefights as well as the daily lives of lower-class sports fans. Further, while past pugilists succeeded solely on the quality of their work (their ability to outlast an opponent), under the Queensbury rules, a boxer's success, hinged on the decision of a referee, that is, unless the fighter possessed knockout power. Like the shift from guilded craftsmen to wage-slave factory worker, the transformation of boxing from London Prize Rules to Queensbury rules represented a "modernization" of the sport to bring it in line with industrialized America. It is not surprising, then, that the best boxers of the Gilded Age were referred to as "fighting machines."[39]

As with so many other aspects of American boxing, the "Great John L." served as the instrument that propelled prizefighting to accept this modernization. After his 1889 bout with Jake Kilrain, heavyweight champion Sullivan announced he would never again compete under the London Prize Rules. By placing boxing's most prestigious title under the control of the Queensbury rules, Sullivan effectively eliminated the final hindrance to full acceptance of the new boxing code and also severed the last connection of wrestling to prizefighting. From this date on, wrestling supporters could maintain that wrestling represented a sport wholly independent of boxing. Sullivan's decision to adopt the Queensbury rules in his subsequent fights derived from both his desire to be viewed as respectable and because he found it increasingly difficult to get in shape for long bouts, rather than for any concern for the freedoms afforded under the London rules. Muldoon, Sullivan's sometime trainer, also recognized the benefits time-limited matches afforded an aging champion.[40]

Although Muldoon never engaged in the sort of dissipation that wrecked Sullivan, the Greco-Roman champion recognized that, as his career continued, his ability to engage in nine-hour matches decreased. Therefore, Muldoon also introduced time limits, often one hour, into his matches during the latter 1880s. These restrictions helped ensure that he did not lose his title to a younger opponent with more "bottom," reduced the amount of effort he needed to retain his title, and allowed for tighter scheduling on his athletic tours. The time-limit match, in fact, became the standard on the tours, with special handicap rules often added to generate excitement; for example, the superior wrestler might be required to throw his opponent a certain number of times within the time limit or pay the challenger simply for avoiding a pin until time expired.[41]

Time limits became popular not only in Greco-Roman matches (where strongmen posing as wrestlers, such as Carl Abs, huffed and puffed after thirty minutes of exertion) but also in the widely held mixed-styles matches. The adoption of time limits also increased the complaints of hippodroming because the time restriction was perceived as a means of ending a match without either competitor emerging victorious. This proved to be a dangerous trend for a sport trying to establish an identity. Concerns over fixed matches and the plethora of styles practiced in professional wrestling had already hampered its growth; time-limit draws served only to add unsatisfactory finishes to the sport's list of difficulties. However, dedicated practitioners of catch, wedded to the notions of fast action and "premodern" bouts grappled to conclusion, doggedly clung to the notion of professional wrestling as an honest sport. It would be these men who helped wrestling survive as a popular sport and ushered in the early twentieth-century recrudescence of wrestling's legitimacy before the merchants of ballyhoo gained complete control.[42]

3

CATCH-AS-
CATCH-CAN

By the late nineteenth century, many aspects of "modern" professional wrestling had developed in this country. The exciting and violent catch-as-catch-can style emerged as the dominant form for professionals. Promotional and touring techniques geared toward maximum publicity and profit replaced the localism characteristic of wrestling through the collar-and-elbow period. A clearer line of succession for national champions (in a welter of weight classes) emerged, which helped give the sport more legitimacy. And, most significantly, the new business models of wrestling ushered in a generation of promoters and performers influenced by the shady practices of carnivals. These men eventually transformed the ancient sport of wrestling into the modern spectacle of professional wrestling. The "catch period," the decades around the turn of the twentieth century, marked the last gasp of authentic, competitive professional wrestling in the United States.

The most obvious alteration in the development of late-nineteenth-century wrestling involved the location of the matches. No longer a rural sport practiced on soft turf or simply a sideline aspect of touring athletic troupes, wrestlers found new ways to protect themselves from the injuries caused by competing on the hardwood floors of theaters. Early attempts to reduce the dangers of matches included wrestling on mattresses or carpets, placing a heavy cloth over thick sawdust, and tumbling mats. The emergence of the catch style, with its reliance on ground wrestling, made the development of safer wrestling environments imperative. By the turn of the twentieth century, most important matches occurred in rings designed for boxing and wrestling, with soft floors covered by taut canvas and ropes to keep the competitors from leaving the ring. Almost all other legitimate matches featured protective mats to prevent both injuries and newspaper editorials that blasted stage wrestling as "scarcely less dangerous to life and limb than the most stubbornly contested prize fight."[1]

The dominant form of professional wrestling also changed during this period. Just as Greco-Roman displaced collar-and-elbow earlier, the catch-as-catch-can style quickly supplanted Greco-Roman as the most popular style for professional battles. With the emergence of catch as the dominant form, mixed-styles encounters also virtually ceased. Greco-Roman was increasingly viewed as an amateur style, with a smattering of American professionals attempting to maintain its presence. A number of factors, including larger cultural issues not directly related to wrestling, facilitated the rise of the catch style.

As the nineteenth century ended, the catch form that emerged in professional wrestling melded rough-and-tumble techniques and jiujitsu onto a base of Lancashire style. With holds below the waist allowed, unlike Greco-Roman, and victories obtained from falls and submission moves, catch proved to be a quick, violent, and exciting style. Although catch matches occasionally dragged out into multihour defensive battles, the style generally avoided the meandering push-and-pull encounters of the more restrictive Greco-Roman matches. John Dizikes cogently argued that the inherent rhythms of American amusements and sports, as early as the nineteenth century, were predicated on speed and immediate results. Catch, therefore, presented a wrestling form more aligned with larger sporting trends than Greco-Roman. The intensity of catch also led physical culturalists, such as Bernarr MacFadden, who wrestled professionally, and Theodore Roosevelt, who held matches in the White House, to promote the style as an integral aspect of the "strenuous life."[2]

Catch also eclipsed Greco-Roman thanks to a virulent strain of late-nineteenth-century nationalism that permeated most aspects of American popular culture. Sports serves as an essential aspect of the developing national culture of the late nineteenth century. As

Steven Pope has noted, it became imperative to develop "nationally-specific" sports. As a result, the fiction developed that American Abner Doubleday invented baseball and that American football owed only a passing debt to European games such as soccer and rugby. Despite its initial tediousness and equipment problems, basketball, a truly American game, rapidly gained a coterie of supporters for the same reason. For athletic boosters of the period, indigenous sports helped shape an American culture distinct from that of Europe. They also believed that sport could serve as a catalyst to unite a multiethnic nation into a society with common interests and values. For this society to be truly "American," homegrown cultural forms, such as basketball, needed to be nurtured and promoted.[3]

Despite its English heritage, and later absorption of Japanese martial arts, catch came to be viewed as an indigenous wrestling form. Contemporary accounts often referred to the style as "American" catch-as-catch-can. The claim of catch promoters that the style was wholly American might have been dubious, but catch did possess a more clearly North American background than Greco-Roman, which, by its very name, appeared "un-American." The promotion of catch style, as the "American" form of professional wrestling, at the expense of "European" Greco-Roman, became one aspect of the larger drive to create an American sporting culture. This notion of styles representing cultures reached its pinnacle in the 1908 world heavyweight championship match between American Frank Gotch and Russian George Hackenschmidt.

Given catch's reliance on speed and technique, rather than the brute strength of Greco-Roman, the style allowed successful smaller wrestlers to emerge. The notion that, regardless of size, anyone could compete in a catch match helped foster the notion that the style was more democratic and therefore more "American." Greco-Roman wrestlers often emerged from a strongman background and few non-heavyweights attempted to establish themselves in the style, but the rise of catch created an opportunity for competitors in all weight classes. As catch came to dominate professional wrestling, the *National Police Gazette* became a clearinghouse for defis for catch stylists as light as one hundred pounds. By the end of the nineteenth century, national catch champions emerged in a variety of weight classes that corresponded with those established in boxing.[4]

Greco-Roman proponents also contributed to the declining status of the style. After William Muldoon's early 1890s retirement, no Greco-Roman stylist emerged that rivaled his popularity. In 1894, German-American Ernest Roeber, Muldoon's handpicked successor, traveled to Europe and defeated all the leading continental contenders, thereby establishing a claim to the world championship vacated by Muldoon. Roeber, however, found it difficult to generate interest in his career because of a lack of worthy challengers. By the late 1890s, Roeber attempted to counter his increasingly marginalized status by facing a series of imported opponents. These matches against foreign competitors, most of whom were "Terrible Turks" imported by wrestling impresario Antonio Pierri, enabled Roeber to connect with the nationalistic overtones of sporting culture. Despite the lackluster performances of many of the Levantine grapplers, public interest in these matches remained somewhat high. However, Roeber's March 1900 loss to Dane Beck Olsen signaled both the movement of the Greco-Roman championship to Europe and Roeber's decline. Without either a title or quality domestic opponents, Roeber spiraled downward, which helped finish Greco-Roman as a viable professional style in this country. Roeber traveled to Europe in October 1900 to attempt to regain the title. Although he failed to defeat Olsen, Roeber returned to the United States claiming he had regained the championship—a quickly uncovered canard that diminished his reputation. Roeber then engaged in aseries of sham bouts that initially generated interest and gate receipts but soon did his career irreparable harm. In a June 1901 defi, Harvey Parker claimed he could throw Roeber, to which the *National Police Gazette* sporting editor retorted "anyone can if he has the price." In the match itself, Parker, a welterweight close to forty years of age, defeated the former heavyweight champion, who "looked as if he quit." Roeber's activities destroyed public confidence not only in him but also in the legitimacy of the Greco-Roman style. After Roeber's fall, Greco-Roman continued primarily among strongman types employed by theaters to meet all challengers and, despite periodic attempts to resuscitate the style, it never again achieved the status it continued to maintain in Europe.[5]

Catch, however, did not escape many of the corrosive influences that befell Greco-Roman. A concern for maximizing profits helped push all professional wrestling, including catch matches, toward showmanship and entertainment and away from athletic competition. This economic factor drove professional wrestling away from legitimate contests (known as "shoots") toward rigged matches with predetermined finishes (known as "works"). The movement away from pure wrestling began as far back as William Muldoon's tenure as champion. Muldoon instituted time limits in his touring matches, a practice that became increasingly common, as a means of keeping his troupe on schedule and to limit the potential for defeat or injury. From this relatively benign alteration, professional wrestling slowly became an exercise in pure entertainment.[6]

This evolution partly derived from wrestling's decreasing status as a sporting pastime. Although it survived the late-nineteenth-century growing pains of the American sporting culture, unlike other popular sports of the time, such as pedestrianism and bicycling, wrestling gradually waned in popularity compared with baseball, boxing, and the burgeoning football cult. Faced with decreased revenues for their matches, wrestlers traversed the country wrestling more frequently in an attempt to offset the reduced income from individual matches. Touring became a means of scheduling matches against other touring professionals, rather than just meeting local challengers. Meeting other touring pros created the opportunity to discuss the match beforehand, which limited the physical risks inherent in the dangerous catch style, and to plan future encounters, which both simplified travel and reduced financial concerns. While touring to face local opponents continued, even this practice became an aspect of the increasingly worked nature of wrestling. Many professionals used an advance man to travel ahead of them to defeat the local champion, thereby setting up a highly anticipated, rigged match when the touring pro arrived.[7]

The shift toward wrestlers working in collusion, and the development of the catch style, emerged from the carnival subculture. The effects of carnivals on the development of modern professional wrestling are immense. Most carnivals and many circuses of the period included an athletic show (or, more commonly, "at show") attraction that included boxers, wrestlers, and strongmen. Carnivals hired these athletes to compete against carnival attendees. At show wrestlers engaged in rough bouts in which a local challenger would receive a monetary prize if he managed to last in the ring until the end (generally fifteen minutes) or successfully pinned the carnival wrestler. Under these circumstances, the wrestlers employed by the carnivals had to obtain falls as quickly as possible. The lumbering

Greco-Roman style, and the potential for a strong local man to hold his own at it, did not provide the carnival operators with the necessary house advantage, hence the faster, more skill-oriented catch style became the standard in at shows. The need to obtain quick victories also led to the development of painful submission holds, which became staples of the catch style. Wrestlers skilled in applying these potentially damaging moves were known as "hookers."[8]

To generate interest in the matches, carnival operators often employed two wrestlers to work together The "inside" man, the carnival champion, met all comers; the "outside" man, or "stick," pretended to be a normal audience member. The stick would volunteer to accept the at show champion's challenge, and the two then engaged in a spirited bout in which the outside man either emerged victorious or lasted the time limit, making the at show wrestler look weak and beatable. Matches of this nature helped wrestlers learn both the catch style and how to engage in believable "works." These skills could then be transferred to ostensibly legitimate professional wrestling matches outside of the carnival circuit. The experience provided by working the at shows proved so effective that these carnival attractions served as training grounds for professional wrestlers into the 1950s.[9]

A mentality about the general public developed among wrestlers who worked in the carnival at shows, particularly those who became promoters. These men developed a carnivalesque perception of paying customers as dupes to be financially swindled. To maintain a veil of secrecy concerning their moneymaking machinations, carnival workers invented a secret slang language, a variant of pig Latin. Wrestlers adopted this terminology and the notion of keeping the business secret (known as "kayfabe") after at show veterans came to dominate the wrestling industry. For example, wrestling promoters maintained the carnival practice of derisively referring to ticket buyers as "marks." To maintain public interest in professional wrestling in the "worked" era, a means of protecting the industry's secrets proved essential. Despite occasional exposés, defections, and governmental investigations, the kayfabe generally held until the 1980s.[10]

A 1905 *National Police Gazette* editorial posited that "nine out of ten [wrestling] bouts...are prearranged affairs." Despite this, undoubtedly correct, assertion, the *Police Gazette* continued to report events in the sport of wrestling and studiously noted those matches clearly "on the level." Therefore, even after the pernicious influence of the carnival entered professional wrestling, legitimate shoots continued to be held. However, these matches became increasingly rare, and only bouts involving two championship-caliber grapplers held the possibility of representing authentic contests. Although the decentralized nature of the sport facilitated the endemic corruption and unscrupulous behavior that created the environment for works to flourish, the lack of a governing body also forced nationally renowned catch wrestlers to engage in shoots with other contenders to protect their status. Once a promotional cartel developed during the World War I era, however, even this meager counter to fakery disappeared.[11]

The sport of boxing, which was more tightly regulated than wrestling, faced similar difficulties at the turn of the twentieth century. A spate of fixed fights involving top contenders such as Jim Corbett and Tom Sharkey created public mistrust of the sport. Nor did national exhibition tours continue to generate interest, as the sporting community no longer wanted "fancy bouts, hippodromes, or exhibitions." Professional boxers therefore sought to augment their income by staging sparring matches promoted as authentic contests; these matches only further eroded confidence in boxing. Outcries over the shadiness of boxing, coupled with lingering concerns over ring brutality, resulted in a number of states, most significantly New York, repealing the laws that had only recently made prizefights legal. Although public concern over wrestling "works" continued to grow, no states banned the sport, which strongly suggests a general, perhaps misguided, perception that grappling matches continued to be authentic contests.[12]

Wrestling, in fact, greatly benefited from the problems of the "manly art." As the *Police Gazette* noted, "while the ban is on boxing, the wrestlers have a chance to bask in the sunshine of prosperity." For members of the sporting community interested in "muscular amusement," wrestling provided the only outlet. Also, cast adrift by the banning of their sport, many boxers became professional wrestlers. Well-known fighters such as Sharkey, Bob Fitzsimmons, Gus Ruhlin, and Peter Maher donned tights to offset lost boxing income. Most of their matches presented very poor representations of the sport and were undoubtedly works, but the publicity surrounding such famous names helped wrestling's popularity. The success of these boxers-turned-wrestlers was a model for later wrestling promoters, who actively sought out washed-up fighters such as Joe Louis, Primo Carnera, and Jack Dempsey to add luster to the grappling game.[13]

Although catch dominated American wrestling only around the turn of the twentieth century, professionals used the style as early as the 1870s. The origins of the catch style can be traced to the influence of English wrestlers, such as Edwin Bibby, Joe Acton, and Tom Connors, who brought the dangerous Lancashire style to this country. Through incessant barnstorming, English wrestlers diffused the style across the United States. The Lancashire style found particular favor in the West, where wrestlers added elements of frontier brawling, the vestiges of rough-and-tumble, collar-and-elbow techniques, and bits of Greco-Roman to it. During the late 1880s a cross-pollination between catch and imported jiujitsu occurred, giving "American" catch its modern form. Although catch's influence became increasingly more difficult to discern as wrestling evolved, the style served as the foundation for all "worked" professional wrestling of the twentieth century.[14]

As practiced in the late nineteenth century, catch proved to be an especially dangerous and violent style of wrestling. Newspaper accounts of catch matches often noted encounters that ended with one combatant seriously injured and unable to continue, a by-product of the ability to earn a victory through submission as well as falls. As catch wrestler Frank Gotch noted, wrestlers in older styles relied on the "mechanical proposition of lever and fulcrum" for success, but catch stylists have "found that there is a more powerful influence toward making a man roll over on his back or simply quit outright... it is pain." Proficient catch wrestlers developed an arsenal of holds to destroy an opponent's will to fight. The most popular submission holds for catch wrestlers included the hammerlock, toehold (sometimes coupled with an arm lock), and the crotch hold and half nelson combination.[15]

Evan Lewis, the first great American catch stylist, established his career on a submission hold so dangerous it eventually became outlawed under *Police Gazette* rules. His use of the "stranglehold earned Lewis both the nickname "Strangler" and a fearsome reputation. Based in Wisconsin, Lewis first came to prominence in the late 1880s. He defeated all of the English catch stylists plying their trades in this country, and, on the basis of an 1887 victory over Joe

Acton, he claimed the catch championship. Lewis blended scientific skills, remarkable lower body strength, and a savage temperament to win matches "in murderous style." Many of his matches devolved into rough-and-tumble affairs in which he simply mauled his opponents into submission. In one representatively savage 1887 affair, Lewis butted, kicked, choked, and punched Tom Connors until the referee finally disqualified the American. The *Police Gazette* noted that the match "seemed like Hades cut loose for a holiday."[16]

Lewis served as the seminal figure in the transition from Greco-Roman dominance of the sport to the ascendancy of catch. As Greco-Roman champion in the immediate aftermath of Muldoon's retirement, Ernest Roeber was recognized as America's finest wrestler; as the finest practitioner of the coming catch style, Lewis represented his most obvious rival. The two met in March 1893, as part of a New Orleans "fistic carnival." To ensure equality, the competitors agreed to alternate falls between their two primary styles, with the first wrestler to win three falls declared the winner. Lewis emerged victorious after a desperate, five-fall match. Although Roeber won two falls in the Greco-Roman style, he struggled mightily to obtain them. Lewis's strong showing in the Greco-Roman style demonstrated his position as the nation's finest wrestler. His success also propelled the popularity of the catch style, which, after this match, gained recognition as both the most exciting and most challenging style of wrestling.[17]

Martin "Farmer" Burns wrested the title of America's best wrestler from Lewis in an April 1895 match in Chicago. A native of Cedar County, Iowa, Burns emerged from the same upper Midwest region as Lewis, the area of the country that developed into the hub of catch wrestling in this country. Born in 1861, Burns began wrestling at age 8 and had earned a strong local reputation by the time he reached young adulthood. During the late 1880s, he faced, and lost to, the touring pros who traveled through Iowa. An 1886 loss to Lewis via the stranglehold led Burns to focus on building his neck muscles. He eventually developed a 20-inch neck atop a frame of less than 170 pounds. Burns later used his remarkable neck strength to develop a carnival trick in which he swung from a hangman's noose without injury. In the spring of 1889, Burns took hogs to Chicago to sell and, while there, wrestled Lewis and Jack Carkeek, who were meeting all comers. With his skills improving,

Burns made a good showing and came to the attention of Tom Connors. The English veteran took the "Farmer," so dubbed because of the overalls he wore in matches, on the road with his athletic troupe. Burns spent the next several years touring the country under the tutelage of Connors. He won the title from the aging and indebted Lewis in a, possibly, worked finish. The indefatigable Burns parlayed this victory into a series of increasingly financially successful tours. He traveled with at shows, worked the state and county fair circuit, and frequently barnstormed with his own troupe of wrestlers. One of his favorite touring gimmicks consisted of facing entire college football or professional baseball teams, one man at a time, with a wager going to the team if any one member defeated him.[18]

Burns also helped popularize the catch style. He opened gymnasiums in Rock Island and Omaha for wrestlers to work out and train. He also developed mail-order courses to instruct young men in catch wrestling. These mail-order programs provided instruction in self-defense and health—Burns was an avid physical culturist—along with explanation of wrestling holds. The Farmer affected professional wrestling's course by training a generation of young catch stylists, often taking promising neophytes on tour with him to help develop their skills. Prominent early-twentieth-century catch wrestlers such as Emil Klank, Bob Mangoff, Sr., William Demetral, Charles Olsen, Jack Reynolds, and Earl Caddock owed much of their success to Burns's mentorship. Like William Muldoon before him, Burns also occasionally helped boxers get into shape. Most famously, he worked with Jim Jeffries before the former champion's 1910 bout with Jack Johnson.

Burns's most famous wrestling pupil proved to be a burly Iowan named Frank Gotch. Born and raised in Humboldt, Gotch developed a local wrestling reputation as an adolescent. In 1898 Gotch, barely out of his teens, lost to barnstorming professionals Dan McLeod and "Farmer" Burns. However, Gotch performed well enough that Burns offered to train the youngster. In the summer of 1901, Burns sent Gotch, under the name "Frank Kennedy," to Alaska with a group of professionals. On this northern tour, Gotch proved his mettle against a series of local opponents and veteran professionals, including an aged Colonel James McLaughlin. His success in the Klondike led Burns to take the young wrestler on tour with him. While on the road with Burns, Gotch both perfected his most feared hold, the stepover toehold, and developed a tendency toward rough tactics.[19]

By 1903, Gotch positioned himself as a legitimate contender for the American catch championship. The current champion was a one-eyed, illiterate former mill worker from Cleveland named Tom Jenkins. He obtained the title by demonstrating his superiority over Dan McLeod, who had previously vanquished Burns, in a series of rough matches. Jenkins approached the sport much the same way as Lewis. He often used dirty tactics and lost a number of matches because of disqualification. Jenkins also developed a modified version of the stranglehold, known as the "jaw lock," to circumvent the banning of Lewis's submission hold.[20]

The rise of Gotch created a golden opportunity for Jenkins. The Ohioan defeated Roeber in a suspect 1901 match and, after his rivalry with McLeod petered out, found himself bereft of viable American challengers. A *Police Gazette* editorial noted that wrestling "was declining in popularity for the sole reason that no aspirants for championship distinction capable of disputing the possessorship of the title...had been exploited." Jenkins's popularity also suffered after a series of disastrous defeats at the hands of a variety of "Terrible Turks." With Gotch looming on the horizon, Jenkins once again had a marketable contender for his title. For Gotch, Jenkins became his first great rival and the opponent upon whom he built his national reputation. Beginning in February 1903, the two grapplers engaged in eight matches over as many years. Jenkins won the first encounter and two 1905 bouts, but Gotch earned victories in five of the contests, including a January 1904 disqualification win referred to by Gotch's biographer as the "roughest wrestling match ever held."[21]

Gotch's May 1906 victory over Jenkins established him as the undisputed American catch champion. Like his mentor Farmer Burns, Gotch toured incessantly, often with Burns and his other protégés in tow. By 1906, he averaged three matches per week, with the *Police Gazette* referring to him as the "busiest wrestler in the country." Gotch briefly lost the American title to diminutive Wisconsin-native Fred Beell in December 1906, but the Iowan won the rematch later that month. After the loss to Beell, Gotch went undefeated for the rest of his career. Having systematically eliminated all legitimate American opponents, Gotch found himself in the same position that had bedeviled Tom Jenkins. With little prospect of substantial financial return from another round of matches with American wrestlers, Gotch dramatically reduced his touring. He spent 1907 buying up Iowa farmland and packing on weight. The American champion only wrestled five times that year. Gotch even toyed with the notion of becoming a professional boxer, especially after the 1906 renewal of prizefighting in New York state (which killed wrestling in New York City, the nation's sporting capital). He avoided this change of occupation by facing his greatest rival of all—George Hackenschmidt.[22]

Known as the "Russian Lion," Hackenschmidt may have been the most famous athlete in Europe during the early twentieth century. After gaining acclaim in Russia as a strongman (he remains a revered figure in bodybuilding circles), Hackenschmidt began training in the Greco-Roman style. By 1901, he had won tournaments in that style held in Vienna, Budapest, Hamburg, Frankfurt, Munich, Berlin, Paris, and numerous smaller cities. The Russian, having earned the title of European Greco-Roman champion, then moved his base of operations to London. He propelled a wave of wrestling popularity in England that pulled American wrestlers across the Atlantic. These touring American pros, such as Jack Carkeek, helped spread the "American" version of catch to the British Isles, where the Lancashire version already possessed many adherents. Hackenschmidt, cognizant of the growing popularity of the catch style, competed in catch matches while in England; the Greco-Roman style, however, always remained his forte.[23]

To solidify his claim to the world championship, Hackenschmidt came to the United States. Although he engaged in a number of minor bouts, the Russian's primary concern rested on defeating Tom Jenkins. In May 1905, Hackenschmidt vanquished Jenkins in a catch match promoted as a world championship bout. Coupled with the Russian's victory over Jenkins in a 1904 Greco-Roman encounter, this win gave the Russian Lion an undisputed claim to the title. During Hackenschmidt's American tour, Gotch repeatedly challenged the Russian. The Russian recognized the inherent dangers of facing Gotch in a catch bout and undoubtedly found the risk outweighed any potential reward, particularly as Gotch had little name recognition outside the United States. Hackenschmidt, therefore, refused all of Gotch's overtures and returned to England that summer.[24]

After returning to Europe, Hackenschmidt wrestled primarily in catch matches, with the occasional Greco-Roman bout as well. His success in both styles waned and created a situation in which he, as subsequently developed with Gotch, his revenues declined because of a lack of worthy challengers. Therefore, by 1908 the Russian Lion had earned a reputation in Europe as unbeatable. His stature and lack of viable European opponents led Hackenschmidt to consider returning to the United States to face Gotch, a decision that stemmed from both financial concerns and anger over Gotch's stinging claims that Hackenschmidt lacked the courage to face him.

Hackenschmidt eventually agreed to the match after wrestling promoter William Wittig offered him $10,000. The Russian wrestler arrived in the United States in March 1908, with the bout scheduled for April 3 in Chicago. Even before Hackenschmidt landed on these shores a massive publicity campaign about the bout began. Many newspaper articles focused on the symbolism of America versus the Old World. Gotch, the Iowa farmboy, seemed to embody the rough-and-tumble nature of American fighting styles/struggles, while Hackenshmidt, staid and mannered, epitomized a classical, gentlemanly European style. Further, Hackenschmidt's victory over Jenkins in the "American" catch style gave Gotch the added significance of serving as the avenger of an earlier national humiliation. While contemporary accounts did not promote the match in the "hero versus villain" mode of later professional wrestling, the seeds of that notion can be discerned from this 1908 encounter.[25]

The bout drew six thousand spectators to Dexter Park Pavilion, with ringside boxes for $20. Gotch's strategy involved a combination of questionable tactics to anger Hackenschmidt ("principally thumbing of the eyes") and defensive maneuvers calculated to wear down the Russian. After more than one-and-a-half hours of wrestling, Hackenschmidt repeatedly offered to call the match a draw; Gotch refused. Just past the two-hour mark Hackenschmidt conceded the match and the world championship, which the Chicago *Tribune* noted now "goes where it belongs." Immediately after the match Hackenschmidt stated that "Gotch beat me and I have to acknowledge it." However, in an attempt to protect his reputation among European patrons, the Russian later claimed that Gotch came to the ring covered in oil, which prevented the Lion from

obtaining holds. Although Gotch blasted Hackenschmidt for ac-
cusing him of cheating, the controversy over the match helped pave
the way for an even more profitable rematch.[26]

The victory over Hackenschmidt brought Gotch to the pinnacle
of his popularity. A natural-born self-promoter, the Iowan parlayed
his world championship into a successful series of exhibition tours
(including one in Europe), profitable title defenses, and a starring
role in the play "All About A Bout," in which he nightly wrestled
Emil Klank. Gotch's post-Hackenschmidt ascension as a national
sporting hero involved far more, than the new champion's good
looks and the vanquishing of a foreign foe. As with so many other
instances in the early history of professional wrestling, the rise of
grappling at the end of the first decade of the twentieth century
hinged on a decline in the sport of boxing. In this instance, Gotch's
fame grew as a counter to Jack Johnson's infamy.

With his defeat of Tommy Burns in December 1908, Texan Jack
Johnson became boxing's heavyweight champion. His victory over
a non-American champion, however, did not prompt the same sort
of patriotic outpouring as Gotch's Chicago success. Race trumped
nationalism in 1908 America, and the African-American Johnson
became an instant national villain. His control of the championship sent boxing into a decline that greatly benefited the contact
sports of wrestling and football. Johnson's physical prowess, gold
teeth, flashy clothes, and white girlfriends (and wives) led to race
riots, the banning of fight films, the passage of the White Slave
Traffic Act (Mann Act), and the champion's departure from this
country to escape federal indictments. The specter of an African-
American heavyweight champion led novelist Jack London to issue
a call for a "great white hope" to redeem boxing.[27]

Johnson's easy disposal of the "white hopes" who endeavored
to wrest the title from him only increased the urgency and des-
peration of racist Americans clambering for a new champion. Not
surprisingly, then, the cry eventually included a plea to Frank
Gotch to fight Johnson, a move the wrestling champion astutely
avoided. Gotch, however, clearly felt the "white hopes" exemplified an important crusade. For example, he and "Farmer" Burns
helped train ex-champion Jim Jeffries, the greatest of all "white
hopes," for his 1910 bout with Johnson. Also, one newspaper reported that his January 1904 match with Jenkins "will not only
decide who is champion of America but the championship of the

Anglo-Saxon race, according to the articles of agreement." Gotch himself wrestled Silas Archer during his Klondike tour, but never again faced another African-American in the ring. While it appears unlikely that Gotch, given his connections to Jeffries, would have given an African-American a shot at his title, wrestling's nineteenth-century color line proved so effective that no African-Americans figured prominently in the sport during Gotch's tenure. Despite his questionable views concerning African-Americans, Gotch did display a willingness to wrestle Catholics, southern European immigrants, and Native Americans—other groups facing open discrimination during this period.[28]

Even with his popularity, the ravages of touring wore on Gotch, and he increasingly limited his public appearances to official title defenses as the decade came to a close. These bouts continued to draw large crowds, but, once again, the lack of publicly acclaimed opponents created concern that wrestling's popularity faced a decline. Gotch's dismantling of his challengers also helped create an air of invincibility around the champion that did little to generate increased excitement in his matches. For example, in June 1910, Gotch pinned the highly regarded Pole Stanislaus Zbyszko in six seconds. The dearth of new American challengers led Gotch to once again enter the ring against the "Russian Lion."[29]

Despite Hackenschmidt's earlier loss to Gotch, the Russian remained highly regarded in Europe. Also despite this defeat, Hackenschmidt represented a potentially lucrative payday against Gotch, thanks to his name recognition and Gotch's defeat of all other contenders. The Russian Lion returned to the United States in late 1910 under the management of Jack Curley, a promoter destined to play a significant role in the creation of pro wrestling's "worked" era. Curley toured Hackenschmidt across the country to generate interest in the Gotch rematch; he then orchestrated a masterful promotional campaign for the September 1911 bout. His ballyhoo swept away all doubts over Hackenschmidt's previous difficulties. Even the Chicago *Tribune*, which curtly dismissed the Russian as a "quitter" after the 1908 match, joined the chorus trumpeting the rematch as a "clash of modern giants" that "resembles [the] match in Homer's 'Illiad.'" The bout, held in Chicago's Comiskey Park, drew a record crowd of thirty thousand and netted promoter Curley $44,000. The match, however, turned out to be a fiasco. Hackenschmidt, hobbled by a knee injured in training and deeply fearful of Gotch, tried to forfeit rather than face the champion. Curley convinced the Russian to enter the ring but declared "all bets were off," an obvious indication to the crowd of chicanery. Gotch scored two falls in less than twenty minutes. Fans in ringside seats heard Hackenschmidt tell referee Ed Smith of his intention to willingly fall backward and yield the second fall to Gotch. With another about-face, the Chicago *Tribune* blasted the "Russian Lamb," noting that "the public had no intimation that he would lie down at the first plausible opportunity, but that, as since discovered, was exactly what he intended to do—and did."[30]

The Gotch-Hackenschmidt rematch fiasco did irreparable harm to professional wrestling. Already reeling from more than a decade of concerns over the legitimacy of matches, the Chicago debacle, occurring in a highly touted world championship bout, destroyed much of the remaining public faith in wrestling. Gotch, who appeared to be innocent of the dissembling in Chicago, continued to defend his title against inconsequential opponents before announcing his retirement in April 1913. The champion declared his intention to leave the ring on several previous occasions but had not, as he did in 1913, ever publicly relinquished the world championship. Gotch's abandonment of the title left professional wrestling without a champion. Several men, seeking to control the sport, then claimed to be champion. The primary victim of this chaotic situation proved to be legitimate professional wrestling. It took several years for order to be restored, and when peace returned, the "worked" era began.[31]

4

THE ART OF DECEPTION

The retirement of Frank Gotch left the greatest prize in wrestling—
the world heavyweight championship—available to any man who
laid claim to it. This chaotic circumstance briefly revived interest
in the sport; with Gotch, perceived as unbeatable, no longer in
the mix, competitive championship matches seemed possible.
However, no American wrestler possessed Gotch's popularity,
reputation, or skills. Coupled with the lack of a national regulatory
organization, this disorder left promoters and wrestlers scrambling
to fill the sport's power vacuum. This battle for control led to a
spate of shooting matches for the title, but once a measure of order
occurred, those in command of wrestling moved to consolidate
their position by ending the unpredictability of shoots. Worked
matches grew throughout the twentieth century and came to be the
norm after World War I. Wrestling's period as a legitimate professional sport had ended. By the late 1930s, wrestling barely resembled the catch-based encounters of the early twentieth century. As
sports commentator Robert Weaver noted, "in recent years wrestling has become a professional sport, which anyone who has seen a
professional bout will admit is pure showmanship."[1]

Although Gotch possessed no concrete powers beyond being
the ostensibly retired champion, he proposed a solution to the
championship confusion. In January 1914, he suggested that Fred
Beell and Gus "Americus" Schoenlein should meet for the world

championship, with Gotch acknowledging the winner as his successor. By this point, Henry Ordemann, Jess Westegaard, and Dr. Benjamin F. Roller had already claimed the title. Less than one year after Gotch's suggestion Charles Cutler, the American champion at that time, also declared himself world champion. To complicate the title issue further, Gotch made sporadic appearances in the ring until breaking his leg during training in 1916. He defeated several of the top wrestlers, including Ordemann and Cutler, thereby demonstrating the second-rate nature of many of the top contenders. The retirement of Gotch, confusion over the title, and lack of a charismatic figure to replace the Iowan all contributed to a dip in wrestling's popularity. The chaotic championship situation probably hurt the sport the most. Not until July 1915 did Joe Stecher emerge as the generally recognized title claimant. Stecher, however, did not possess the name recognition or charisma of Gotch.[2]

Born in Nebraska, Stecher turned pro in 1912 and quickly established himself as one of the preeminent wrestlers in the Midwest (the leading pro wrestling region at the time). Trained by B. F. Roller, Stecher developed a fearsome body scissors as a submission hold. Stecher's victory over Cutler in July 1915 restored order somewhat to the championship picture. Despite a loss to John Olin that established a short-lived title branch, Stecher remained consensus champion until 1917. Stecher was probably the last champion to engage in a scheduled shooting match to defend his title. The struggle to claim the championship propelled a short burst of nonworked matches, as the various claimants battled for the title and its concomitant financial rewards. These matches, however, helped demonstrate that the public quickly tired of long, slow matches. In what may have been the last title shoot, Stecher and Ed "Strangler" Lewis pushed each other around an Omaha ring for more than five hours in July 1916 before the referee mercifully called the match a draw. With no wrestler able to generate the excitement of Frank Gotch and the attendance figures dwindling, professional wrestling faced a dire circumstance. To survive as a economically viable operation, the sport fundamentally altered. No longer a legitimate sporting contest, wrestling became pure entertainment under the guise of an athletic endeavor.[3]

A handful of promoters, managers, and wrestlers were the driving force behind this shift. Many of them emerged from carnival backgrounds and displayed the influence of that business's view of customers as "marks" to be duped and exploited. Chief among the promoters who transformed professional wrestling stood Jack Curley. Although he began his career as a turn-of-the-century Chicago boxing promoter, Curley soon moved into the lucrative (and less regulated) world of wrestling. He managed B. F. Roller and promoted many of Frank Gotch's matches (including the 1911 bout with Hackenschmidt). Curley befriended Jack Johnson and promoted many of the boxing champion's title defenses, including the 1915 match in which the Texan lost his title to Jess Willard. Displaying the determination to embrace profits over personal loyalties that made him so successful, Curley abandoned Johnson and became Willard's manager. His new charge toured as an attraction with the Sells-Floto Circus, with a newly-retired Gotch in tow. Curley's time with the circus proved short-lived, thanks to Willard's surly disposition, but his experience proved enormously significant for the future of wrestling.[4]

Recognizing the economic potential of professional wrestling, Curley abandoned boxing to promote wrestling matches exclusively in late 1915. His efforts focused on establishing promotional control of matches in the northeast, with his base being New York City's Madison Square Garden. Curley successfully spent the next few years building a promotional empire along the East Coast. His efforts to reestablish wrestling in the industrial northeast benefited greatly from the hindrances facing professional boxing, which suffered from periodic banning and convoluted regulations regarding bout decisions. Curley, however, faced difficulties in sustaining his gains because of the lack of prominent eastern wrestlers. The Plains, which produced Gotch, Burns, and Stecher, remained the locus of the sport. To create a vast and sustainable wrestling empire, Curley needed to develop ties to the wrestling powers of the Midwest.

In the West, Gene Melady dominated wrestling promotions. A former Notre Dame football player, Melady made a fortune in the livestock business and parlayed his earnings into a successful career promoting wrestling in the Midwest. While Melady lacked Curley's grand vision, he did control the new world's champion, Earl Caddock. The son of Jewish immigrants and raised in Iowa, Caddock turned pro only in 1915, but, thanks to the promotional work of manager Melady, he rose rapidly in public opinion. Melady dubbed Caddock "the man of a thousand holds" and greatly improved the young wrestler's skills by sending him to Gotch and Burns for training. In April 1917,

Caddock met Stecher for the championship in a Melady-promoted Omaha bout that drew almost eight thousand fans. After the men split the first two falls, an exhausted Stecher refused to return to the ring for the third and forfeited the title to Caddock, who spent the rest of the year defending his new title.[5]

Curley's planned promotional demesne required an agreement with Melady and the western promoters. The New York promoter recognized that the decentralized nature of the wrestling business, the tediousness of long shoot matches, and the independence of wrestlers all contributed to wrestling's declining status as a form of entertainment. Curley recognized that, as historian John Dizikes later noted, the inherent rhythms of American amusements were predicated on speed and immediate results. The excitement engendered by boxing knockouts, motion pictures, and the startling home run power of Babe Ruth demonstrated to Curley that professional wrestling required a dramatic overhaul to stay competitive in the box office market. Curley and the other promoters, therefore, agreed to a variety of rule changes, including the adoption of time limits, referee's decisions (to alleviate the public anger over time limit draws), and the increasing usage of one-fall matches. Most important, they recognized that through cooperative effort promoters could dominate the sport and effectively eliminate the bargaining power of independent-minded wrestlers. As the controlling force in wrestling, promoters could maximize profits by carefully establishing new stars and through selective scheduling of matches. For this plan to succeed, "works" had to be an integral part of professional wrestling. However, by virtue of their authority over wrestling, the promoters could skillfully organize matches with a view toward long-term benefits and avoid destroying the wrestling market in a town the way the "crossroaders" of traveling troupes, with their crudely fixed betting schemes, had in the past. The machinations of Curley and the other promoters did not go completely unnoticed at the time. An unnamed editor of *Baseball Magazine* decried both the worked nature of wrestling and that "the soft, big-bodied, fat-faced men who live by wit and by the straining sinews of far better men [have] laid their fell claws upon the wrestling game." Attacks such as this one, however, failed to either curb the power of promoters or dissuade many Americans from attending wrestling matches.[6]

One aspect of Curley's plan to manipulate wrestling involved establishing a champion wrestling fans in the urban East would recognize. To that end, he staged a December 1917 tournament in New York that drew the nation's leading matmen. Curley may have intended the tournament to serve as a springboard for developing Caddock into a national drawing power. However, after a disagreement over the Nebraskan's demand that he be billed as the world champion during the tournament, Caddock left the event early in the proceedings. Curley then crowned Stanislaus Zbyszko's younger brother Wladek as the new champion. Zbyszko defeated Ed "Strangler" Lewis in the tournament final, thereby positioning himself as the heir to a disputed title lineage that originated with John Olin's 1916 victory over Joe Stecher. Curley's control of a "champion" then allowed him to leverage Caddock into cooperating with the promoter.

Western promoters, however, engaged in a bitter struggle with Curley to retain their dominance in the business. After much wrangling, the rival promotional factions agreed to stage the May 1918 Zbyszko-Caddock bout in Des Moines. Caddock solidified his claim to the championship by defeating the Pole in three falls before a crowd of eight thousand. In keeping with Curley's notions of streamlining, the bout had a time limit and Caddock won the third fall via referee's decision. The prematch disagreement over location, however, led Curley to develop plans to circumvent (and eventually undermine) the power of the western wrestling promoters, rather than attempt to involve them in a wrestling cartel. Curley's efforts to destroy Melady and Oscar Thorson improved when the United States entered World War I. Caddock, Stecher, and other leading wrestlers, having been drafted into military service, could not continue the wrestling careers for the duration of the war, which enabled Curley to establish another personal world champion without facing challenges from the bereft-of-talent western promoters.

Curley once again placed the title on Wladek Zbyszko, whom a military doctor ruled unfit for service due to the loss of hearing caused by the wrestler's "cauliflower" ears. In early 1919, Stecher's military service ended, and he allied himself with the New York promoter. Stecher and Zbyszko met several times in Curley-promoted matches during 1919, with the title freely exchanged back and forth. The combined success of the Stecher-Zbyszko battles and his Madison Square Garden matches enabled Curley to provide wrestlers and assistance to promoters throughout the eastern United States.

Curley maintained control over a multitude of compliant wrestlers whom he sent to wrestle for aligned promoters. This promotional network allowed Curley to both assert his authority beyond his New York base and helped establish larger reputations for wrestlers in his organization.

Along with Stecher and Zbyszko, Curley used Ed "Strangler" Lewis for many of his main event matches in the postwar period. Born Robert Fredericks, Lewis co-opted the name of the original "Strangler" Lewis in the early 1910s. Lewis eventually mastered a feared stranglehold but met with only moderate success in his early career. While competing in Kentucky in 1914, Lewis became associated with promoter-manager Billy Sandow (who previously wrestled as "Young Muldoon"). By the late 1910s, Lewis had established himself as one of the leading wrestlers in the country (and also claimed a version of the world championship). During 1919, Curley used Lewis as a foil for Zbyszko and Stecher in matches across the country. Having established reputations for all three of these men, Curley made them the main attractions at a late 1919 New York tournament to crown a world champion; Stecher emerged with the title.[7]

Earl Caddock did not receive his military discharge until mid-1919 and did not compete in the New York tournament. However, despite a wartime claim of retirement and injuries suffered during a phosgene gas attack, Caddock announced his return to the ring and sided with Curley in his war with western promoters. In January 1920, Curley promoted a Caddock-Stecher unification bout that proved to be one of the most successful wrestling matches in history. The bout drew ten thousand people to Madison Square Garden, and Curley claimed the gate topped $75,000. Stecher won both the match and a claim to the undisputed world championship. The Caddock-Stecher match, however, marked the peak of Jack Curley's wrestling dominance. He successfully promoted matches throughout the eastern United States, but events in New York sapped Curley of much of his power. The newly organized New York State Athletic Commission, with William Muldoon as a member, exerted increased control over boxing and wrestling in the Empire State. Their decrees included one-fall matches, a banning of punishing holds (including Lewis's stranglehold), and mandatory licensing of promoters. Curley dominated New York wrestling, but the watchful eye of the commission restrained his freedom of activity. Even more damaging to the wrestling czar, he lost a power struggle with boxing promoter George "Tex" Rickard, which dislodged Curley as the ruler of Madison Square Garden. While wrestling shows continued to occur at the Garden, Curley no longer had his choice of dates and faced an ever-present danger, of losing his right, at the whim of his great rival, to promote matches in the venue.[8]

Curley compounded his miseries by making an enormous tactical error. In December 1920, he instructed Stecher to drop the title to Ed Lewis. Curley's decision was based in part on a serious injury Stecher suffered earlier in the year that reduced his touring abilities, but Lewis's taste of power as undisputed champion led him to plot to break Curley's control of wrestling. Lewis also felt that Curley betrayed him by not standing up to the New York commission when that body made Lewis's headlock illegal. The Strangler dutifully lost the title to Curley's friend Stanislaus Zbyszko in May 1921, but this appears to be the end of his kowtowing to the promoter. Lewis's manager Billy Sandow conspired with Zbyszko to desert Curley, and the Polish wrestler obliged by losing the title to Lewis in a November 1921 Madison Square Garden match promoted by Tex Rickard. Curley lost the title, control of wrestling, and his most prominent venue in the aftermath of this bout. Although Curley continued to dominate wrestling in New York, he no longer had the leverage to dictate to promoters across the country. And after Rickard oversaw construction of the "new" Madison Square Garden in 1923, Curley found himself closed out of Manhattan's sports mecca.[9]

Sandow, Lewis, and a bulky "Farmer" Burns–trained wrestler named Joe "Toots" Mondt, who served as their all-around troubleshooter and idea man, used their control of the title to position themselves as the major force in wrestling. This group, later dubbed the "Gold Dust Trio," recognized, in ways that initially eluded Curley, that the worked nature of professional wrestling could be used to generate more excitement. The trio developed elaborate means of ending matches that ensured large crowds for return bouts (known in wrestling as a "program"). Finishes that became staples of professional wrestling, such as out-of-ring count outs, double count outs due to head bumps, and "broadways" (time-limit draws that ended just as one wrestler was about to win), all originated with the Gold Dust Trio. The group also skillfully developed interest in Lewis title defenses by building up the reputation of

potential challengers. Title contenders engaged in carefully orchestrated series of matches calculated to establish them as legitimate opponents for the champion. Influenced by the entertainment
rhythms of vaudeville, they sought to end matches "with a flash."
The Sandow combine, however, did not possess Curley's promotional connections and also feared that the promoter might find a
devious means of stealing back the title if they ventured into New
York City. As a result, Lewis defended his title mostly in the Midwest, to reasonably large crowds, but could not fully exploit his
position as champion by scheduling matches in the urban areas of
the Atlantic seaboard.[10]

Wrestling's power brokers clearly learned the benefits of controlling the heavyweight championship by observing the example
set by Jack Dempsey's handlers. Nothing more than a tough but
mediocre western heavyweight willing to take dives in his early
career, Dempsey fortuitously allied himself with manager Jack
"Doc" Kearns, also a sometime wrestling manager, who promoted
the fighter as a "man killer." Dempsey and Kearns eventually caught
the eye of New York promoter George "Tex" Rickard, who used his
control of Madison Square Garden to make the "Manassas Mauler"
into a contender. Kearns and Rickard skillfully selected opponents
for Dempsey to ensure that he maintained the title, which kept
them at the forefront of the boxing business, and they used a vast
promotional machine to generate excitement over these mis-
matches. Wrestling's power brokers simply adopted the same
methods, made easier by the worked nature of wrestling matches,
and kept the heavyweight title on whomever seemed capable of
generating the most revenue.[11]

Wrestling champions, however, did not draw the million-dollar
gates that Rickard organized for Dempsey, which meant they had
to defend the title more frequently than their wrestling counter-
parts. Despite the Sandow group's effective means of building
contenders for Lewis's crown, the pool of skillful wrestlers pro-
motable as contenders was limited. By 1925, Lewis's dispatch of
the nation's leading wrestlers made it difficult to find recognizable
opponents to draw profitable gates. Sandow's answer proved to be
one of the turning points in the history of professional wrestling.
With a wrestler's grappling skills no longer the determining factor
in match decisions, Sandow recognized that a charismatic individual, with little or no actual wrestling ability, could be built into

a champion. He solved the dilemma of a dearth of marketable title challengers by orchestrating the rise of Wayne "Big" Munn. Already known in sporting circles thanks to his football career at the University of Nebraska, Munn's six feet six, 260-pound frame allowed Sandow to promote the wrestling neophyte as a giant capable of battering more experienced wrestlers into submission.[12]

In January 1925, Munn defeated Lewis for the championship. Sandow's ultimate plan involved developing a "program" between Lewis and Munn, with Lewis winning the title back in a return match to set up a final showdown (the part of a "program" later known as the "blow off"). This scheme, however, never came to fruition. In one of the most famous double-crosses in wrestling history, Stanislaus Zbyszko turned his April 1925 match with Munn into a shoot (a legitimate contest) and won the title. During the match, Sandow berated Zbyszko for his duplicity but to no avail. The slippery Zbyszko had personal ties to Curley (although that did not prevent his 1921 defection) and also harbored resentment toward the Gold Dust Trio for ordering him to lose (known as "jobbing") a number of matches in 1924. The aging Zbyszko, contemplating retirement from the ring, decided to couple revenge on the Trio with a payoff from Curley and steal the title. The Pole dropped the title to Stecher in St. Louis the next month, and the Gold Dust Trio's period of dominance ended.[13]

Joe Stecher's title win returned control of wrestling to the promoters. Although Curley did not dominate the business as he did in the immediate postwar period, he represented an integral part of the wrestling trust that developed during Stecher's title run. Along with Curley, promoters from across the country such as Lou Daro, Tom Packs, and the champion's brother, Tony, again began to work in concert. The trust's extensive network exerted a control over wrestling east of the Mississippi River that once again tipped the balance of power toward promoters and away from individual wrestlers. This arrangement proved highly successful for the promoters, who, generally, worked together to maximize profits. With individual trust members operating out of different regions, an informal division of wrestling markets occurred, in which trust-affiliated promoters agreed to not book shows within regions controlled by other promoters. By 1925, wrestling developed the notion of territories (areas of the country as the exclusive domains of specific promoters) that would serve as the foundation of the business until Vince K. McMahon's systematic destruction of wrestling regionalism in the 1980s.

With the champion expecting nothing more from his matches than a worked finish, however, the trust faced the dilemma of potential double-crosses from title challengers. It became imperative to ensure the loyalty of any wrestler granted a match with the champion. The extensive reach of the trust allowed it to present the potentially career-ending threat of blacklisting for any wrestler unwilling to lose on demand. Those wrestlers still wrestling outside the trust found it difficult to survive financially with trust-controlled venues closed to them, and they often supported themselves by working the at shows or appearing on cards in the less-regulated Far West. The continued operation of small, nontrust promoters provided the "trust busters" with reasonably steady bookings, but these independents could not offer the same level of financial remuneration as trust promoters. These trust busters also used the press in attempts to leverage the trust into giving them title shots. By portraying these wrestlers as legitimate contenders, sportswriters forced the promotional cartel to find methods to silence the trust busters.

The most obvious means of deflecting trust buster accusations involved co-opting these independent operators and convincing them to follow the dictates of the trust. Although working for the trust held the potential of championship laurels, the most fundamental benefit for former trust busters involved steady work and a guaranteed income outside the vicissitudes of independent promotions. For a trust buster such as Marin Plestina, joining the trust represented the only option for effectively supporting his family while working as a professional wrestler. Active since the 1910s (and trained by Farmer Burns), Plestina generated little public excitement because of his plodding, defensive style, but his mat skills made him a dangerous opponent for trust-controlled champions. His manager J. C. Marsh trumpeted Plestina as the uncrowned world champion, but the wrestler's refusal to engage in works left him with no option but to work either for independent promoters or on barnstorming tours. Broke and widowed with four children, Plestina signed on with the trust in April 1926 out of financial necessity. Thereafter, he obtained steady work but suffered the humiliation of jobbing to wrestlers with less skill but more charisma.[14]

Those trust busters who proved unwilling to kowtow to the promotional cartels' whims presented a more complicated problem. The trust eventually solved this situation by developing a cadre of tough and loyal wrestlers known as "policemen." The trust presented well-known independents too successful to be ignored the opportunity to wrestle "policemen." For a trust buster, wading through the "policemen" meant establishing his reputation as a legitimate title contender; for the trust, victory by a "policeman" over an independent meant discrediting the trust buster. The trust's most ferocious "policeman" of the 1920s was John Pesek. Known as the "Nebraska Tigerman," Pesek was the perfect "policeman" for the trust (he previously performed similar duty for the Gold Dust Trio). A master of the double wristlock–head scissors combination hold, he coupled great wrestling skills and unswerving loyalty to the trust with a nasty ring disposition. The Tigerman defeated all of the leading trust busters, including Plestina, Charles Hansen (another Burns protégé), Jack Taylor, and former Olympian Nat Pendleton. Pesek also appeared to enjoy injuring opponents, and his reputation for brutality dissuaded many independent wrestlers from challenging the trust.[15]

The trust managed to maintain control of wrestling until the late 1920s. Stecher proved to be an able champion, who could handle potential double-crosses. However, by 1928, he had repeatedly defeated all the leading contenders, and the promoters recognized that the public began to grow tired of his reign. Stecher also wanted to scale back his wrestling career to spend more time at his Nebraska ranch. With the approval of the western-most trust promoters, Stecher lost the title to Strangler Lewis in St. Louis in February 1928. Lewis, chastened by the decline of his influence after losing control of the title, became part of the trust to support himself. Although Lewis's loyalty seemed suspect, the nature of the business had changed to such an extent by 1928 that the trust did not fear a potential double-cross from him. Even if Lewis wanted to use the championship to regain dominance of wrestling, the trust's control of venues and wrestlers made such a move impossible. And as the most recognizable name in the sport, Lewis represented the most obvious choice to replace Stecher as champion.

Lewis's fame came not only from his long career and previous tenure as champion but also from the benefits of positive press coverage by sportswriters of the period. The 1920s status as the "golden age of sports" in this country rests, to a significant degree, on the promotional work of newspaper sportswriters. These newspapermen, thanks to the editorial independence of many sports sections, presented hyperbolic portraits of athletes that helped develop public images of these individuals as superhuman characters engaged in titanic sporting struggles. Sportswriters engaged in a symbiotic relationship with athletes in which the ballyhoo of writers helped increase ticket sales for sporting events, while the athletes colluded with sportswriters in creating public images for the "physically famous," which drove the interest of the reading public. Figures such as Babe Ruth, Jack Dempsey, and Red Grange benefited from the publicity to become national celebrities even nonsports fans recognized. Although no wrestler achieved the fame of these three, the sporting press did help construct national reputations for leading grapplers. For example, Strangler Lewis, the nation's best-known wrestler of the decade, found himself courted by the trust and able to obtain lucrative bookings despite his checkered past relations with the promoters due in part to the way friendly sportswriters portrayed him.[16]

The trust may have benefited from the loyalty of sportswriters, but it collapsed because of the duplicity of its own members. Lewis, in a move similar to the treachery he suffered at the hands of Zbyszko, accepted a payoff from Paul Bowser, the trust's Boston promoter, and lost the title to Gus Sonnenberg. Given that the promoters based their business on falsely presenting a rehearsed form of entertainment as an authentic sport to an audience they considered gullible and contemptuous, Bowser's underhanded actions are not surprising. To Curley and the marginalized Midwestern promoters, however, the theft of the title and Bowser's declaration of independence were unexpected. Bowser's machinations instigated a shuffling of alliances within the now broken trust, as promoters attempted to remain vital by maintaining connections with promoters outside of their home territories. Curley, for example, allied himself with Mondt and Philadelphia promoter Ray Fabiani.

One aspect of Curley's plan to parry Bowser involved reviving a tactic he pioneered during Earl Caddock's absence from the country: declaring his own champion. As part of making Sonnenberg champion, Bowser gave the new titlist a belt and declared him to be champion of the newly constituted American Wrestling Association (AWA). Curley and his associates countered by convincing the

National Boxing Association, the collective of state athletic commissions that regulated boxing, not only to organize a wrestling division subsequently named the National Wrestling Association (NWA) but also to recognize a champion put forth by the New York wresting king. Dick Shikat, a burly German import managed by Mondt, then became the first NWA heavyweight champion. The creation of multiple champions not only hindered the popularity of wrestling but also illustrated to the promoters that, with the wrestling world once again splintered, control of the most popular wrestlers would determine which promoters succeeded.[17]

Initially, Bowser maintained the upper hand in the struggle between promoters. Strangler Lewis not only worked for his promotion but the Boston promoter possessed the more popular of the two competing world champions. A distant antecedent of Bill Goldberg, Gus Sonnenberg first achieved fame as a member of the Dartmouth football team. Because of his superior physical skills and charisma, Sonnenberg succeeded in the role that the Gold Dust Trio attempted with Wayne Munn. The AWA champion helped forge a link between professional wrestling and the burgeoning national cult of college football. Just as football's governing bodies made that sport more exciting by changing the rules, Sonnenberg adopted a ring style based on constant movement and flash. His lack of wrestling knowledge forced him to use this approach, but the liveliness of Sonnenberg's style thrilled fans, turning a necessity into a benefit. Sonnenberg also reinforced the connection between his two sports by adapting football techniques to the ring. For example, he frequently scored pinfalls by first flattening his opponents with a flying tackle. His success led to a wave of former college football players flooding promotions across the country. For the promoters, the addition of clean-cut, college-educated athletes with preexisting name recognition proved to be a gold mine they continued to excavate for the rest of the century.[18]

Bowser's success with Sonnenberg, however, proved short-lived. Curley and his associates began to import not only their own former college football players but, after an unsuccessful run with Hans Steinke, they found a champion even more marketable than Sonnenberg. Although he turned pro in 1917, and proved to be a good draw throughout the 1920s, Jim Londos never earned the title because of his small size. Promoters during the Republican Decade felt that the public would not accept that he could defeat much larger heavyweight wrestlers. However, by the end of the 1920s, the success of Sonnenberg and poorly trained ex-footballers indicated that ring skills (and believability) no longer represented the most significant factor in wrestling. Londos possessed a drawing power that more than overcame his very average mat skills. Nicknamed the "Golden Greek" thanks to his bronzed skin and chiseled physique, Londos provided professional wrestling with its first sex symbol. His matinee good looks drew hordes of female fans to his matches, sold newspapers, and led to lucrative advertising contracts. Curley insured continued positive press for his star by donating the proceeds of several shows a year to Mrs. William Randolph Hearst's Free Milk Fund for Babies. The promoter's machinations led sportswriters to spew streams of hyperbole on the "Adonis of ancient Argos," whose shirtless photos helped sell newspapers. After winning the NWA title from Shikat in August 1929, Londos became the biggest draw in wrestling. His New York City title defenses, staged in large venues such as Madison Square Garden and Yankee Stadium, regularly drew in excess of ten thousands fans.[19]

The popularity of Londos and the college football players led promoters to recognize the potential windfalls associated with creating personas for wrestlers. This notion eventually became codified into a Manichaean system of rule-abiding good guys ("babyfaces" or "faces") and despicable villains who resorted to tactics not according to Hoyle ("heels"). For wrestling, a sport lacking home teams or an established "season," the development of personas was an essential aspect for drawing fans to matches in which they had no vested, personal interest. The influx of ex-college football players partially offset this difficulty, by bringing in wrestlers associated with schools for which fans felt a particular allegiance, but not enough of these athletes competed to fill the nation's wrestling cards. Wrestling promoters, therefore, created their own personas for wrestlers as a means of generating interest in matches. Although no hard rules existed for determining personas, promoters usually pushed handsome or former college star wrestlers as clean-wrestling faces, while older, fatter, or foreign-born (who became somewhat less common thanks to the immigration laws of the 1920s) wrestlers often became heels. By the early 1930s, promoters across the country adopted the technique, and it became a standard aspect of professional wrestling. Because of this development, the first few years of the 1930s proved to be highly lucrative for wrestling promoters.[20]

The growth of heels and faces represented a logical evolution of professional wrestling. To a certain degree, the notion of good wrestler versus bad wrestler can be discerned throughout the history of the sport. In the Gilded Age, out-of-town shooters, at show inside men, and wrestlers known for dirty tactics played the role of embryonic heels. Imported wrestlers, particularly the welter of Terrible Turks, also presented foils for homegrown wrestlers in front of parochial crowds. As with their stranglehold on the boxing heavyweight championship, the activities of Tex Rickard and Doc Kearns exemplified the benefits of presenting athletic encounters as representations of larger issues. Rickard generated excitement for Dempsey bouts by promoting his title defenses as archetypal struggles. Most famously, he created a flurry of excitement over the July 1921 bout between Dempsey and Georges Carpentier. Rickard promoted the match as representing a battle between the draft-dodging Dempsey and the patriotic French war hero Carpentier. The scheme worked so well that Rickard adopted it whenever possible for future matches. Dempsey's 1926 defense against Gene Tunney, for example, was promoted as a struggle between the primitive, anti-intellectual westerner versus his brainy, scientific counterpart. That Tunney also possessed patriotic military credentials only added another layer to Rickard's ballyhoo.[21]

Wrestling promoters simply adopted the Rickard model, albeit in a typically less subtle form, and built reputations for wrestlers. Although physical attractiveness often proved to be the deciding factor in determining a wrestler's persona, other factors often played a role. Londos's success led promoters to apply (often false) ethnic identifications to wrestlers to generate interest among fans of the same ethnic group. In one typical example, Lutheran Paul Boesch found himself not only promoted as a Jew but scheduled to meet Sammy Stein for the "Jewish Heavyweight Championship." This practice allowed promoters to avoid forcing wrestlers into the straightjacket role of rule breaker by pitting them against grapplers from other ethnic groups. While purposefully pitting Greeks versus Italians or Jews versus Catholics appears cynical and calculated to stir racial prejudices, such overt manipulation of audiences helped sustain wrestling during the economic difficulties of the Depression. Nor were the wrestling powers alone in using divisive means to attract fans; boxing promoters of the period engaged in the same practice.[22]

The adoption of heels and faces also reflected developments in other entertainment forms. Motion pictures of the 1920s, constrained by the lack of sound and a desire to appeal to the poorly educated, also presented oversimplified representations of good and evil. Perhaps most important, motion pictures brought bad guys to life. Film "heavies" often adopted readily identifiable visual clues that immediately established them as villains. Physical appearance became a means for determining good and evil in ways not fully developed in popular culture previously. This notion became so pervasive that actors found themselves stereotyped as heroes or bad guys in all of their films. The career of Joe Bonomo represents an intriguing connection between film and wrestling public images. After gaining recognition as a bodybuilder, Bonomo became an actor and stuntman for Universal Studios in the mid-1920s. A lifelong wrestling fan, Bonomo moonlighted as professional wrestler "Joe Atlas." The pseudonym, however, failed to keep his identity secret and newspaper accounts of his matches typically referenced his true identity. To protect the good guy screen image Universal cultivated for him, the studio informed Bonomo that he could continue to wrestle but only if he won all his matches and always wrestled clean. Under these guidelines Bonomo continued to wrestle until the end of the decade, retiring only after contracting trachoma, a potentially blinding eye disease that proved to be the scourge of professional wrestlers.[23]

The cinema was a great friend to wrestling during the Depression era. The simple morality play of wrestling's good guy versus bad guy adapted well to motion pictures (and pulp magazines). Wrestling films represented a significant aspect of Hollywood's sports-related melodramas. Typically, the wrestling films served as the second feature (often derisively known as "programmers") on a cinema's bill. Motion pictures also provided additional income for many wrestlers. As large men already trained in the ways of making fake fights look legitimate, wrestlers were ideally suited to work as stuntmen or actors in action sequences. While most wrestlers, such as Joe Varga and Stanislaus Zbyszko, made only a few appearances in films, others became regulars in Hollywood productions. The ill-fated George Kotsonaros starred in a number of silent features, usually playing a boxer or wrestler. Well-known trust buster Nat

Pendleton started working in films in 1930 and eventually appeared in more than one hundred movies. No wrestler, however, made the transition to film better than Mike Mazurki. He became one of Hollywood's most prominent "heavies" in a career that lasted more than forty years.[24]

Londos's success once again made Curley a dominant figure in the wrestling business, but the bickering among grappling's power brokers again wreaked havoc on the industry. Personal animosities led to a rift between Londos and Mondt, which resulted in a further splintering of the title picture. At various times in 1933, Londos, Lewis, Henri Deglane, Jim Browning, Ed Don George, and Sonnenberg clone "Jumping" Joe Savoldi all staked their claim as world champion. The confusion over the title and the disruption to efficiency caused by the factionalism of promoters led to the development of yet another promotional trust. While the original trust controlled wrestling east of the Mississippi River, the new trust remarkably, given the animosities and mutual mistrust of the promoters, actually extended control across the entire United States. By the end of 1934, tentacles of the promotional cartel reached from Los Angeles to Boston. The new trust proved even more profitable than the old one; its increased size and the cooperation it engendered allowed the title situation to be clarified. Londos initially regained recognition as champion, but, with the public beginning to tire of him, Danno O'Mahoney emerged as wrestling's new draw. Irish-born O'Mahoney benefited greatly from the prevalent ethnic identification of the period, which Bowser used to make the former shot-putter a star in Boston. To solidify O'Mahoney's claim to the title, he defeated all the other claimants during 1935.[25]

For the second trust, the disruptive influence emerged from the outside. Just as the trust busters blasted away at Curley and his cronies in the late 1920s, a cluster of disaffected promoters closed out of lucrative trust promotions launched a public campaign against wrestling's rulers. Although Columbus, Ohio, promoter Al Haft helped propel the antitrust crusade, Jack Pfefer became the force that eventually destroyed the trust. A Polish Jew born near Warsaw, Pfefer came to the United States in 1921 and quickly moved into the wrestling business. During the 1920s, he managed a string of imported wrestlers and eventually became one of Curley's lieutenants. As part of the 1933 power struggle, Pfefer found himself ostracized by the new trust. He then launched a massive public campaign to discredit the trust in particular and professional wrestling in general. Pfefer used his connections to stay abreast of the trust's moves and then fed the information to reporters and state athletic commissions. He routinely passed the prearranged results of matches to New York *Daily Mirror* sports editor Dan Parker, who gleefully published the results in evening editions issued shortly before the bouts occurred. Pfefer made his vitriolic attacks more effective by openly admitting his own role in the fleecing of the public. Despite continuing to promote professional wrestling matches, Pfefer always maintained that he provided entertainment, not athletic contests.[26]

As one writer noted, Pfefer's "greatest asset is his high nuisance value." This asset helped drive down the trust's profits. Newspapers decreased the space they devoted to wrestling coverage. Many of the papers also openly derided the wrestlers and presented wrestling as a laughable exhibition for the uneducated. For example, a newspaper account of a Steve Casey–Lou Thesz title match ended by noting "with no small display of pomp and panoply, the sometime fisherboy from the Roaring Water received due recognition of his triumph when he was presented the gaudy buckler, emblematic of the corn belt supremacy, by Mrs. Bob Gregory, blonde wife of the main bout referee and daughter of the Rajah of Sarawak." The embarrassing newspaper coverage so angered Washington, D.C., wrestlers that they staged a brief strike in March 1937. State athletic commissions also noticed Pfefer's pronouncements and scrutinized the actions of the promoters. The New York commission, for example, examined Curley's business practices and decreed that all wrestling matches, save title defenses—which the commission mistakenly believed to be on the level—must be promoted as "exhibitions."[27]

Pfefer's most damaging attack on the trust, however, began with yet another title match double-cross. Pfefer worked in concert with Al Haft, a bitter foe of Curley since the mid-1920s, to convince Dick Shikat to shoot on O'Mahoney in a March 1936 bout, an event doubly galling to Curley as it occurred in Madison Square Garden. Curley and the trust immediately responded by convincing the NWA to strip Shikat of the title for missing scheduled defenses. The convoluted justification for this move revolved around a 1934 management contract Shikat signed with Paul Bowser associate Joe

Alvarez. Under the terms of the contract, Alvarez possessed exclusive control over Shikat's bookings. Alvarez hastily scheduled defenses for Shikat, without bothering to notify the new champion, and then used these missed dates as the basis for stripping him of the title. In New York, where the commission often operated independently of the NWA, Curley made a desperate bid to convince the authorities to order Shikat to defend his title against the old warhorse Strangler Lewis; his plan came to naught. The trust was left with the uncomfortable situation of their handpicked champion being beaten by a man no longer under their control. In a move fraught with pitfalls, Alvarez, with the trust's blessings, filed a breach of contract suit against Shikat in Columbus. The April 1936 trial threatened to expose all of the business's secrets and undoubtedly increased public awareness of the trust, but, in the end, the cautious testimony of both sides led to little more than the confirmation of much already suspected. Curley became the first witness, and he refused to break the kayfabe, a pattern followed by subsequent witnesses. Given that Pfefer, Haft, and allied promoter Adam Weissmuller of Detroit faced the possibility of losing the case, which meant losing control of the stolen title, they ordered Shikat to drop his title to Ali Baba (a fez-wearing native of Fresno, California, named Harry Ezekian) in late April. Newspapers cynically noted this "was the natural development in a sequence of odd events—a quick turning of tables which leaves certain big wigs of the wrestling trust, in the East, and Missouri, gasping for breath." Early the next month federal judge Mell Underwood, at Alvarez's request, terminated the Alvarez-Shikat contract and dismissed the case.[28]

The Columbus trial proved to be the end of the line for the new trust. With a publicly recognized champion not under their control, trust members scrambled to protect their territories. Curley's lack of influence to maintain the cohesion of the trust, suspected after his failure to pressure the New York commission into sanctioning a Shikat-Lewis match, became obvious in May when Pfefer and Haft booked the Shikat-Baba rematch into Madison Square Garden. Curley, the former undisputed czar of wrestling, could no longer prevent rivals from holding shows in the most prestigious venue in his home city. The anti-Shikat campaign also led to a splintering of the championship. With the NWA and various state commissions recognizing a cluster of different title claimants, the brief era of one nationally recognized world champion (which represented only the man viewed as champion in this country) ended. Former trust members once again began to promote their own "world" champion within their territories as a means of attracting fans. In 1936 alone, the title claimants included Shikat, O'Mahoney, Baba, Dave Levin, Daniel Boone Savage, Vincent Lopez, Everett Marshall, Dean Detton, Yvon Robert, and Cliff Olsen. Any hope of reorganizing the trust to clear up the title mess ended in July 1937 when Curley died.[29]

The combined effects of the Columbus trial, the fracturing of the trust, the plethora of "champions," and the newspaper disclosures of the business resulted in a sharp decline in attendance during the late 1930s. External factors also worked against wrestling. The downturn in gate receipts corresponded with the "Roosevelt Recession" of 1937–1938. With the nation's disposable income sharply reduced, many former followers of wrestling spent their remaining dollars on other forms of entertainment. Professional wrestling found itself in the uncomfortable position of increasing marginalization in a bad economy. To make matters worse, recent events had shattered public assurance in the honesty of wrestling. For example, in his 1939 study of American amusements and sports, Robert B. Weaver noted that "there is less confidence in wrestling as a sport today than in any other of our major sports activities." Those newspapers that continued to note developments in wrestling did so in tones of condescension that suggested only the very young, the very old, and the very gullible attended the matches. The Boston *Globe's* reference to wrestling as "entertainment" for "the yokels, both those who live in hick towns and those who strut in great metropolitan centers" proved to be a common refrain as the 1930s drew to a close.[30]

To counter these developments, the promoters clung to the kayfabe and made moves to insure the survival of their personal fiefdoms. One tactic that emerged in the aftermath of the spate of championship double-crosses involved the selection of champions. Recognizing that the "workers" (as the wrestlers were known) could not be trusted and that the era of "policemen" had also passed, promoters faced the potential of double-crosses without the ability to threaten a national blacklisting as they had during the peak of the trust (which was not successful even then). To alleviate the threat of double-crosses, some promoters moved to put their titles on men with both legitimate wrestling skills and, hopefully, a sense of loyalty. Tom Packs, controller of the lucrative St. Louis market, for example, made a strapping young Missouri native of German-Hungarian ancestry named Lou Thesz his champion. Blessed with lightning quick reflexes and expertly trained by former veteran wrestling coach George Tragos, Thesz, who turned pro in 1935, rose very quickly through the wrestling ranks. After becoming a professional, Thesz received supplemental training from Ray Steele and "Strangler" Lewis, which resulted in him winning Paul Bowser's AWA title in 1937. Well-versed in classic catch wrestling, Thesz represents a significant transitional figure in the history of professional wrestling. Part of the last generation of wrestlers to receive intensive catch instruction before becoming a successful pro, Thesz remained a vital figure in the business through the first television era of the 1950s and continued to campaign actively during the territorial era of the 1960s and 1970s.[31]

Wrestlers of Thesz's skills, however, were rare. Many worried promoters did not have any wrestlers under contract who combined mat skills with drawing power like the handsome young Missourian. For the bottom-line-driven promoters, the danger of a double-cross mattered little if no one attended their shows. Faced with declining revenues, the promoters made the fateful decision to focus on developing wrestlers who possessed drawing power, with increasingly little regard given to knowledge of holds. While most promoters continued to place their title belts on men with competent ring skills, cards became filled with wrestlers who exhibited little in the way of catch wrestling holds. Recognizing that much of the public now viewed professional wrestling as an entertainment form rather than an honest sport, the promoters simply gave the public what they believed it wanted. As Strangler Lewis noted, fans "want that kind of show—hippodroming and clowning rassling stuff—and I'm always willing to oblige." Matches became more comical and outlandish as promoters introduced gimmick matches and bizarre wrestling personas. Wrestling survived as a business, but all vestiges of catch-style legitimacy fell away in the gaudy new spectacles. Unwittingly, however, the ballyhoo promoters of the 1930s altered the form of professional wrestling into something perfectly suited for a new medium set to sweep the nation.[32]

Greco-Roman champion William Muldoon pioneered many of the barnstorming techniques that led to worked wrestling. Courtesy of wrestlingreview.com

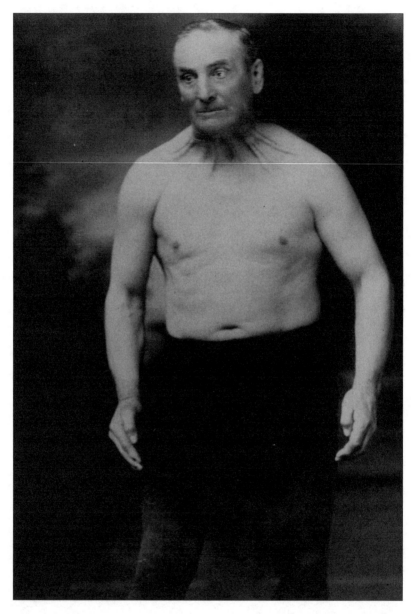

Martin "Farmer" Burns engaged in more than 6,000 matches. He also trained many of the top wrestlers of the early twentieth century. Courtesy of wrestlingreview.com

Gotch CHAMPION

Frank Gotch solidified the dominance of the catch style. His matches
with George Hackenschmidt brought increased attention to the sport.
Courtesy of wrestlingreview.com

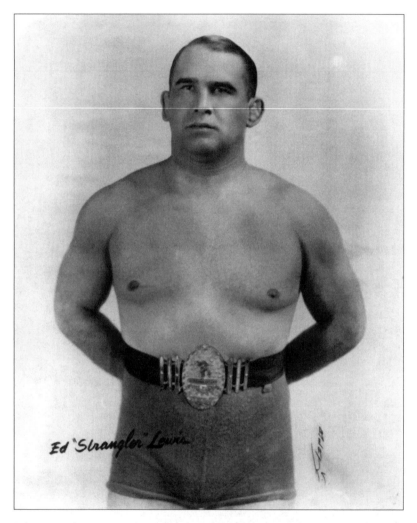

Ed "Strangler" Lewis served as wrestling's perennial champion in the 1920s and 1930s.

Joe "Toots" Mondt developed many of the dramatic conventions that helped enliven wrestling during the 1920s. He continued to be a significant power in the wrestling business until the 1960s. Courtesy of wrestlingreview.com

Wrestling's first sex symbol, Jim Londos helped bring increased numbers of American women to wrestling shows. Courtesy of wrestlingreview.com

Gus Sonnenberg led the wave of college football players who entered wrestling rings in the 1920s. Courtesy of wrestlingreview.com

Lou Thesz melded showmanship and legitimate wrestling skills. His success helped establish the National Wrestling Alliance (NWA) as the nation's leading wrestling organization. Courtesy of wrestlingreview.com

Buddy Rogers pioneered the narcissistic heel persona. He became
Lou Thesz's main rival during the 1950s. Courtesy of wrestlingre-
view.com

Former collegiate wrestling champion Verne Gagne utilized his success in pro rings to establish his own American Wrestling Association (AWA). Courtesy of wrestlingreview.com

The most successful heel champion in wrestling history, Nick Bockwinkel dominated the AWA during the late 1970s and early 1980s. Courtesy of wrestlingreview.com

Bruno Sammartino helped build the World Wide Wrestling Federation into an East Coast rival to the NWA. Courtesy of wrestlingreview.com

Although he never served as a long-time champion, Andre the Giant operated as a phenomenally successful special attraction. Courtesy of wrestlingreview.com

Ric Flair coopted much of Buddy Rogers' persona to become the NWA's standard bearer during the 1980s. Courtesy of wrestlingre-view.com

Hulk Hogan established the World Wrestling Federation's preeminence during the 1980s. He parlayed success in wrestling into status as a cultural icon. Courtesy of wrestlingreview.com

The anti-hero New World Order (nWo) propelled World Championship Wrestling's challenge to World Wrestling Federation dominance in the mid-1990s. Courtesy of Michael Lano.

Steve Austin's angry blue-collar persona resonated with working class fans during the late 1990s. Courtesy of Michael Lano.

Third-generation wrestler Dwayne "the Rock" Johnson utilized wrestling as a springboard to a motion picture career. Courtesy of Michael Lano.

5

GIMMICKS AND TELEVISION

The complete transformation of professional wrestling from worked catch-style matches to a pure "spectacle of excess," in Roland Barthes's famous phrase, involved a years-long evolution of the sport, just as the shift from shoots to works, but the transmutation represented the logical (perhaps, inevitable) progression of affairs in the business. The move away from authentic contests during the Republican Decade provided opportunities to establish men as contenders based solely on their drawing power. By the early 1930s, wrestlers climbed through the ranks, in large measure, on the basis of either their good looks, their ethnic identification, or their ability to believably engage in illegal activities in the ring. While the rise of heels and faces set the stage for the development of more flamboyant wrestlers, this progression received a spur from the declining gates of the mid-1930s. Forced to find ways to fill empty arenas, promoters resorted to gimmick matches, over-the-top personas, and special attractions. Although older wrestlers who possessed true catch skills may have found these alterations reprehensible, the changing nature of the business forced all to adapt or perish. Even the proud and dignified Lou Thesz, a respected shooter whose career began at the cusp of the gimmick era, resorted to the ridiculous "airplane spin" as his finishing move.[1]

Like the beginning of the worked era, no specific date irrefutably relates to the birth of the gimmick era. Having emerged out of the carnival culture, wrestling promoters always used gimmicks of various types as part of their promotional arsenal. From the "sultan's favorites" who stormed these shores as the "Terrible Turks" of the late nineteenth century to the proliferation of Masked Marvels in the wake of Mort Henderson's initial turn as that hooded character in the mid-1910s, gimmicks helped sell wrestling even during the catch era. By the early 1930s, promoters relied on falsified identities of wrestlers to generate interest in Irish, Jewish, Italian, or Polish neighborhoods, a clear example of the mixture of duplicity and ballyhoo that gave rise to the gimmick era. However, the economic necessities of the mid-1930s propelled gimmicks to the forefront of the business. Therefore, just as the July 1916 Stecher-Lewis match reasonably marks the date the catch era ended, Ali Baba's emergence as world champion in April 1936 can be viewed as the beginning of the gimmick era.[2]

Although all promoters found themselves faced with financially circumscribed circumstances that forced them to use gimmicks, some promoters more readily embraced this shift. Chief among the promoters who exploited gimmicks stood Jack Pfefer. After Jack Curley's death, Pfefer reestablished himself in the New York market (in an alliance with "Toots" Mondt) and promoted increasingly bizarre wrestling characters as the decade progressed. Given that Pfefer never claimed to promote anything but pure entertainment, his shift to complete spectacle did not surprise others in the business. As A. J. Liebling later noted, "the difference between Pfefer's productions and Curley's was like that between avowed fiction and a Hearst news story." As a self-proclaimed showman, Pfefer not only relied on gimmick wrestlers to sell tickets but also took great pleasure in publicly acknowledging how he used them to dupe the gullible public. In 1938 Pfefer told a reporter from *Collier's*:

> Freaks I love and they're my specialty. I am very proud of some of my monstrosities. You can't get a dollar with a normal-looking guy, no matter how good he can wrestle. Those birds with shaved, egg-shaped heads, handlebar mustaches, tattooed bodies, big stomachs—they're for me! Dopes who wear Turkish fezzes and carry prayer rugs into the ring with them, kurdled Kurds, bouncing Czechs—all those foreign novelties I import for my stable. None of these atrocities of mine can find their way out of a phone booth or sock their way out of a cellophane

sack, but that's not important. I teach 'em their routines and ship 'em out. The suckers think they're hot stuff—haw.[3]

The development of gimmick wrestlers undoubtedly benefited from the carnival experience of many involved in professional wrestling. Pfefer referred to his gimmick wrestlers as "freaks," exactly the same term carnival operators used to describe their human sideshow attractions. Many of the gimmick wrestlers of the period faithfully followed formulas successful at attracting crowds to the sideshows. For example, wrestlers who could contort themselves, such as Fritz Kley, or tightwalk on the ropes and perform acrobatic tricks, such as "Count" George Zarynoff, translated circus moves directly into the ring. Also, a wave of obese wrestlers, reminiscent of carnival and circus "fattest man in the world" attractions, established themselves in the 1930s. Some, such as "Wee" Willie Davis and Man Mountain Dean, who had been an active wrestler under the name Frank Leavitt since the 1910s, possessed legitimate wrestling skills. Others, such at Martin "Blimp" Levy, performed only the most rudimentary holds. Most obese wrestlers of the period developed some version of a "splash" move, which involved dropping their enormous girth across the midsection of a prone opponent.[4]

The most popular conversion of freak show attraction to wrestling involved individuals with facial deformities or, more frequently, simply spectacularly unattractive countenances. The trend began with the importation of Maurice Tillet, who became known as the "French Angel." Tillet suffered from acromegaly, a glandular dysfunction that left his facial features bloated and distorted. His abhorrent appearance proved to be an enormous box office draw. Paul Bowser made him American Wrestling Association (AWA) champion in 1940, and Tillet helped keep that promotion solvent during the dark days of World War II. Tillet's success spawned a number of imitators. Swedish, Polish, and Czech (among others) "Angels" flooded the country during the 1940s. Tor Johnson, the most successful of the later "angels," wrestled as the Super Swedish Angel before embarking on a successful acting career (including a feature role in the legendary *Plan Nine from Outer Space*). In the late 1950s, Jack Pfefer even attempted to promote the Lady Angel, a bald woman allegedly unable to speak English.[5]

Wrestlers without obvious physical draws became caricatures of familiar figures from comic books and action movies. Wrestling rings around the country became inundated with cowboys, Native Americans, and members of the English nobility. Russian-themed wrestlers became "red menace" heels in the late 1940s, but during the 1930s Sergei Kalmikoff, Ivan Rasputin, and others portrayed simple peasants or Cossacks. The cowboy, Cossack, and hillbilly characters reflected a trend during the Depression decade for Americans to seek out the myths and folklore of the rural, pioneering spirit in an attempt to counter the industrialization and urbanization that became negatively linked to the nation's economic dislocation. Wrestling promoters astutely connected this archetype with rule-abiding wrestling styles to further their appeal. Cowboys, Native Americans, and hillbillies always appeared as faces; not until the middle of the century did wrestlers adopting these characters compete as villains. This nostalgic sentiment helped propel the enormous popularity of hillbilly Daniel Boone Savage and football star Bronko Nagurski, whom fans often compared to a wild beast in the ring due to the moonlighting Chicago Bear's strength and viciousness.[6]

Excessive wildness and out-of-control behavior also became a hallmark of heels of the period. This gimmick proved highly profitable for countless wrestlers of the 1930s and beyond, with none benefiting more during the Depression Decade than a family of wrestlers known as the "Dirty" Duseks. Rudy, Joe, Emil, and Ernie Dusek, who competed in singles matches and in various combinations as the "Riot Squad," became major heels by generating constant in-ring chaos during their matches. Although the Duseks' matches often came closer to barroom brawls that catch wrestling contests, even they could not match the frenzy of Ted "King Kong" Cox. A protégé of Pfefer, Cox pioneered many of the actions that became staple aspects of heel behavior for the rest of the century. He tore the shirts off unfriendly referees, used ringside props (water bottles, buckets, and chairs) on his opponents, often continued beating on his opponents as he dragged them to the dressing rooms, bled regularly, squirted "ammonia" in other wrestlers' eyes, and taped his knuckles to signify added punching power. Cox eventually won a version of the world title in 1938 (wrestling as the Masked Marvel) and continued to be a major draw into the late 1940s.[7]

The late 1930s also witnessed a resurgence in women's wrestling. Female wrestlers competed on a regular basis during the late nineteenth century, but few remained active into the catch era. Cora Livingston, who later married promoter Paul Bowser, claimed the women's world championship in 1920, but a dearth of quality opponents eventually derailed her career. Promoters returned to women's wrestling in the midst of the Depression as a means of providing sexual titillation for male customers. Many of the female wrestlers of the 1930s possessed only the most rudimentary of wrestling skills, but the novelty of women in skimpy clothing rolling around in the ring proved very lucrative. Appearance, not in-ring ability, proved to be the key to success for most women wrestlers of the period. In this regard, their circumstances were not all that different from those of male wrestlers during the period. However, the promoters stressed looks among the women even more than they did for the male wrestlers. As Pfefer told a reporter, "a girl what has a svell [sic] shape, a good-lookin' face and wants to be in pictures should foist be a rastler."[8]

However, as with the men, gimmick-type female wrestlers drew crowds, but promoters felt uncomfortable giving them title belts. Mildred Burke, a woman with legitimate wrestling skills, therefore, became the first women's world champion of the worked era. Managed by (and later married to) promoter Billy Wolfe, Burke began her career wrestling men in carnival "at shows." She quickly developed both solid catch wrestling skills and a remarkably muscular physique. Burke won the women's championship in a Columbus, Ohio, tournament in 1937 and successfully defended the title until 1954 when she lost to June Byers (a wrestler trained by Burke's then ex-husband Wolfe). Burke achieved a level of success and proficiency that prevented promoters from establishing any viable alternative champion. Her dominance of women's wrestling stemmed in part from Burke's relentless travel schedule. Although Burke based her operations out of Al Haft's Ohio promotion, she defended her title across the country, often wrestling twice a week.[9]

Burke's greatest opponent proved to be state athletic commissions. Concern over the impropriety of the often openly sexual content of women's matches, coupled with sexist attitudes related to the need for female protective legislation, led many states to ban the holding of women's matches (a move applauded by, among others, the Roman Catholic Church). In other states, commissions permitted only matches in which the competitors remained standing. Significant wrestling markets such as New York, Illinois, Michigan, and California remained closed to Burke during portions of her career. Sports historian Donald Mrozek has persuasively argued that these attempts to restrict women's athletic endeavors represented an "especially vivid and concrete" example of generalized male fears concerning loss of identity and purpose. These fears lay at the heart of the creation of separate male and female spheres. Women's movement into the "male" spheres of sports, politics, and the workforce only gained significant strength and legitimization in the post–World War II period. Wrestling reflected this development in that court challenges resulted in the restrictive statutes' removal in some states during the 1950s. For example, in 1955 wrestler Rose Hesseltine successfully challenged the Illinois prohibition. However, residual fears limited opportunities for female wrestlers. Jerry Hunter lost her case against the state of Oregon the same year that Hesseltine won her case. And the lucrative New York market did not become open to women until 1972. Male wrestlers often fought against the encroachment of women into the "male" sphere of the ring. Longtime NWA champion Lou Thesz noted "most male professional wrestlers resent the intrusion of women into the field of what men feel is their exclusive sport, [and] I must confess that I'm in the majority."[10]

Gimmick wrestlers may have been lucrative for the promoters, but they left promoters in the uncomfortable situation of relying on the wrestlers to either develop into marketable characters or possess exploitable physical characteristics. Resourceful promoters eventually established means of building the gimmicks directly into the matches, making the wrestlers secondary to the process. With the types of wrestlers in the ring undergoing a transformation, promoters recognized that crowds could be attracted by transforming the ring itself. During the late 1930s, gimmick matches with wrestlers competing in a ring filled with unusual substances became a standard technique among promoters. The first of these type of matches, mud wrestling, became the longest-lived, but promoters attempted countless variations. Matches took place in ice, ice cream, and piles of fish. To attract crowds, promoters had wrestlers compete in rings filled with substances linked to their local economies; matches were held in rings filled with blueberries, tomatoes, molasses, coal, and iron shavings. Melding two new attractions, promoters began staging women's mud wrestling matches by early 1938.

Resourceful promoters sought increasingly outlandish new types of matches to draw crowds. One technique involved pitting a human wrestler against an animal. Although promoted as a new gimmick during the period, bear-baiting and similar practices possess an ancient lineage. Traveling entertainment impresarios often organized animal versus human matches in the mining camps of the West during the nineteenth century, which continued to be popular entertainment at carnival sideshows. Desperate wrestling promoters simply brought the bears indoors and made them part of special attraction matches on regularly scheduled cards. Ginger, the most famous wrestling bear of the period, began competing in 1940 and continued to perform as a special attraction throughout the decade. For the protection of her opponents, she wore a muzzle and gloves during the matches.[11]

Tag-team matches proved to be the most lasting successes of all the 1930s gimmick matches. Recognizing that matches slowed down (and crowds grew restless) as wrestlers became winded late in matches, promoters began holding matches in which two teams of two wrestlers competed. Initially dubbed, in a bit of false exoticism, "Australian" tag-team matches, these types of encounters kept the in-ring action well paced, allowed heels to carry out their assigned role through illegal double teaming, and presented opportunities to have four wrestlers in the ring at once. Further, tag-team matches appealed to an underlying, but significant, aspect of American's self-image: as Allen Guttmann noted, the stressing of both rugged individualism and voluntary cooperation. With the rise of tag-team matches, wrestling tandems who competed only in these types of matches developed. These specialized teams, and the popularity of tag-team matches, allowed promoters to create new tag-team championships, thereby giving themselves the opportunity to promote even more cards with title defenses. Not surprisingly, promoters found ways to combine tag matches with other new attention-getting techniques. By the early 1940s, women's and midget tag-team matches made their way onto wrestling cards.[12]

All of these maneuvers helped sustain the industry during the late 1930s, but the next decade brought a new challenge for wrestling—a wartime lack of wrestlers. With millions of American men called into military service, wrestling promoters faced a significant manpower shortage. Travel restrictions and gasoline rationing also made it difficult for wrestlers to maintain their prewar wrestling circuits. This situation resulted in significant alterations to the business of sports, including professional wrestling. Promoters had to rely on local performers consistently, with few opportunities to bring in national figures. Although cards scheduled in areas with defense plants or military bases drew respectable crowds, in many areas the fan pool significantly shrank. The number of cards promoted, therefore, decreased during World War II. Those cards that continued to be held often circumvented the dearth of wrestlers by containing only three singles matches and a tag-team main event with wrestlers who had already appeared in the earlier singles encounters.[13]

With champions such as Lou Thesz and Steve Casey drafted into the military, promoters followed boxing's lead and froze all major titles. However, bottom-line-driven promoters created "duration" champions to maintain interest. Given that the duration champions faced significant problems arranging transportation to defend these belts, the temporary titles proved only marginally successful in maintaining public interest. Some of the prosperous prewar territories managed to continue their profitability, especially St. Louis (where the NWA world title resided during the war) and Los Angeles (temporary home of the light heavyweight championship), but many other areas faced economic difficulties. These circumstances led promoters to not only continue working the gimmick matches of the late 1930s, but, as did baseball's controlling interests, to turn to the infirm and the aged. "Wild" Bill Longson, unfit for service due to back injuries, spent the war years touring as the NWA world champion. Old stars exempt from military service, such as Dick Shikat, Bronko Nagurski, and John Pesek returned, once again, to positions as championship contenders. Even an aged Strangler Lewis, badly out of shape and suffering from trachoma, returned to the ring and captured the Midwest Wrestling Association's heavyweight championship.[14]

Given the large number of professional wrestlers drafted, it is not surprising that many made significant contributions to the war effort. Thesz helped train military police guard dogs before becoming a hand-to-hand combat instructor. Paul Boesch the most decorated wrestler of World War II, received numerous commendations, including Silver and Bronze Stars, the Purple Heart, and the French *Croix de Guerre*. He later wrote a well-received book, *Road to Huertgen*, about his experiences. Stars such as Gus Sonnenberg, Joe Pazandak, Steve Casey, and Joe Savoldi (who allegedly engaged in secret missions in the European theater), along with many others, served on active duty during the war. Wrestlers also engaged in specially arranged matches at camps and hospitals as entertainment for the troops. A United Service Organizations (USO) plane crash in March 1945 killed five wrestlers touring Europe for the benefit of the armed forces.[15]

On May 17, 1939, W2XBS (NBC's experimental television station in New York) televised a baseball game between Columbia and Princeton. The approximately one thousand owners of television sets in the New York metropolitan area complained that the players appeared to be white dots and that the ball proved impossible to see, but the era of televised sports had begun. Before the year ended, the RCA mobile unit responsible for broadcasting this baseball game also covered boxing and wrestling matches on an irregular basis. World War II temporarily halted the development of television, but the immediate postwar years witnessed the birth of America's fascination with the "magic window." By 1946, four national networks began offering prime-time network programming. With videotape not yet perfected and Hollywood uneasy over providing a new rival with material to broadcast, the networks relied heavily on live programming. The networks quickly recognized that sports programs offered an opportunity to fill their schedules with exciting and popular entertainment and sports constituted 40 percent of the prime-time programming during 1946. However, the primitiveness of television technology made team sports contested on large playing fields both difficult to cover and aesthetically unpleasing for viewers. Arena sports, however, not only fit perfectly with television's need for exciting programming but could also be broadcast in an effective manner despite the medium's technological limitations. Easy to film with one or two stationary cameras and occurring in well-lit arenas, boxing and wrestling became staples of early television. The two sports, especially wrestling, also appealed to television networks because they were cheap to produce and readily available. Further, they both dovetailed with wartime developments regarding strength, physical fitness, and an increasing connection between masculinity and America's global power.[16]

In 1945, KTLA in Los Angeles began the first weekly wrestling television program. Hosted by veteran entertainment industry hustler Dick Lane, the show initially broadcast from a Paramount sound stage, then moved to the ten-thousand-seat Olympic Auditorium. The program was an immediate success, and other stations soon included professional wrestling in their weekly programming. With the advent of prime-time network programming the next year, wrestling became a network staple. By 1948–1949 professional wrestling could be found in the prime-time schedules of all four networks. Local channels also offered their own wrestling programming, and, at its peak, weekly wrestling programs could be found on over two hundred stations. As other programming became available (and the "rules" of television developed), the networks moved sports programs to the weekends and out of prime time. The cash-strapped Dumont network, however, doggedly kept wrestling in its prime-time lineup and wrestling did not completely disappear from the prime-time hours until 1955. This move out of prime time, however, did not end wrestling's connections to television as local channels continued broadcasting weekly programs late at night and on Saturday mornings.[17]

The advent of wrestling's first television era also brought significant changes to the sport (as it did to boxing as well). A focus on the need to attract viewers and keep them interested led wrestling promoters to push their product into new, gaudier forms with increasingly stylized and uncontrollable mock violence. The trend toward promoting wrestlers with distinctive characters and personas that began in the late 1930s accelerated dramatically. With wrestlers now plying their trade on television, a new emphasis on wrestlers who could perform compelling live interviews also developed. Concomitantly with the development of live television interviews came the growth of a fraternity of wrestling announcers who themselves became an integral part of the programs. Perhaps, most significantly, television introduced wrestling to a new audience previously unexploited by the promoters—American women.[18]

Despite the occasional sex symbol wrestler, such as Jim Londos, women represented a relatively minor portion of the wrestling audience prior to the first television era. The postwar success of wrestling pushed live cards, in many places, out of smoke-filled arenas viewed as male preserves and into larger, more respectable venues in which women felt both more welcome and comfortable. As Chad

Dell noted, postwar American women sought new ways to articulate their identities in the face of pressures to return to banal domesticity after the rush of freedom provided by their contributions to the war effort. Professional wrestling offered women a classic story of the clash between good and evil performed by often attractive, atheticized men in abbreviated attire. Going to live matches, or watching it on television, gave American women, according to Dell, a chance to demonstrate freedom, sexuality, and assertiveness at a time when increasingly restrictive societal pressures reduced women's ability to express themselves. By 1950 women represented 60 percent of the audience at wrestling shows. The increasing numbers of women attending shows helped spur a dramatic increase in total attendance throughout the country. Between 1942 and 1950, attendance at wrestling cards increased by 800 percent.[19]

The television era also created a new occupation related to the wrestling industry—ringside announcers. Unlike boxing and baseball, wrestling did not prosper on the radio. The in-ring action and multiplicity of holds translated very poorly in an audio-only medium. Although television represented a far more conducive media form, some sort of contextualizing commentary proved necessary. Ringside announcers, therefore, became an essential aspect of wrestling programs. They functioned as mediators, interpreters, and interviewers, ensuring that the program flowed smoothly and understandably. Because they guided the proceedings every week, the announcers became a familiar and comforting aspect of wrestling programs. The best offered not only continuity and simple play-by-play commentary but also heightened the excitement of matches and helped build interest in future encounters by skillfully directing interviews. Dick Lane became the first announcer to establish himself as a significant aspect of a wrestling program, but Dennis James of the Dumont network achieved an even higher level of popularity during the early 1950s. James borrowed techniques from radio dramas and used props such as bones, blocks of wood, and balloons to accentuate the authentic match sounds emanating from the ring. Although they did not attain the popularity levels of James and Lane, Harry Carey, Steve Allen, and Jack Brickhouse, later prominent in sports and entertainment, also worked as wrestling announcers during this period.[20]

With television bringing wrestling into a period of fantastic profitability, a recognition developed among promoters that, just as it had in the 1920s, centralization and cooperation among them might be in the best interest of those controlling the business. To that end, Midwest promoter P. L. "Pinkie" George organized a meeting of promoters from across the country in July 1948. At this meeting the promoters hammered out a deal that created the National Wrestling Alliance (NWA). George had used this name for his territory since the early 1940s and, as the initially dominant force within the organization, successfully lobbied for its adoption. The acronym also helped create continuity within the business (and for wrestling fans) as the National Wrestling Association's title continued to be the belt most highly regarded. George and the new NWA ultimately hoped to wrest control of the title from the Association. In this endeavor, they benefited from the increasing uneasiness with which state athletic commissions (the organizations that constituted the National Boxing Association and its wrestling wing) viewed professional wrestling. Although athletic commissions continued to view the licensing of wrestlers as their responsibility, many state officials viewed recognizing champions in a "fake" sport as dishonest and unseemly. The alliance came about when control of the business (and title) proved available and when profits from the burgeoning television boom made that control more lucrative than any time in wrestling's history. NWA-aligned promoters moved quickly to consolidate their power and, despite some significant challenges, managed to retain their dominant position within the industry until the 1980s.

Although the NWA promoters agreed to work cooperatively and recognized the benefits of collusion, memories of the territorial wars and double-crosses of the past led to a generalized wariness of each other. To alleviate these concerns, the NWA established by-laws geared specifically toward protecting the sanctity of member's territories and to guarantee that the Alliance never lost control of the title. Under NWA rules, promoters who poached wrestlers from other aligned promoters or scheduled cards within the territory of another NWA member faced ejection from the Alliance. Promoters understood that, once outside the protection of the NWA, their territories would be viewed as fair game for a new, NWA-sanctioned promotion. With the weight of the Alliance behind him, the new promoter in the region could win any territorial war that might ensue. Over the years, promoters' power within the Alliance not only stemmed from their control of a current champion but also from their perceived ability to leave the federation and successfully withstand an NWA-sponsored war.[21]

The long history of promoter-instigated in-ring double-crosses in title matches also led to the development of specific NWA rules. To ensure the NWA champion would follow the Alliance's directives, wrestlers provided the federation with a championship belt "deposit" upon obtaining the title. Also, no title changes could occur without the consent of the NWA board of directors. The issue of a championship surety bond became significant almost as soon as the NWA organized. Orville Brown, reigning champion in George's territory, was recognized as the new NWA's initial champion. As part of the plan to eliminate the National Wrestling Association's authority, the NWA contracted with Lou Thesz, who owned the Association's championship, to engage in a title unification match with Brown in 1949. Before the match, however, Brown suffered serious injuries in an automobile accident and Thesz received Alliance recognition as their champion. Before this a Thesz-controlled group battled with NWA-aligned promoter Sam Muchnick for control of the St. Louis territory. Although Muchnick and Thesz settled their dispute and began cooperating, some within the NWA feared that Thesz would take the title, break with the Alliance, and establish himself as the head of a rival organization. Once Thesz made the belt deposit—in his case $25,000, as opposed to the $5,000 put up by Brown, who was perceived as more compliant—this fear proved illusory. In fact, Thesz proved to be such a successful, and pliant, champion for the NWA that he retained the title until 1956.[22]

With an acknowledged NWA world champion in place, promoters moved both to establish local titles for their individual promotions and to position wrestlers as drawing cards for the periods when the NWA champion defended his title in their territory. The recognition that they could maintain their own local champions, coupled with the growing authority of the NWA, pushed even the most independent-minded promoters to affiliate with the new combine. Veteran promoters, such as Al Haft in Ohio and Paul Bowser in Massachusetts, recognized the NWA's strength would only increase with the television exposure given to the organization's champion, making any struggle against the NWA futile. While these older, established promoters maintained some measure of autonomy and initially possessed the freedom to maneuver outside of NWA regulations,

even they conceded rights to the "world title" to the NWA. Thesz
engaged in a number of matches during his early championship reign
in which he defeated various promotional claimants to the title,
thereby establishing the validity of the NWA title, while promoters
scrambled to create local titles for their personal champions. Bowser,
for example, abandoned the notion of an AWA world title, with a
lineage back to 1929, and began promoting his champion as possessor
of the Eastern States title.

The establishment of the NWA may have also reflected promoters' concerns that the star-making capabilities of television
might create a celebrity wrestler too powerful for them to control.
Certainly the difficulties caused by the independent-minded Jim
Londos remained fresh in their memories. Television did, in fact,
propel the popularity of wrestling's greatest ever draw. George
Wagner, a Nebraska native raised in Houston, demonstrated little
of the charisma early in his career that eventually made him
wrestling's most famous personality. During the 1930s and early
1940s, Wagner received steady work from promoters, but he did not
establish himself beyond the level of a mid-card-level heel. By the
mid-1940s, however, Wagner recognized that his lack of success
reflected his lack of a distinctive ring persona. As one newspaper
reporter noted, Wagner discovered "a couple of years back that the
louder the act the bigger the house." Wagner began wearing elab-
orately sequined robes and died his hair a series of unusual colors.
He eventually bleached his hair with peroxide and adopted the
name Gorgeous George, a move that made him not only the nation's most famous wrestler but also a prominent figure in the
larger popular culture.[23]

Wagner developed a ring character that established several of the
nonverbal clues fans recognize as denoting a heel; a character so
successful it continues to be copied today. Promoting himself as
the "Human Orchid," Wagner grew his hair long and then had it
bleached and marcelled. Heels ever since have used peroxide as
shorthand for rule breaker. Wagner also pioneered the elaborate
ring entrance. Before he even emerged from the dressing room, his
valet entered the ring and placed a rug on the mat for George to
clean his feet, then sprayed "Chanel No. 10" from a large atomizer.
Only then did George, to the strains of "Pomp and Circumstance,"
deign to enter the ring, invariably wearing an elaborate robe and
responding to hecklers. He refused to begin his matches until the

valet had carefully removed George's hairnet and robe, an effete move calculated to enrage blue-collar fans by playing on their homophobic tendencies. George's portrayal of what Patrice Oppliger termed the "feminine male" provided a template for generations of heels. As George himself noted, "I kept thinking: Gorgeous, you've added something to your profession."[24]

Wagner, who legally changed his name to Gorgeous George in 1950, benefited immensely from television. He buttressed his startling appearance with highly effective interviews in which he preened and ridiculed both his opponents and wrestling fans. While television proved the perfect medium for George, he astutely recognized the benefits of newspaper coverage. George always remained in character for his interviews, a task that proved difficult for many later wrestlers, and engaged in a symbiotic relationship with the press in which they gained sales and he expanded his role as a celebrity. In keeping with his character, George never acknowledged this relationship or expressed any gratitude toward reporters. He always maintained that he only performed these duties as a courtesy to his inferiors. As George told one reporter, "I do not read the sports pages because my mind is otherwise culturally employed." George seeped into the nonwrestling public's consciousness in a manner no previous wrestler achieved. He starred in his own movie, the wretched *Alias the Champ*, and became recognizable enough to be the punch line in jokes by Red Skelton, Bob Hope, Milton Berle, and other comedians. Muhammad Ali would later acknowledge that he copied his brash style and glib tongue from George.[25]

Although George's activities in the ring became almost secondary to his celebrity, he continued to wrestle, and promoters throughout the country sought his services. After a hugely successful run at Los Angeles's Olympic Auditorium in 1946, George began touring the country. His success culminated in a headlining appearance at Madison Square Garden in 1949, the first wrestling show at that arena in twelve years. During the early 1950s, George used his vast ring earnings to purchase an enormous turkey ranch east of Los Angeles and earned extra income by selling food and trinkets (including the legendary gold-plated "Georgie pins" used to hold his hair in place) to tourists and curiosity seekers. His career, however, skittered downward in the mid-1950s just as the popularity of wrestling in general faltered. George continued to wrestle into the next decade and exploited his gimmick by engaging in matches in which he shaved his head if defeated, but alcoholism and decades of toiling on the road took their toll. He died penniless in 1963.[26]

George won a disputed claim to the AWA title in 1950, and was NWA Southern champion in 1953, but he never won a major championship. This lack of titles partly derived from George's constant movement between promotions, borne of concerns that his gimmick would not continue to draw if it were overexposed in a territory, but also reflected that George's focus was on fame and wealth, not championships. George can be viewed as the first modern professional wrestler in that he abandoned antiquated notions of striving to become world champion to achieve celebrity. George told one reporter "I don't want to be a millionaire, I just want to live like one." With the championship title now merely a prop to be exploited by promoters, and all vestiges of catch-style legitimacy forever gone, wrestlers such as George truly became entertainers, as opposed to athletes. In the NWA era and beyond, wrestlers continued to fight and struggle to obtain the world championship but did so because it reflected their success in drawing a large gate and putting on a good show, not because it signified their status as the world's best wrestler.[27]

The remarkable success of Gorgeous George led wrestlers to the development of increasingly elaborate characters as others sought to emulate his achievements. It also pushed promoters to search the globe for wrestlers they could build into similar stars for their promotions. Just as former college football players filled wrestling rings in the late 1920s, former boxers pursued wrestling during the first years of television. Ring veterans such as Joe Louis and Tony Galento became wrestlers, while former heavyweight champions Jack Dempsey and Rocky Marciano often worked as special referees. Primo Carnera, however, made the most successful transition from boxing to wrestling. Carnera became boxing's heavyweight champion in the 1930s, thanks to a string of fixed bouts, before his lack of ability caught up with him. He returned to his native Italy after his boxing career but returned to the United States in 1946 at the behest of wrestling promoters in southern California. Carnera possessed enormous name recognition and a six-foot-six frame that promoters hoped would make his transition to the wrestling ring believable. The novelty of a former boxing heavyweight champion competing as a wrestler proved immediately successful, despite the

"Ambling Alps" knowledge of "only two or three holds," and Carnera became one of wrestling's biggest attractions in 1947.[28]

Despite their popularity, wrestlers such as Carnera, Thesz, and Gorgeous George did not ever represent the most significant challenge to NWA control of wrestling. The surety bond for the championship belt helped keep NWA champions honest, but in many respects it proved unnecessary. The era of an independent-minded wrestler taking the title and breaking with the promotional cartel to strike out on their own effectively ended in the 1930s. Centralization and cooperation among promoters ensured that no independent champion could continue to tour nationally with a renegade title. Promoters also gained an added layer of protection from double-crosses because of the changed nature of wrestlers' success. With catch skills downgraded in importance, few of the major professional stars of the 1950s possessed the ability to protect themselves if an underhanded opponent turned a match into a shoot. Without these skills, an independent champion faced little chance of success. Despite his advancing age, Lou Thesz remained the most feared shooter in the business during the 1950s, a circumstance clearly recognized by the NWA. Thesz's skills and popularity made him the only wrestler capable of succeeding on his own, which undoubtedly contributed to the NWA's decision to allow him to remain undefeated for almost eight years.

Although individual wrestlers provided no real threat to NWA control, other challenges loomed in the Alliance's future. Primarily, the danger derived from promoters who felt slighted in the selection of champions or the scheduling of the titleholder's appearances. An alienated promoter with a popular local champion could break away from the Alliance far more easily than a disgruntled wrestler. One promotion that eventually broke ranks and contested NWA hegemony controlled the lucrative New York market. Based in Washington, D.C., Capitol Wrestling owned the NWA rights to lower New England and the Chesapeake region. Most importantly, they controlled the wrestling shows at Madison Square Garden. After wrestling's return to the Garden in 1949, the historic arena became an important wrestling venue. Although Capitol's owners, second-generation promoter Vince J. McMahon and the ubiquitous "Toots" Mondt, remained loyal NWA members during the 1950s, their prosperity during the decade laid the seeds of the promotion's eventual severance. They, as with the business in general, began to suffer in the middle of the decade, but, even with this downturn, New York remained a lucrative wrestling center. Part of Capitol's success during the early years of the NWA reflected the promotion's ability to establish their wrestlers as major stars. In the late 1940s, they brought Carnera to New York and used his notoriety as the means of rebuilding the New York market. Carnera's lack of wrestling skills, poor command of the English language, and taint of underworld connections from his boxing days soon combined to limit his success. Once the novelty of witnessing a former heavyweight boxing champion compete evaporated, Carnera's liabilities proved overwhelming. Capitol struck gold, however, with Antonino Rocca, an Argentinian of Italian descent. Discovered in his homeland by wrestler Nick Elitch, Rocca parlayed good looks and the athletic maneuvers of an acrobat into wrestling fame. He knew very few legitimate wrestling holds, but his charisma and electrifying moves captivated audiences. McMahon, Mondt, and partner Ray Fabiani soon recognized that Rocca's appeal brought Italian-Americans, long a significant part of the wrestling community, to arenas but also attracted Hispanics in record numbers. As a result, Capitol began to hire Hispanic wrestlers such as Miguel Perez, Pedro Escobar, and Enrique Torres to fill their cards. These moves created a vibrant promotion, distant from the NWA's hub of St. Louis, operating with homegrown stars in the country's largest urban area; a situation destined to cause difficulties for the Alliance.[29]

Like all promotions, Capitol relied on gimmick wrestlers and matches during the first television era. Television, in fact, sped up wrestling's shift toward gimmicks. As television programming became more diverse, professional wrestling found itself in an increasingly competitive marketplace. The threat posed by other types of programming pushed wrestling toward a television style characterized by increasing reliance on barroom brawl action and stylized personas. Women's matches were heavily featured on television programs, and bouts with midget wrestlers, often engaging in embarrassing comic relief encounters, enjoyed a brief vogue. Male wrestlers also adapted and developed increasingly vibrant and distinctive characters. They adopted costumes and attitudes reflective of superheroes (The Golden Superman, Steve "Mr. America" Stanley, "Spaceman" Frank Hickey), comic book villains (The Bat), and arrogant bullies ("Nature Boy" Buddy Rogers). Although wrestling's faces, to a certain extent, changed during the period, heels underwent the most significant alteration.[30]

The shift in heel personas reflected the diverse demographics of television audiences. Television moved the audience for wrestling beyond the immediate observation of the promoters. In the past, promoters tailored their villains to match the prevailing attitudes of those filling the arena. This sort of place-specific booking helped give rise to the practice of changing wrestlers' names and ethnicities for different venues. With the audience watching the matches now dispersed across the country, promoters could no longer rely on local prejudices to draw "heat" (crowd anger) for their heels. In response to this development, promoters turned toward heels who displayed their villainy either with flagrant violations of the rules (in the manner previously exemplified by the "Dirty" Duseks) or who used nonverbal appearance clues to immediately establish themselves as heels. Wrestlers entering an arena wearing a fez, monocle, flamboyant robe, or bleached-blond hair made clear their status as blackguards even before they stepped into the ring.

The ethnic factor, however, did not entirely disappear. Rather than play on localized animosities, promoters developed heels who represented evil to all Americans. Conditioned to mistrust Asians because of popular culture villains (Fu Manchu, Ming the Merciless) and World War II, all wrestlers of Asian ancestry became evil Japanese. Harold Sakata proved to be the most successful of these heels. Initially, he wrestled as Tosh Togo, but, after his appearance in the film *Goldfinger*, Sakata became known as Oddjob. While Japanese heels played on the legacy of World War II, their success at keeping wartime animosities alive paled in comparison to the achievements of wrestlers who promoted themselves as Nazis. Goose-stepping, swastika-emblazoned heels with bad German accents swelled wrestling's ranks during the 1950s. Karl Von Hess pioneered the gimmick, but Hans Schmidt more profitably used the persona; his ability to generate heat spawned countless imitators. Many of the later wrestlers adopted ridiculously melodramatic monikers such as Otto Von Krupp and Fritz Von Goering to guarantee fans recognized their connections to the Third Reich. Although Nazi wrestlers continued to operate into the 1970s, they faced competition from men with gimmicks related to a more immediate danger—Communism. Television brought the threat of Communism directly into America's homes. With governmental investigations into Communist subversion of the media fostering blacklists and threatened boycotts, television executives adopted a staunchly nationalist approach that regularly and routinely demonized Communism. As such, the simple-minded Cossack wrestling characters of the 1930s gave way to un-American Soviets, such as the "brothers" tag teams the Kalmikoffs and the Koloffs, as part of the burgeoning Cold War's influence on popular culture. The connection of Communism to "un-American" rule-breaking tactics proved so strong that it eventually spread to include alleged Cuban villains as well.[31]

Foreign menaces dated back to the "Terrible Turks" of the late nineteenth century and proved to be a profitable means of developing challengers for Jim Londos in the 1930s. However, the number of foreign menaces, the manner in which they directly linked their "other" status to villainy, and the visceral reaction they generated among fans all sharply escalated during the 1950s. According to Jeffrey Mondrak, this change reflected the intensely nationalistic, chauvinistic, and xenophobic sentiments that dominated American society at the time. Wrestling, therefore, not only adapted to reflect larger societal trends but also reinforced national, racial, and political stereotypes through its heel personas. This absorption of Cold War values spurred wrestling's recrudescence during the late 1940s and early 1950s. With its simple Manichaean dichotomy that linked those espousing alien ideologies to rule breaking and the eternal guarantee of retribution for those who promoted un-American values, wrestling offered a simplified version of the Cold War in which the good guys always emerged victorious. With wrestling operating within prevailing nationalist rhetoric, not surprisingly, narcissistic American heels captured major titles, but foreign menaces managed only to obtain minor or tag-team championships.[32]

This close connection between the politics of professional wrestling and the second Red Scare may partially explain the sharp drop in wrestling's popularity during the mid-1950s. Although Communism continued to operate as America's political bogeyman, the fervor of anti-Soviet sentiment lessened with Stalin's death and the discrediting of the nation's leading red-baiter, Joseph McCarthy. However, other factors also affected wrestling. The rush to exploit the new medium of television proved devastating in the long run. Oversaturation resulted in decreased live gates and eventually public weariness with the product. As technology advanced, other sporting options became available on television. By the end of the 1950s, baseball and football, now easily televised, nudged wrestling out of the limelight and came to dominate the decreased hours the networks devoted to sports programming. Network executives also moved to limit wrestling's coverage out of concerns over "television fatigue," a much-publicized theory that viewers would tune out if confronted with the same type of programming over an extended period. Wrestling survived on television, but only as a local product dedicated solely to convincing viewers to attend live matches. The decline of the mid-1950s also reflected another round of exposés aimed at discrediting the validity of matches. While many wrestling fans already recognized the showmanship involved in matches, newspaper accounts (and Herman Hickman's widely publicized breaking of the kayfabe) trimmed away some of the audience. Further, as NWA members scrambled to adapt to this return to localism and decreased revenue, court cases jeopardized the Alliance's ability to maintain control of wrestling. Just as investigations into the business practices of promoters destroyed the trust in the 1930s, governmental scrutiny would bring an end to the NWA's goal of a national wrestling cartel.[33]

6

HOLDING THE LINE

The flush of success experienced by professional wrestling in the late 1940s and early 1950s proved short-lived. Beset by external pressures and conflicts within the business, wrestling became one of the casualties of what Benjamin Rader termed the "great sports slump" of the 1950s. While football and baseball survived the slump because of their increasing popularity as television staples, which to a degree offset the losses in gate receipts, wrestling found itself edged out of the crowded television sports market as networks came to view it as an outdated fad. With attendance at arenas down as well, wrestling was marginalized, similar to the experience of the late 1930s. No longer an attraction featured in popular periodicals and prime-time television, wrestling survived as an entertainment form on the fringes of popular culture. Maligned and ridiculed by social critics, wrestling nonetheless proved to be seemingly indestructible.[1]

Wrestling endured, in part, because the promoters learned that television could be harnessed as a tool to increase live gates, not reduce them. Wrestling helped establish television as a viable medium in the United States, and wrestling also prospered because of its relationship with the networks. However, the unfettered availability of wrestling shows on television eventually resulted in a significant decrease in live gates. As early as 1950, promoters expressed concern about the oversaturation of wrestling on television.

In February 1950, Los Angeles promoters instituted a ban on the telecasting of local matches on channels in that city. As part of this battle to preserve live revenues a wrestlers' strike developed. Unwilling to lose this lucrative programming, Los Angeles stations negotiated with local promoters and agreed to limit the number of wrestling programs broadcast each week. The deal, however, did not affect the channels' ability to show out-of-town cards, which continued to hurt live gates in Los Angeles.[2]

Television overexposure across the nation propelled the wrestling slump of the mid-1950s, and the slump, in turn, helped push wrestling out of network prime-time lineups. Wrestling promoters, however, believed that television, a medium perfectly suited for wrestling, was a vital tool for the industry. Their efforts to develop television into a positive influence on the industry benefited from the economic circumstances of local television channels. Local network affiliates significantly increased the hours of weekly programming as the 1950s progressed. Moreover, wrestling, a type of programming cheap to produce, and with a proven track record of success, offered a useful means of filling local channel airtime. Shunted away from prime time, professional wrestling became a staple of Saturday programming. The Saturday shows typically fit two categories: live morning broadcasts from a studio or taped arena cards shown late at night. Weekend wrestling programs proved so successful that, by 1974, local channels offered 235 different shows weekly.[3]

Saturday wrestling programs became a valuable weapon in the arsenal of promoters. Learning from the mistakes of the early 1950s, promoters did not allow marquee matches to be part of the programs. Rather, the programs served to inform fans of current feuds and storylines, to keep established stars in the public eye, and to introduce new featured performers. The Saturday shows helped promoters "push" (the wrestling term for a focused promotional effort to establish a wrestler as a headliner through frequent victories and on-air attention) their stars, thereby increasing the attractiveness of seeing these men in live performances. Television "pushes" often revolved around "squash" matches, in which a star performer easily defeated an inept and unknown opponent (wrestlers known as "jobbers"). The television matches provided fans with a taste of a featured wrestler in the hope that they would then pay to see him compete at a local arena. Long before the recognized creation of television "infomercials," Saturday wrestling programming served as a long-form advertisement for local promoters.[4]

The almost universally negative coverage wrestling received from mainstream newspapers and magazines, and the eventual disappearance of wrestling coverage in local papers, also forced wrestling's powers to find new ways of keeping fans informed. Wrestling responded by developing its own dedicated magazines. These organs allowed wrestling to overcome the decrease in coverage by mainstream news outlets and ensured that fans received their wrestling information from a source sympathetic to the industry. While some respectable sporting journals, most significantly *Ring Magazine*, continued to offer balanced (but kayfabed) coverage of wrestling, the ballyhoo-filled wrestling magazines came to be the main source of printed information for devotees. Many of these magazines served as the printed equivalent of Saturday wrestling programs and offered readers carefully edited accounts of wrestling news and thinly veiled promotional "articles." *Wrestling Life*, *Wrestling As You Like It*, and *Official Wrestling* (the NWA's house journal) were the most successful wrestling magazines of the 1950s.[5]

Changing patterns in television and print media affected the manner in which the business operated, but these alterations represented relatively minor distractions compared with the legal difficulties faced by the NWA. Just as the wrestling trust of the 1930s found itself attacked for monopolistic practices, the Alliance ran afoul of the Department of Justice in the mid-1950s. The NWA's legal problems stemmed in part from the organization's success in regulating the wrestling industry. By 1956, thirty-eight regional promotions in the United States belonged to the Alliance, with the group's tentacles also reaching into Mexico, Canada, and Australasia. With affiliated promoters in every significant wrestling market, the NWA positioned itself to squeeze out any potential rivals. To eliminate threats from independent ("outlaw," in NWA parlance) promotions, the Alliance adopted strict rules that pushed the organization into actions later determined to be in restraint of trade. Alliance bylaws divided the nation into specific territories to prevent the wars that damaged the business in the 1930s—a move that kept affiliated promoters in line—but the NWA also regulated the movement of wrestlers as a means of combating independent operators. Like many businesses and governmental agencies of the 1950s, the NWA created a blacklist. Wrestlers who worked for independent promoters, publicly criticized their NWA-sanctioned promoter, or failed to uphold their contract faced the possibility of losing their ability to work for NWA promoters across the country. When an independent promotion challenged an NWA promoter, the Alliance would rush star performers into the area to prop up their promoter and also make clear that any wrestler who worked for the independent could no longer expect employment with NWA affiliates. The size and strength of the Alliance made these moves highly effective, but this success came at a price. With nothing left to lose, promoters and wrestlers victimized by the NWA's monopolistic practices brought these maneuvers to the attention of the authorities.

The NWA's legal difficulties began with a Department of Justice investigation of activities in southern California. In 1953, a war between NWA promoters and independents so intensified that not only did the independents find themselves driven out (an NWA victory hastened by the wrestlers' strike previously mentioned) but the NWA group controlling the region also fractured. John Doyle, a Los Angeles booker-promoter with NWA membership, left the southern California combine in disgust but later returned to the wrestling business. In 1955, Doyle started an independent promotion in Los Angeles and discovered that his former affiliation with the NWA provided no protection from the group's cutthroat business practices. He found himself unable to book top talent and also soon learned that those wrestlers working for him had been blacklisted by the NWA. After appeals to NWA president Sam Muchnick failed, Doyle retaliated by informing the Department of Justice of the Alliance's illegal practices. An investigation followed that discovered the NWA operated in a similar fashion across the country.[6]

In October 1956 the U.S. Attorney General's office filed a civil suit against the NWA in an Iowa federal district court. Interestingly, boxing, a sport long connected to wrestling and one that also prospered in the television era, also faced Department of Justice scrutiny. In that sport, the International Boxing Club (IBC) operated in a manner similar to wrestling's NWA. However, the Attorney General filed criminal, rather than civil, charges against that organization because of its ties to organized crime. Although NWA members avoided the possibility of prison sentences, the government's suit posed a significant challenge to the organization. The suit alleged that the NWA violated numerous antitrust statutes. Specific violations included the NWA's recognition of individuals as exclusive promoters and bookers in a designated territory, prevention of promoters and bookers from doing business in other territories, restriction of matches to certain areas and only to bookers or promoters affiliated with the NWA, and the requirement that bookers schedule matches exclusively through NWA promoters. The abundance of evidence related to these charges ensured the government's success in the suit, a circumstance that might have led to the complete dissolution of the NWA.[7]

Faced with the potential destruction of the NWA's wrestling empire, and a trial fraught with danger for a business built on worked matches, wrestling's controlling interests, unlike boxing's powers, decided to quietly settle with the government. The NWA members signed a consent decree acknowledging past antitrust violations and agreed to cancel all NWA bylaws found to be in restraint of trades. NWA members pledged to end the practice of allocating exclusive territories to promoters, to end the blacklisting of wrestlers who worked for nonmembers, to admit to membership any booker or promoter, and to allow wrestlers to be booked by non-NWA members. The decree effectively ended the federal government's concern over professional wrestling. For Muchnick, the decree saved both the NWA and the kayfabe.

Although the NWA consistently violated the decree's terms in the future and complaints continued to be filed with the Department of Justice, few legitimate attempts to investigate the business developed. This ambivalence stemmed both from the Department of Justice's need to allocate limited resources to cases involving national security or consumer safety and from perceptions of professional wrestling as an inconsequential and harmless form of entertainment. The removal of professional wrestling from prime-time television and the sport's retreat into regionalism during the 1960s and 1970s, helped foster this notion. Just as boxing's declining popularity allowed that sport's corruption to continue unabated after the IBC prosecutions, wrestling found itself marginalized to a degree that left it low on the list of federal investigators' concerns. The belief that the NWA did not possess the power to engage in monopolistic practices led to court victories for the Alliance in the infrequent cases in which it found itself challenged by those outside the organization.[8]

Although the NWA continued to be the dominant organization in wrestling, the federal investigation dealt a significant blow to the alliance's strength and prestige. With the NWA, legally at least, enjoined from engaging in the business practices that initially attracted members, promoters within the organization questioned the necessity of remaining tied to the Alliance. The promoters, always a fractious and self-absorbed group, developed a sense of independence in the wake of the court case, borne from the recognition that the benefits of NWA membership no longer outweighed the dangers of independence that threatened to cripple the Alliance. With business slumping and the NWA staggered, the possibility of challenges to alliance control increased. NWA president Sam Muchnick tried desperately to keep all of the member promoters within the Alliance but to no avail. In the end, maneuvers by the Alliance paved the way for the organization's rivals.

The most significant schisms in the Alliance developed over the issue of the world championship. Lou Thesz, the Alliance's standard-bearer since 1949, dropped the title to Leo Nomellini via disqualification in early 1955, but the NWA ruled that the title could not change hands in a match with a disqualification finish. Thesz officially lost the title to "Whipper" Billy Watson in March 1956, ostensibly so that the longtime champion could take an extended break from wrestling, with Thesz regaining the title in December of the same year. In one of the most confusing episodes in the history of professional wrestling, Edouard Carpentier defeated Thesz in June 1957 when Thesz injured his back and could not continue the match. Carpentier initially gained recognition as the new NWA world champion, but the Alliance later ruled that the title cannot change hands through an injury and gave the championship back to Thesz. However, in two subsequent draws with Thesz during the summer of 1957, Carpentier received billing as the NWA champion. With the "injury" rule in place, Thesz also defended the NWA title throughout the year, before losing to Dick Hutton in November. Quite possibly Muchnick planned the confusion over the championship to increase revenues by having two champions engaged in title defenses across the continent and to generate excitement for unification bouts, but this plan backfired.

Carpentier's claim to the title legitimized a number of championships outside of the Alliance. The NWA's 1956 legal difficulties emboldened several former members to break with the organization and strike out on their own. This confusion over the title proved to be the catalyst for many of these moves. With the NWA not offering the public a clear championship picture, independent-minded promoters recognized they could establish their own championships. Carpentier's title claim provided these promoters the opportunity not only to establish their own champions but to legitimize their new titles. A calculated risk at best, Muchnick's decision to promote simultaneous world champions might have succeeded in generating public interest in the NWA had all members cooperated. However, Eddie Quinn, Carpentier's promoter in Montreal, became one of the first to break with the crippled NWA in the wake of the court case. Quinn's move toward independence created an environment in which other promoters, seeking to leave the NWA, could exploit the title muddle.

By 1958, promoters in Montreal, Boston, and Omaha established their own "world" champions through Carpentier. All three of these cities possessed strong promotions and therefore represented significant losses to the NWA, but the greatest setback to the Alliance during this period occurred in the lucrative southern California market. Los Angeles promoters Jules Strongbow and Cal Eaton remained within the NWA after the court case, but they eventually broke with the Alliance over scheduling world title defenses in their territory. Unhappy with the NWA's refusal to send the world champion to the West Coast more regularly, they broke with the Alliance in late 1959 and declared Carpentier champion of the new North American Wrestling Alliance. After reorganizing under the name World Wrestling Association (WWA), the California promotion (along with Roy Shire's "outlaw" organization in San Francisco) developed into a vibrant challenger to NWA attempts to control the Pacific Coast. The WWA succeeded during the 1960s, in large measure because of the work of "Classy" Freddie Blassie. Possessing fantastic microphone skills, Blassie established himself as one of the most hated heels in the country. Eventually hobbled by knee injuries, Blassie later became a successful manager and commentator. The WWA struggled to maintain its independence in a changing Los Angeles market during the late 1960s and rejoined the NWA in late 1968.[9]

Although the Los Angeles promotion eventually returned to the NWA fold, other promoters used the Alliance's late 1950s difficulties to establish long-lived rivals to NWA hegemony. The NWA remained the business's dominant federation until the 1980s, but it never again exercised the high level of control the Alliance maintained in the early 1950s. Schisms within the Alliance propelled promoters to break with the NWA, and the success of these non-aligned promotions hampered the organization's ability to dictate terms to those promoters still affiliated. That the NWA, under these difficult circumstances, continued to be the largest organization in the country reflected the successful guidance of Muchnick. The Carpentier-Thesz title fiasco hurt Muchnick's reputation, and the NWA board forced him to resign the presidency in 1960, but his successors (Frank Tunney and Fred Kohler) proved incapable of providing comparable leadership. Muchnick once again became the Alliance's president in 1963 and continued in the post until 1977. The NWA's decision to reinstate Muchnick in 1963 reflected a recognition that the Alliance faced significant threats that the St. Louis promoter was best equipped to combat. At the beginning of his second tenure as NWA president, Muchnick was confronted with two organizations seeking to usurp the NWA. The territorial era of the 1960s and 1970s would be marked by the struggle by each of these three organizations to expand their market shares at the expense of the other two.[10]

Carpentier's title claim laid the foundation for the first of these NWA rivals—the American Wrestling Association (AWA). In June 1957, Omaha promoter Joe Dusek recognized Carpentier as world champion in his territory. Verne Gagne obtained the promotion's version of the world championship in 1958 after defeating Carpentier. Gagne's mixture of wrestling skills and business acumen led to the creation of the AWA. An all-American football player at the University of Minnesota and two-time National Collegiate Athletic Association (NCAA) wrestling champion, Gagne possessed immediate name recognition, legitimate shooting ability, and enormous ambition. With his claim to a version of the world title established, Gagne pushed for a chance to wrestle NWA champion Pat O'Connor. After the NWA refused, not surprisingly, to give an "outlaw" champion a shot at their title, Gagne and Minneapolis promoter Wally Karbo established the AWA in August 1960. Based in Minnesota, the AWA eventually controlled a territory that included the upper Plains, Chicago, and Winnipeg, with sporadic attempts to establish connections with promoters in the eastern Midwest and Mississippi Valley. Gagne not only ran the

AWA but also served as the federation's public face. He won the AWA championship for the ninth time in August 1968 and did not relinquish it until November 1975. Gagne finally retired in 1981 (during his tenth title run). Although Gagne frequently held the title, the AWA often gave the championship to well-known heels, who could then serve as foils for Gagne. During the 1960s, villains such as Dick the Bruiser, "Crusher" Lisowski, and Maurice "Mad Dog" Vachon held the organization's title. In this regard, the AWA offered a significant alternative to the NWA, which consistently kept its championship belt on high-drawing-power babyfaces. The AWA also gained a reputation as the organization most wedded to providing matches that stressed legitimate catch holds and less brawling. This reflected Gagne's views on offering the most believable product; he therefore maintained a roster of wrestlers weighted toward those with amateur wrestling backgrounds.[11]

During the 1970s, the AWA expanded its territory throughout the upper Midwest and into western cities such as Denver, Las Vegas, and San Francisco. While Gagne continued to be the company's standard-bearer for the first half of the decade, he built a strong federation through the skillful use of rivalries with heels such as Ken Patera, "Superstar" Billy Graham, and the Iron Sheik. In 1975 Gagne lost the AWA championship to Nick Bockwinkel. A second-generation wrestler, Bockwinkel turned pro as a teenager in the 1950s. In keeping with Gagne's traditional views, Bockwinkel possessed the legitimate wrestling skills necessary to both fend off a potential double-cross and provide fans with a believable match. With the exception of a few brief periods, Bockwinkel remained the AWA's champion until 1984. Although Gagne exhibited a willingness to give heels the AWA title throughout his career, Bockwinkel's long run as champion represented a stark departure from Gagne's, or other promoters', prior practices. Heel champions typically enjoyed only short tenures between the longer reigns of popular babyfaces; hence, Bockwinkel's almost decade at the top made him the most successful heel champion in wrestling history.

The NWA also lost control of the Northeast after a dispute with Vince J. McMahon, "Toots" Mondt, and Ray Fabiani of Capitol Wrestling. Capitol, based in Washington, D.C., used its control of Madison Square Garden to build a successful television-era territory around Primo Carnera and then Antonino Rocca. The organization's break with the NWA developed out of a rift over the most successful heel of the 1950s, "Nature Boy" Buddy Rogers. Born Herman Rhode (he later legally changed his name to Buddy Rogers), the Nature Boy developed a persona even more widely copied than that of Gorgeous George. In fact, Rogers' character can be viewed as a hypermasculinized version of George Wagner. Rogers bleached his hair like Wagner, wore elaborate robes and trunks, had valets, and strutted in the ring. However, Rogers converted George's techniques into pure narcissism and machismo. Rogers' gaudy ring attire often involved animal prints to connect him to safaris and hunting; instead of male attendants, he hired attractive young women to serve as his valets. While his interviews, like those of Wagner, typically involved frequent references to his beauty and wrestling skills, Rogers presented himself as the archetypal bully. Gorgeous George preened with the air of a dandy, Rogers preened with swagger. The Nature Boy and his solipsism shtick proved so successful at drawing fans that the NWA made him their champion in June 1961.

By the early 1960s, however, Mondt served as Rogers' booker. In attempting to shift the Alliance's balance of power to the East Coast, Mondt resisted booking Rogers west of the Mississippi River. Fearful that Capitol might break with the Alliance and take the NWA's championship with them, Muchnick brought Thesz out of semiretirement to regain the title in January 1963. Under threat of not refunding Rogers' belt deposit, the NWA convinced the Nature Boy to relinquish the title. Angered over losing the title, McMahon and Mondt refused to recognize Rogers' one-fall defeat to Thesz in Toronto, claiming that NWA championship matches had to be scheduled for best of three falls, broke with the NWA, and established the World Wide Wrestling Federation (WWWF).[12]

In May 1963, Rogers became the WWWF's first world champion, after allegedly winning a fictitious tournament in Rio de Janeiro, but he suffered from significant health problems that prevented Capitol from building their new federation around him. The same month he lost the title in forty-eight seconds against Bruno Sammartino. Born in Italy, but raised in Pittsburgh, Sammartino possessed only marginal wrestling skills, but his bodybuilder physique and charisma made him the standard-bearer for the new WWWF. The WWWF used Sammartino in a number of memorable feuds, including a bitter rivalry with much-traveled monster heel Walter "Killer" Kowalski. Sammartino's ascension reflected the changed environment in which professional wrestling operated during the 1960s and 1970s. When the national audience of the early 1950s ebbed, wrestling found itself buoyed by a fan-base similar to that of the pretelevision era. The very young, the very old, blue-collar workers, and minorities became wrestling's core audience. This situation led the WWWF to tailor its shows to appeal to these groups. Sammartino remained WWWF champion until early 1971 partly because he became a hero to working-class Italians. His success pushed the WWWF to promote other Italians, such as Dominic DeNucci and Antonio Pugliese, as well as make appeals to other ethnic groups. The WWWF proved especially adept at attracting New York's large Puerto Rican population. Capitol had attempted to increase its Hispanic attendance during the 1950s; however, the efforts increased in the ensuing decades. McMahon brought in a Rocca clone—"Argentina" Apollo—and several significant Hispanic performers, including Victor Rivera, Carlos Colon, and Mil Mascaras. The culmination of this appeal occurred in February 1971 when Pedro Morales became the WWWF world champion.

In 1972 the New York State Athletic Commission rescinded the ban on women's wrestling and McMahon booked ladies' matches in Madison Square Garden beginning in July. The Fabulous Moolah (born Lillian Ellison) became the main attraction of these matches. A protégée of Jack Pfeffer, Moolah began her career in the wrestling business as a valet. In the mid-1950s Moolah replaced June Byers as the recognized women's world champion. As a feared heel, Moolah held either the NWA or WWWF women's title for most of the remaining century. She eventually parlayed her in-ring success into a lucrative operation that provided female wrestlers for promoters across the country. Undoubtedly, the most important female wrestler in American history, the indestructible Moolah continued to wrestle into the twenty-first century.[13]

Shortly after Morales obtained the WWWF belt, McMahon rejoined the NWA. This move helped McMahon by making it easier to bring new talent into the area and benefited the NWA by giving them the ability to claim the eastern seaboard as Alliance territory. However, while McMahon officially demoted the WWWF belt to a regional title, the NWA never completely controlled the territory. The same independent-mindedness that led McMahon to first leave the Alliance thwarted NWA attempts to bring the promotion in line. McMahon, for example, steadfastly maintained the WWWF's preeminence in Madison Square Garden, the single-most important venue under his control. Not until 1979 did McMahon allow an NWA title match to occur in the historic arena.

While the return of women's wrestling to New York and McMahon's officially rejoining the NWA served as significant developments within the WWWF, the emergence of McMahon's son Vince Kennedy McMahon would prove to be the most historically important event of the decade. Vince K. (often erroneously referred to as Vince Junior) first became part of the family business by serving as the announcer for the *All-Star Wrestling* television program at the dawn of the "Me Decade." In 1973 his father gave him control of the WWWF's promotion in Maine. From the very beginning of his career in the wrestling business, Vince K. promoted the idea of experimenting with new techniques to increase the visibility of professional wrestling. McMahon proved to be one of the staunchest advocates of making wrestling more brawl than catch style. He encouraged wrestlers to bleed, to take their fights out of the ring and into the crowd, and to attempt flashy, high-risk maneuvers.

Vince K. also promoted the use of closed-circuit television as a way to both increase revenue and to make WWWF product available in more areas. He first attempted to use closed circuit as a moneymaking venture by organizing Evel Knievel's 1974 jump of the Snake River. In 1976, McMahon financed an ambitious plan to offer closed-circuit viewers a spate of boxer versus wrestler matches from various cities, which culminated in the Antonio Inoki–Muhammad Ali bout from Tokyo. The Inoki-Ali main event proved to be a dull disaster, but McMahon presciently recognized that emerging technology could be harnessed to drag professional wrestling back into the cultural mainstream. As the 1970s progressed, and Vince J. moved closer to retirement, the younger McMahon took on increasingly more responsibility within the organization. It was Vince K. who successfully lobbied for the holding of NWA title matches in the Garden in 1979, and he led the push for the adoption of the less unwieldy World Wrestling Federation (WWF) name that same year.[14]

The changing nature of wrestling audiences also affected the NWA. While the Alliance continued to revolve around its St. Louis hub, the loss of the Northeast and upper Plains left the NWA strong in the nation's heartland and South, with other centers located in a few industrial centers of the East. The blue-collar base of professional wrestling allowed the NWA to maintain this eastern presence even with the difficulties in controlling the WWWF territory. Loyal NWA promoters kept the Alliance active in cities such as Columbus, Buffalo, and Detroit. In Buffalo, promoter Pedro Martinez followed McMahon's lead and offered fans local favorites, such as Dick Beyer (before he turned heel as the Destroyer) and Italian-American hero Ilio DiPaolo. A rust belt promotion based in Detroit also proved successful. As with Gagne and the AWA, the Michigan promotion operated under the auspices of its leading ring performer, Ed Farhat. As the Sheik, Farhat established himself as the promotion's perennial champion and became one of the nation's most hated heels. Farhat knew only a handful of holds, but he developed a very marketable ring style. He launched a frenzied attack on his opponent as soon as the match began, pummeling them with kicks, punches, chokeholds, and foreign objects. The Sheik's matches invariably became bloodbaths that ended within five minutes.[15]

While the NWA maintained successful territories in the North, the Alliance's power during the 1960s and 1970s derived primarily from the highly lucrative promotions of the American South. The South became the Alliance's base after the defections of the early 1960s and continued to provide the NWA's strongest territories until the organization crumbled in the 1980s. Professional wrestling became a staple of working-class southern entertainment during the 1960s. This partly reflected the sport's general appeal to law-and-order blue-collar Americans willing to embrace wrestling's simple good versus evil dichotomy, but the South's unique position in the 1960s also contributed. Wrestling retreated from prime-time television and the North, in part, because of the expanding popularity of team sports, particularly professional football and basketball. With the exception of the burgeoning metropolis of Atlanta, the South was overwhelmingly excluded from hosting teams in major professional sports. Southern sports fans, therefore, possessed fewer choices in their quest to attend live events; college football and professional wrestling became the beneficiaries of this circumstance. By the 1970s, the South provided most of both the NWA's wrestlers and live match attendees.[16]

The troubled history of championship double-crosses led the NWA to be especially careful in selecting world champions during this period. Although all titleholders were still required to post a belt deposit, the NWA made sure the title rested on men completely loyal to the Alliance. Also, to reduce the potential for in-ring double-crosses, the NWA champions of the period all possessed legitimate wrestling skills. When the aging Thesz lost the title for the final time in 1966 he gave way to a cluster of champions who both possessed the ability to defend themselves in the ring and who fit the NWA's image of a champion. The NWA believed strongly in a championship formula that involved young, handsome stars who wrestled as baby-faces. This led to title runs for Gene Kiniski, Dory Funk Jr., and Harley Race. However, Jack Brisco, NWA champion from 1973 to 1975, represented the epitome of NWA-style champions. He worked well on the microphone, won an NCAA championship in 1965, and possessed dark good looks. From his professional debut in 1966 on, Brisco clearly fit the NWA championship mold. Most tellingly, even the gimmick-driven promoters immediately recognized Brisco's abilities and, despite his being a Native American from Oklahoma, did not force an "Indian" character on him.[17]

Although the NWA ran shows in Japan, Mexico, and Australia (and even did occasional cross-bookings with the AWA and WWWF), these champions spent most of their time touring the Alliance's southern promotions. In terms of title changes that occurred in the United States, no city north of St. Louis witnessed the crowning of a new champion from Thesz's 1963 defeat of Rogers until 1987. The NWA maintained its strongest territories in Texas, Florida, Georgia, and the Carolinas. As these territories came to the fore (and younger promoters took charge of them), Muchnick's ability to dominate the Alliance from his St. Louis base slowly eroded. While Muchnick's reputation and longevity earned him the respect of all NWA members, a significant shift in power occurred during the 1970s as the aging Missouri boss found himself challenged by young promoters in lucrative territories. The southern promoters who gained the upper hand within the Alliance proved far more willing to place the title on wrestlers who offered successful gim-micks, with increasingly less reliance on catch skills. As wrestling columnist Dave Meltzer noted, "the quiet babyface who was a technician and wrestled a legitimate-looking wrestling match on top like Mr. Wrestling, Brisco and Funk Jr. were losing ground to wilder-talking, brawling babyfaces who got by more on charisma, squirming their bodies and dancing, like [Mr. Wrestling] II, Wahoo McDaniel, and Dusty Rhodes."[18]

Wrestling's biggest draw of the 1970s also reflected the changing nature of babyfaces. In prior decades an oversized, foreign wrestler with misshapen facial features would have been, as with Maurice Tillet, promoted as a heel. Because he suffered from the glandular disease acromegaly, Andre Rousimoff grew to a remarkable six feet ten inches and weighed around four hundred pounds. As a young man, Rousimoff demonstrated fantastic athletic skills for a man his size, and he became a professional wrestler (and, briefly, a boxer) as a teenager. His bulk made Andre a fantastic special attraction, and his affable manner led promoters to push Rousimoff, against type, as a good guy. After wrestling in France and Canada in the 1960s, Rousimoff, renamed Andre the Giant by Vince J. McMahon, became a huge draw in the United States during the next decade. To prevent his gimmick from growing stale, Andre traveled throughout the country, spending only a few weeks at a time in any territory. Typically promoted as the "eighth wonder of the world" (and as seven feet four inches, five hundred pounds), Andre became the "most in-demand wrestler in the world." Although his illness, and lifestyle, reduced his physical capabilities as the decade progressed, Andre continued to be a significant draw and a significant player in the rise of the WWF during the 1980s.[19]

The strongest NWA territories during the 1970s included those in St. Louis, Texas, Florida, Georgia, and the Carolinas. With Muchnick's advancing age becoming a factor, promoters in these areas sought to increase their power within the Alliance. While battles for control and influence raged in the Alliance from its inception, the fights of the 1970s presented Muchnick with new challenges. Many of the younger promoters respected Muchnick but felt he no longer understood young fans or the changing nature of the business. The drift away from catch-style matches that Meltzer noted reflected the changes in fan attitudes recognized by the Alliance's younger members. To keep the fans interested in NWA product, promoters lobbied for champions who presented believable brawling styles. The increasing power of the younger promoters can be seen by the board's championship selections during the period. In 1975, Terry Funk, son of Amarillo promoter Dory Funk Sr., became the NWA champion. Although Funk possessed legitimate wrestling skills, his style reflected the influence of barroom fights rather than the teachings of Lou Thesz. Funk lost the title to Harley Race. Again, Race knew how to engage in catch-style matches, but he built his reputation on a rugged, tough guy persona and a surly disposition. Race, except for brief intervals, remained NWA champion until 1981.

During his reign, Race lost the title to Dusty Rhodes on two occasions. No wrestler better represented the changing nature of NWA champions than Rhodes. Born Virgil Runnels, Rhodes became the leading attraction of Eddie Graham's Florida promotion during the 1970s. Promoting himself as the "American Dream," Rhodes connected perfectly to the blue-collar fans of the 1970s. His spittle-filled, non sequitur–laced interviews often made little sense, but Rhodes perfectly understood his audience. He shouted, pointed, and threatened without ever losing sight of what his fans wanted to hear—that Dusty loved America and beating people up in equal measures. With his expansive beer belly, badly dyed hair, and scarred forehead, Rhodes looked like a guy who just stepped out of the crowd, which only furthered his linkage to the fans. As later commentators noted, Rhodes was "urban and blue collar, a southern 'embodiment' of the silent majority yet clearly within the 'good ol' boy' mold of regional stereotypes." Despite his popularity, Rhodes' lack of wrestling skills would have prevented him from becoming champion in previous decades, but the changing of the guard within the NWA allowed him to ascend to the title. Rhodes' promoter Eddie Graham served as NWA president during the late 1970s, and his power within the Alliance helped push Rhodes on a national level.[20]

While promoters such as Graham, Dallas's Fritz von Erich, and Bob Geigel of Kansas City helped push the NWA's championship into a new direction, two other promotions came to affect the organization in even more significant manners. The thriving promotions in Georgia and the Carolinas became the bases for promoters who not only transformed the nature of the NWA but who also laid the foundation for the destruction of the Alliance. Both of these promotions did well during the 1950s and 1960s, but they became even more lucrative during the 1970s. Significantly, both areas came under the control of new promoters during the 1970s. Jim Crockett Jr. inherited the Carolina promotion from his father. In Georgia, a bitter wrestling war developed that eventually left James Barnett in control of the area. Crockett and Barnett used their power in these territories to leverage control of the Alliance itself, with Crockett eventually gaining the strength to break the NWA and establish his own wrestling empire.

"Big" Jim Crockett operated the Carolinas territory from 1953 until his death in April 1973. During his tenure, the promotion focused on tag-team wrestling but adopted a singles championship as well at the beginning of the 1970s. After Crockett's death, his son Jim, only 24 years old at the time, took over the promotion. Crockett Jr. continued to support a competitive tag-team division but also increasingly stressed the singles title, which he renamed the Mid-Atlantic title. His Mid-Atlantic promotion blossomed in the 1970s because of the developing population and economy of his territory, Crockett's willingness to spend money to recruit wrestlers, and the genius of his booker, George Scott. During the 1970s the Mid-Atlantic territory became the NWA's most vibrant promotion. Crockett and Scott brought in established stars such as Johnny Valentine, Wahoo McDaniel, Jack Brisco, and Ole and Gene Anderson to rebuild the territory but also exhibited remarkably sound judgment by hiring younger performers as well. Wrestlers such as Jimmy "Superfly" Snuka, Ricky Steamboat, and Greg Valentine helped attract young fans by bringing fast-paced styles into the region.[21]

The biggest new star to develop out of the Mid-Atlantic territory, however, promoted a persona straight out of the 1950s. Bodybuilder Ric Flair established himself in the region by co-opting Buddy Rogers' character. Flair adopted the nickname "Nature Boy," strutted, wore flamboyant robes, and finished opponents with Rogers' figure-four leglock. Despite the initial derivativeness of his character, Flair succeeded because his own abilities amplified the Nature Boy gimmick beyond even Rogers. Flair melded a masterful understanding of the psychology of matches with tremendous stamina and athletic ability to elevate many of his in-ring encounters to a fevered, dramatic pitch. He coupled this with fantastic microphone skills, which Flair used to create a jet-setting, international playboy persona.

In the Carolinas, Flair initially teamed with veteran Rip Hawk, but he established himself as a singles wrestler during the mid-1970s. In September 1975, he captured the Mid-Atlantic heavyweight title by defeating McDaniel in a "hair versus title" match. Flair regularly built excitement for matches by stipulating that he would shave off his long blond hair if defeated, just as Gorgeous George did twenty years before. Flair clearly understood the root of George's appeal to wrestling fans. Although Rogers served as his primary influence, Wagner also inspired the new Nature Boy. Flair not only engaged in George-style hair matches, but he also wore robes of sequin, rhinestones, and fur that resembled Wagner's elaborate ring wear. Flair's persona, then, mixed aspects of Wagner's dandified character with the narcissism of Rogers. His career, however, almost ended just two weeks after he won the Mid-Atlantic title. On October 20, 1975, a plane carrying Flair and several other wrestlers crashed near Wilmington, North Carolina. The crash ended the careers of Johnny Valentine and Bob Bruggers and left Flair with a broken back. Despite the severity of his injuries, Flair recovered sufficient strength to return to the ring in February 1976. The torch was somewhat passed in 1979 when Flair engaged in a series of Nature Boy bouts against Buddy Rogers, who came out of a more than decadelong retirement. Flair continued to be a top draw (and perennial champion) in the Mid-Atlantic territory and elsewhere throughout the 1970s before becoming the NWA's main attraction in the early 1980s.[22]

By the dawn of the 1980s, the success of the Mid-Atlantic promotion made Jim Crockett Jr. the most powerful single promoter in the NWA. However, it would be events in the Georgia territory that set the stage for Crockett's eventual dismemberment of the NWA. In Atlanta, the ABC Booking Company (controlled by Paul Jones, Lester Welch, and Ray Gunkel) owned the NWA rights to the territory. In August 1972, Gunkel, who wrestled as well as promoted, died of a heart attack. His death led to a power struggle over the territory between Jones and Welch and Gunkel's widow, Ann. Within days of Gunkel's death, the two sides organized separate promotions, with both vying for NWA recognition. The NWA sided with the Welch faction and funneled top talent into the territory in an attempt to run Ann Gunkel out of business. Atlanta wrestling fans found themselves treated to Friday night cards that included stars such as Brisco, Kiniski, Thesz, Mr. Wrestling, and "Cowboy" Bill Watts. The NWA also brokered deals that gave some stars, such as Brisco, small ownership portions in the Georgia territory as a way to keep them involved in the area.[23]

In mid-1973, Jim Barnett bought out the Welch faction. As a well-educated patron of the arts and an open homosexual, Barnett little resembled the grizzled huckster stereotype of wrestling promoters, but he used keen business sense to establish himself as an important player in the NWA. Barnett first became involved in wrestling during the 1950s, when he worked for Chicago promoter Fred Kohler. He later partnered with Johnny Doyle to operate promotions in Indiana and Australia. Barnett also purchased part of Eddie Graham's Florida promotion in 1973, and, in early 1974, he convinced Ann Gunkel to sell her struggling "outlaw" promotion to him for $200,000. These southern developments helped make Barnett a national power within the NWA. Barnett became an NWA board member in 1974, and later served as vice-president and secretary-treasurer. He also held the important position of booker for the NWA champion.[24]

The purchase of Gunkel's operation provided two direct benefits to Barnett. First, it gave him complete control of the Georgia territory, thereby ending the costly war for the region. But even more important, by owning Gunkel Enterprises Barnett controlled that company's local television program on WTCG in Atlanta. In 1971, maverick entrepreneur Ted Turner purchased the struggling UHF channel WJRJ and immediately renamed it WTCG. Desperate for programming, Turner scooped up ABC Booking's *Georgia Championship Wrestling* program when WQXI decided to move wrestling to a lesser time slot. *Georgia Championship* ran on Turner's station on Saturdays at 6 p.m., and the show was an immediate success. When the war for Atlanta broke out, Ann Gunkel persuaded Turner to show her *All-South Wrestling* at 5 p.m. on Saturdays, with *Georgia Championship* following it. Therefore, when Barnett bought out Gunkel, he obtained a two-hour block of Saturday night programming. Control of two hours of Saturday night television gave Barnett an unrivaled opportunity to publicize his stars, angles, and live gates, and the Georgia territory flourished in the mid-1970s.[25]

In December 1976, as one of the pioneering satellite "superstations," Turner took his station national. Renamed Turner Broadcasting System (TBS), little WTCG suddenly seeped into homes across the nation. Turner, despite going national, did not fundamentally alter his programming and *Georgia Championship Wrestling* maintained its two-hour block on Saturday nights. Part of Turner's move to uplink his channel to a satellite derived from his determination to make the Atlanta Braves (which he owned) a more economically viable baseball club. Turner's decision to broadcast his station on the Satcom 1 satellite converted the local into the national; the Braves became "America's team," and *Georgia*

Championship became the nation's most-watched wrestling program. Host Gordon Solie and the wrestlers appearing on Barnett's television program gained national exposure and fame. Wrestling fans across the country, too distant from Georgia or the other areas Barnett promoted to attend his live shows, now followed the storylines and stars of his promotion.

Outraged NWA members complained bitterly that Barnett had electronically invaded their territories and that the local availability of his TBS program drove down their live gates. However, promoters in territories close to Georgia, such as Graham in Florida and Crockett in the Mid-Atlantic, benefited from *Georgia Championship Wrestling*, as their location made it easy to get their stars to Atlanta for television tapings. Wrestlers gained notoriety from appearing on the program and returned to their home promotions as bigger attractions. With the balance of power already shifted toward the South, promoters in that region successfully kept the NWA from forcing Barnett off the national airwaves. And *Georgia Championship Wrestling* served only to further strengthen the position of the promoters operating profitable southern territories. For Barnett, the success and exposure of the television program allowed him to expand his territory. By the early 1980s, he booked shows in Ohio, West Virginia, Tennessee, Alabama, and parts of Pennsylvania. Reflecting this growth, the Saturday night television show became *World Championship Wrestling*.[26]

While the southern territories of the NWA continued to be profitable ventures, wrestling slipped in both respectability and visibility throughout the country. During the 1970s, professional wrestling came to be viewed as a crude "morality play with muscles." The mainstream media outlets, although willing to accept advertising dollars from promoters, increasingly ridiculed or ignored wrestling, leaving the long-lived entertainment form thoroughly marginalized and roundly denigrated. The entrée of eccentric comic Andy Kaufman into wrestling best represents the state of the business at the dawn of the 1980s. In the late 1970s, Kaufman proclaimed himself "intergender" world champion and began wrestling women on talk shows and during his stand-up appearances. Kaufman then attempted to break into professional wrestling proper and, through a connection with wrestling writer Bill Apter, started appearing on shows booked by the NWA promotion in Memphis. Promotion owners Jerry Jarrett and Jerry "the King" Lawler initially had

Kaufman wrestle women and then established a feud between the comedian and Lawler. Their matches in 1982–1983 sold out arenas throughout the mid-South, and the publicity spilled over into a joint appearance on the *Late Show with David Letterman*. That a star of the television show *Taxi* dabbled in wrestling represented the only knowledge many Americans possessed about the current state of affairs in the business, a clear demonstration of how far wrestling had slipped from the public consciousness. Even more telling with regards to the fan base of wrestling, Kaufman managed to generate enviable heat from crowds through his incessant attacks on hillbillies and other southern stereotypes.[27]

At the dawn of the Reagan Decade, wrestling found itself cut off from significant elements of the American public and struggling to maintain its reduced status. Although strong in the southern part of the country, even the successful NWA promotions in that area faced challenges in the early 1980s. The new decade would bring prosperity to wrestling, but at the cost of enormous upheavals. By the early 1980s, Crockett, whose territory expanded almost as much as Barnett's, positioned himself to become the dominant influence within the NWA. The vehicle with which he could establish that preeminence proved to be cable television. Barnett's success in parlaying national television exposure into profitability and the opening of new markets demonstrated that the medium could be exploited by a promoter looking to swallow up territory from less successful promotions. When Barnett and those controlling Georgia Championship Wrestling stumbled financially in the early 1980s, the expansionist-minded Crockett swooped in to build on the advances made by Barnett. Crockett's efforts would eventually finish the NWA as a national organization as he struck out on his own, but the NWA-aligned promotion that controlled New York broke the Alliance even before the Mid-Atlantic kingpin served the coup de grâce. Just as "Toots" Mondt and Jack Curley changed the face of wrestling before him, Vince K. McMahon permanently altered wrestling during the 1980s.

7

THE RISE OF VINCE McMAHON

At the dawn of the 1980s, the AWA, NWA, and WWF all continued to vie for dominance of the wrestling business. As the oldest and, in terms of territory controlled, largest of the three, the NWA appeared to have the upper hand. And with Vince J. McMahon's return to the Alliance fold, the AWA stood as the only truly independent rival to the NWA. However, just as television shifted the balance of power within the business in the 1950s, the expansion of cable television in the 1980s decisively altered the wrestling world. The mid-1970s' battle over *Georgia Championship Wrestling* seeping into the territories of other NWA members proved to be a bitter fight, but it did not pose a challenge to the NWA's existence. In the 1980s, however, a promoter with visions of ruling wrestling independently of the Alliance used cable to declare war on all other promotions. The machinations of Vince K. McMahon, coupled with disastrous business practices by NWA promoters, proved that the fragile Alliance, with its individual fiefdoms, could not withstand a committed opponent. Through slick production, savvy marketing, and forceful performers, McMahon's promotion brought wrestling to the peak of its popularity in American history. After a desperate battle, he also managed to bury his competition. By the end of the century, only one truly national promotion remained in operation.

During the early 1980s, the WWF lagged behind the NWA promotions in Georgia, the Carolinas, and the AWA. However, business decisions within those promotions gave Vince K. McMahon opportunities to build his operation at the expense of his leading opponents. Both the Georgia and Carolinas promotions crumbled from a combination of mismanagement and McMahon's tactics. Those two NWA promotions offered significant obstacles to McMahon's plan to control American wrestling, and both attempted to expand beyond their traditional boundaries to position themselves as market leaders. In both cases, the promotions overextended themselves, rendering them even more vulnerable to the WWF's attacks. Further, both the Jim Barnett and Jim Crockett promotions proved susceptible to internecine warfare that hampered attempts to keep the promotions viable. In the AWA, Verne Gagne lost most of his talent to McMahon in the early 1980s, and the aging Minnesota promoter never fully recovered. Gagne attempted to counter his marginalization by obtaining a cable television contract and co-opting WWF techniques to modernize the AWA, but these efforts could not save his underfunded organization.

In 1980 Georgia Championship Wrestling parlayed the exposure offered by its weekend programs on TBS into a territorial expansion. The Barnett promotion began booking shows in towns where the local cable companies carried Ted Turner's station. By early 1981, Georgia Championship offered live cards throughout Ohio and in parts of Michigan and West Virginia. With their television programs providing free advertising, the promotion even found it profitable to stage one-off shows in small towns such as Athens, Ohio. This northern push placed Georgia Championship into direct competition with the Sheik's Detroit-based NWA promotion and Vince J. McMahon's WWF (in cities such as Cleveland, Baltimore, and Pittsburgh). The Sheik's promotion, already staggering toward oblivion, closed during this period, but the encroachment into McMahon's territory posed a more serious challenge. Although Vince J. McMahon gave Georgia Championship his blessing to run shows in some cities, Barnett's violations of the supposed sanctity of other NWA promoters' territories undoubtedly influenced the actions of Vince K. McMahon. The younger McMahon recognized not only that the NWA did not possess the power to hold ambitious promoters in check but that cable television could serve as a wedge to splinter other promotions.[1]

While Georgia Championship's management proved astute in its usage of cable television's power, they thoroughly mismanaged the company's finances. Inflated salaries, wasteful spending, and the welter of incidental expenses involved in operating such a far-flung promotional territory slowly sank the company as it expanded into the Ohio Valley. These financial difficulties translated into significant internal problems as the company's largest stockholders began to squabble over Georgia Championship's future direction. By 1984 two warring factions—Barnett and the Brisco brothers versus Ole Anderson and Fred Ward—developed within the company, which made daily operations almost impossible. In the spring of 1984, the Briscos and Barnett made the fateful decision to sell their majority of the company's shares to Vince K. McMahon. The WWF boss's decision to purchase Georgia Championship represented merely one aspect of his larger drive to eliminate all of his wrestling rivals.[2]

McMahon had developed an increasingly large role in the operations of the WWF at the end of the 1970s. By early in the Reagan Decade McMahon supplanted his father as the driving force behind the federation. In the spring of 1983 he officially purchased the company from his father. While Vince J. McMahon continued to be part of the WWF, both his health and his interest in the business declined. Although Vince J. had maintained a solid working relationship with the NWA throughout his career, the aging promoter made no attempt to curb the ambitions of his son. In fact, in one of Vince J. McMahon's final acts with the WWF, he officially pulled the promotion out of the NWA in August 1983. This move came in response to Alliance members' demands that the WWF stop running their cable television program in other promoters' territories. The WWF's departure from the NWA eliminated any lingering doubts that the Alliance faced a very real threat from the McMahon promotion. While Vince J. McMahon and the AWA's Gagne maintained working relationships with the NWA and at least a grudging acceptance of territorial boundaries, Vince K. McMahon refused to accept wrestling's established business methods. The old-guard promoters, complacent and assailable, found themselves confronted with a renegade promoter unwilling to respect the NWA's divisions of wrestling's spoils.[3]

While McMahon recognized the NWA posed the most serious threat to his efforts, Verne Gagne's AWA offered an easier initial target. Central to McMahon's plans to develop the WWF into a national organization stood the need to build a roster of "superstars" capable of generating excitement over McMahon's product in new markets. Despite being a clear second to the NWA in popularity, the AWA possessed a remarkable strong stable of performers in the early 1980s. McMahon therefore began his attempts to improve the quality of WWF product by raiding the AWA for talent. He initially offered to simply buy the AWA from the aging Gagne. Rebuffed, McMahon then offered AWA performers significantly more money than Gagne could afford to pay them. The WWF chief eventually co-opted more than two dozen AWA wrestlers. The more significant early pilferings included announcer "Mean" Gene Okerlund, manager Bobby "The Brain" Heenan, Jesse "The Body" Ventura, Rick Martel, and Adrian Adonis. To add insult to injury, McMahon started booking WWF shows in Minneapolis, Gagne's base, in 1983. These WWF cards often included wrestlers recently acquired from the AWA.[4]

However, a blond former bodybuilder proved to be McMahon's most important acquisition from the Gagne promotion. Terry Bollea began wrestling in 1978. After being discovered playing bass in a Tampa bar band, Bollea went to work for Eddie Graham's Florida promotion, then moved to Memphis to wrestle for Jerry Jarrett and Jerry Lawler. Following the pattern of all young wrestlers in the pre-McMahon era, Bollea then spent short stints working for various promotions, including Georgia Championship. In January 1980, Vince J. McMahon hired him to wrestle in the WWF. Before this move, Bollea wrestled under the names Terry "The Hulk" Boulder and Sterling Golden; McMahon changed his name to Hulk Hogan. In August 1981, Hogan moved again and began working for Gagne's AWA. During Hogan's stint in the WWF, he landed a part in the Sylvester Stallone vehicle *Rocky III*, which premiered in May 1982. The film proved to be a box office success and Hogan ("Thunder Lips" in the movie) suddenly became one of the most recognizable wrestlers in the country. Gagne exploited this renown by making Hogan the top babyface in the AWA. However, Gagne continued to cling to the notion that his world champion must possess legitimate wrestling skills. While Hogan looked great, bristled with energy, and proved himself adept at coining interview catchphrases, the hulking Floridian knew very few actual holds. As the AWA's top draw, Gagne found himself compelled to keep Hogan involved in a program with champion Nick Bockwinkel, but he refused to let Hogan ever win the title. The disgruntled Hogan, therefore, left the AWA for the WWF in December 1983.[5]

McMahon needed Hogan and the other AWA wrestlers for his own cable-television programming. In October 1983, the USA Network, which began life as a dedicated sports network, dumped Joe Blanchard's *Southwest Championship Wrestling* from San Antonio over an on-air incident involving wrestlers hurling animal feces at each other. As a replacement, they turned to McMahon and the WWF, who immediately launched *All-American Wrestling*. USA reached 24 million homes by early 1984, and this national coverage turned the WWF into the most-watched wrestling federation in the nation. McMahon's greatest success, however, proved to be *Tuesday Night Titans*, a prime time USA show with McMahon and "Lord" Alfred Hayes as hosts. *Titans* presented an alternative universe version of the *Tonight Show*, with wrestlers sitting on a coach chatting with the hosts, sophomoric comedy sketches, and footage from recent WWF matches. McMahon also repackaged tapes for three other shows sold in syndication. The trickle of WWF programming that caused such consternation at the NWA's annual meeting in 1983 had, by 1984, turned into a flood that washed over the entire country. Even with its two-hour block on Saturday nights Georgia Championship could not compete with the expansive reach of the WWF. For the other NWA promoters, whose stars only gained national exposure by appearing on the Georgia promotion's show, any attempt to generate countrywide interest in their product as a counter proved impossible. They did not possess the resources, nor could they stomach the idea of breaking the NWA's territorial code. McMahon played on this reluctance, moved into their territories in the wake of his television shows, and picked the NWA promoters off one by one.[6]

Because of his slick product and marketing, McMahon undoubtedly would have positioned himself as the dominant wrestling presence regardless of NWA actions, but a legitimate effort by NWA members to work in concert might have slowed his progress. However, the Alliance found it impossible to agree on a united counter to McMahon's assault. In March 1984, NWA promoters and Verne Gagne met to discuss means of cooperating in an effort to stop the WWF. They discussed pooling of talent and developing national NWA television shows, but they could not agree on who would be empowered to run the operation. Gagne, Jim Crockett, and Bill Watts, among others, all lobbied for the right to control the newly centralized NWA. Gagne and Crockett briefly operated a syndicated TV show, *Pro Wrestling USA*, but the program quickly fizzled. For most members, however, relinquishing control of their territories to an all-powerful promoter under the NWA banner appeared no different that McMahon taking over their territories. The decision to keep their individual fiefdoms and fight McMahon, rather than surrender their territory to the NWA, proved fateful. Localized and underfunded, most of the NWA promoters stood no chance against the WWF juggernaut.[7]

Only the largest NWA promotions offered any real challenge to McMahon. With its TBS television program, Georgia Championship represented the only one of these promotions that possessed fully national exposure; therefore, it became a primary target of McMahon. In that endeavor, he benefited from the internal struggle that wracked the expanding, but economically fragile, promotion during the early 1980s. Barnett and the Brisco brothers, who together held the majority of the company's stock, recognized earlier than most that the WWF's momentum made the NWA's survival highly unlikely. Armed with that knowledge, they decided to accept a buyout from McMahon before he completely bankrupted their promotion. In April 1984, McMahon purchased the majority interest in Georgia Championship (and Barnett and the Briscos obtained employment with the WWF). For McMahon this not only eliminated one of the few promotions that could derail his efforts but also gave him control of the company's TBS time slots. Overnight the WWF became the only wrestling promotion with national coverage.[8]

As part of the agreement between Ted Turner and McMahon, the WWF boss pledged to tape live Saturday matches for the TBS show formerly controlled by Georgia Championship. On "Black Saturday," June 14, 1984, the WWF debuted in the old Georgia Championship time slot on TBS. McMahon, however, found it impossible to get his workers to Atlanta every Saturday, so, in violation of his agreement with Turner, the WWF program relied heavily on tapes of matches from the Northeast. Turner responded by pressuring McMahon to increase the number of tapings held in Atlanta and contracted with "Cowboy" Bill Watts to air his *Mid-South Wres-*

tling Hour on Sunday afternoons. Their dispute came to a head eight months later when Turner refused to allow McMahon to sell advertising time on the Saturday night program. Turner threatened to sue McMahon for breach of contract, which forced McMahon to find a way out of Atlanta. Barnett then brokered a deal between McMahon and Jim Crockett Promotions (JCP) for the sale of Georgia Championship. Turner agreed to allow Crockett to run his own show during the Saturday night slot and even agreed to assist Crockett by dropping Watts's show off the Sunday schedule. As part of the shift toward a national audience, Crockett dropped the Mid-Atlantic name (and title) from his company and began calling it World Championship Wrestling (WCW).[9]

By the time Crockett purchased Georgia Championship, his promotion stood as the most successful of the remaining NWA territories in the country. He parlayed this status into appointment as NWA president for much of the 1980s. As president, he wielded the power to make his main attraction, Ric Flair, the NWA champion. Crockett and his booker, Dusty Rhodes, also demonstrated a willingness to embrace new business practices that kept JCP viable at a time when other NWA members faltered. On Thanksgiving night 1983, they promoted wrestling's first major closed-circuit event, *Starrcade*, from Greensboro, North Carolina, to venues in three states. The show, which featured Harley Race versus Ric Flair in a steel cage, was an enormous success. With a national television deal to follow up this triumph, JCP positioned itself as both the face of the NWA and the WWF's most significant rival.[10]

However, JCP, even with its accomplishments, found itself consistently outmaneuvered by McMahon. The loss of Georgia Championship represented the only blip of difficulty for the WWF during the period McMahon battled with Crockett for preeminence. In December 1983, McMahon replaced Bob Backlund, whose winsome do-gooder character had outlived its usefulness, with the Iron Sheik as WWF champion. The Iranian served merely as a caretaker champion until the ascension of Hulk Hogan in January 1984. McMahon planned to build his WWF around Hogan. With his chiseled body, boundless energy, and arsenal of catchphrases, Hogan perfectly fit the mold of the new generation of professional wrestlers. McMahon also recognized that Hogan's in-ring limitations threatened to dampen fan excitement, so the two men developed an appealing formula for the times when Hogan had to actually wrestle. His matches, whenever possible, would be short, with Hogan's heel opponent, controlling the action until the WWF star made a miraculous recovery (fueled by fan excitement) and quickly dispatched the villain. As one critic noted, Hogan's "entire repertoire consists of the [Survivor song] *Eye of the Tiger*, a shredding muscle shirt, a few minutes of inept brawling and the infamous leg-drop finish out of nowhere."[11]

The WWF's success stemmed, in large measure, from the promotion's success in selling characters such as Hogan. With slick production values, mass marketing, and a mind-numbing array of merchandise, WWF wrestlers possessed a vibrancy lacked by the blander AWA or southern-tinged NWA performers. McMahon's characters certainly possessed no more depth or nuance than those of other promotions, but the WWF's promotional techniques magnified each wrestler's dominant trait to the level of semi-cartoon-ishness. Cultural critic John Fiske linked professional wrestling to the folk carnival, with both exhibiting "an institutionalized form of popular spectacle . . . [and a dedication to] the centrality of the body, to excess, exaggeration, and grotesqueness." Although professional wrestling always exhibited carnivalesque aspects, McMahon's WWF brought this connection to full fruition. Sergeant Slaughter, for example, exhibited a blind patriotism that rendered him a cari-cature of a Marine drill instructor. As with many of the WWF characters, Slaughter's proud American routine offered nothing particularly new or original (and McMahon had Hogan and "Hacksaw" Jim Duggan working related gimmicks), but no previ-ous wrestling organization promoted their characters with such well-paced and slickly produced television programming. With Slaughter and other WWF wrestlers playing their roles completely straight, the absurdity of much of the WWF's product reached the level of high camp. By not allowing WWF wrestlers to appear that they were in on the joke, McMahon allowed everyone to be in on the joke. The poker-faced ridiculousness of the WWF made it acceptable for wrestling to be embraced by ironic hipsters with disposable in-comes.[12]

McMahon brilliantly played on his expanded audience by cre-ating a spectacle that appealed to the ironists and blue-collar fans alike. His wrestlers came to the ring in elaborate costumes, often with props in hand. Their introductions typically included pyro-technics and personalized theme songs (available for purchase on compact disks) to stir the crowd's interest. These moves revolutionized the precontest rituals of American sporting events. Flashy WWF-style entrances became the norm in boxing (especially for flamboyant 1980s fighters such as Hector "Macho" Camacho and Jorge Paez) and arena team sports (such as the National Basketball Association). McMahon also recognized that, as John Dizikes noted, throughout American history "the crowd and the sporting event were thought of as equal parts of a moment in history." The WWF chief, therefore, made the crowd part of the spectacle. He broke completely with wrestling tradition and turned on the house lights during shows. WWF fans became part of the show. They held up placards, mugged for the TV cameras, and proudly displayed their WWF merchandise.[13]

To attract younger fans McMahon developed connections with the music industry. A chance encounter between singer Cyndi Lauper and WWF heel manager "Captain" Lou Albano led to the WWF performer appearing in her "Girls Just Want to Have Fun" music video. In the spring of 1984, the video went into heavy rotation on Music Television (MTV), the explosive new arbiter of teenage culture. McMahon and Lauper's management then built a feud between Lauper and Albano over his alleged sexist attitudes. Both cut promos that ran on WWF programs and MTV. The cross-promotion helped both sides. Lauper's album sold 6 million copies, and the WWF broke out of the wrestling ghetto and into mainstream popular culture. McMahon proclaimed his product "Rock 'n' Wrestling" and built the Lauper-Albano feud into a major wrestling event. The feminist angle eventually led well-known figures such as Gloria Steinem and Geraldine Ferraro to make public statements in support of Lauper. On July 23, 1985, the match between Lauper's proxy, Wendi Richter, and the ageless Fabulous Moolah, drew the largest audience in MTV history.[14]

The success of the Lauper-Albano angle pushed McMahon to attempt to undercut JCP by staging his own closed-circuit event. To generate interest in the show McMahon developed a storyline that broke the WWF ranks into pro- and anti-rock music camps, with Lauper as the titular head of the pro-rock music faction. In January 1985, MTV broadcast the blow-off match of the feud live and in prime time. McMahon's ambitious plans heightened public consciousness of the WWF, but at the cost of almost bankrupting the company. His efforts, however, propelled a wave of interest that allowed the WWF to benefit from free advertising. In late December 1984, the ABC newsmagazine *20/20* did a special on pro wrestling that grabbed headlines when wrestler David Schults physically assaulted reporter John Stossel. In March 1985, the month of both the closed-circuit event and McMahon's sale of Georgia Championship, Hogan gained notoriety for injuring talk-show host Richard Belzer, and Hogan and *A-Team* star Mr. T, himself involved in a WWF storyline, appeared as the hosts of *Saturday Night Live*. Not since the heyday of Gorgeous George had professional wrestling seeped this deeply into television culture.

Wrestlemania I, held in Madison Square Garden, validated McMahon's vision beyond all expectations. The performance not only included wrestling matches but also a spate of celebrities as accoutrements. Muhammad Ali, Billy Martin, Mr. T, and Liberace, among others, appeared on the show. All of the preshow promotion led to an enormous audience, as the converted and curious alike paid $15 each to watch the production in theaters across the country. The main event featured Hogan and Mr. T defeating the team of Roddy Piper and Paul "Mr. Wonderful" Orndorff, but the actual wrestling seemed almost inconsequential to the overall spectacle. Those who watched witnessed the culmination of a revolutionary cross-pollination of sports, music, and television, with the concoction held together by professional wrestling. McMahon grossed a staggering $4 million for the event. During the show, announcer (and future Minnesota governor) Jesse Ventura neatly summarized the event's significance to professional wrestling: "*Wrestlemania* is making history."[15]

Wrestlemania not only sparked a revitalization of wrestling thirty years in the making but also ensured McMahon's eventual supremacy over the NWA and AWA. In the wake of the closed-circuit event, NBC contracted for a once per month *Saturday Night Live* replacement program. *Saturday Night Main Event* eventually ran on the network for five years. By early 1987, the WWF had regular time slots on NBC, USA, as well as three hundred buyers for its syndicated programs. To increase its market share, the WWF developed strategies to attract children to their product. Pioneering methods later widely adopted by motion picture studios and sports leagues, the WWF flooded the marketplace with branded merchandise. To help sell the WWF to those too young to stay up and watch their prime-time shows, McMahon developed a Saturday morning cartoon, *Hulk Hogan's Rock 'n' Wrestling.* Hulk Hogan became not just an entertainment entity but an "icon-as-commodity." School-age children could spend their entire day immersed in the WWF. From pajamas and bedsheets, to toothbrushes, lunch boxes, books, and toys, Hogan's muscular image and the WWF logo graced the possessions of millions of "little Hulk-amaniacs." Through television and merchandising, McMahon created "an entire culture of wrestling which proposed, in effect, that there's a whole universe out there centered on these [wrestling] matches." By 1988, merchandise added $200 million annually to the WWF's coffers.[16]

For JCP, the explosive growth of the WWF made competing with McMahon's company a difficult proposition. Crockett faced dwindling attendance for his live and television shows as the WWF continued to expand into new markets. Part of Crockett's problem stemmed from the work of his head booker, Dusty Rhodes. The "American Dream," given almost free reign by Crockett, used his power to keep himself at the forefront of JCP productions. Unwilling to lose clean to NWA champion Ric Flair, for whom Dusty possessed a deep personal animosity, Rhodes engaged in incessant championship matches with the Nature Boy in which Rhodes appeared to win, only to have the result overturned later on some technicality. Very similar to Gagne's manner of handling the Bockwinkel-Hogan feud in the AWA, these screw-job finishes became so common in the NWA that insiders later dubbed matches of this type "Dusty finishes." The Flair-Rhodes rivalry, although real, generated little interest and paled in comparison to the angles developed by McMahon during the mid-1980s.[17]

Crockett recognized that, to compete with the WWF, he needed to expand his product into new markets as a counter to the national reach of McMahon. This necessity forced him into a spending frenzy that brought JCP perilously close to bankruptcy. In March 1987, Crockett purchased Championship Wrestling from Florida. In the same month, he scooped up Bill Watts's moribund Universal Wrestling Federation (UWF). The UWF acquisition in particular demonstrated the unsound business practices of JCP. Because of its complete insolvency, the UWF stood on the brink of closing by early 1987. If JCP had simply waited a few more months, they could have moved into the territory for free. As Jim Crockett's brother David noted, the purchase "was our downfall." JCP also moved its headquarters from North Carolina to an elaborate office complex in Dallas the same year. The pattern of overspending and over-extension adopted by Crockett and Rhodes by 1987 made it essential for the company's survival that *Starrcade '87* prove profitable.[18]

By 1987, technological advances meant that wrestling promoters no longer needed to convince viewers to leave their homes and visit local venues for closed-circuit broadcasts for premier cards. With the development of pay-per-view (ppv) technology fans could watch special live events from the comforts of their own homes. McMahon first used ppv for *Wrestlemania II*, and, despite some technical issues, the show made clear that ppv soon would succeed closed circuit in the wrestling marketplace. McMahon fully exploited ppv at 1987's *Wrestlemania III*. The show marked the peak of wrestling's 1980's revival. Headlined by a match featuring Hogan and the returning (and gravely ill) Andre the Giant, *Wrestlemania III* attracted more than seventy thousand fans to Detroit's Silverdome (WWF propaganda placed the number at more than ninety thousand). While the live attendance proved staggering, McMahon's profit derived largely from the home audience. *Wrestlemania III* grossed more than $10 million from ppv buys. For the thinly stretched Crockett, the rise of pay-per-view appeared to offer a glimmer of hope for his promotion.[19]

In response to McMahon's success in a northern city, Crockett made the fateful decision to move *Starrcade* from Greensboro to Chicago in 1987. Intended to demonstrate the national power of JCP and the NWA, the Thanksgiving Day show drew poorly. Even this difficulty would have been mitigated had *Starrcade* drawn a significant ppv buy rate. However, McMahon undercut the Crockett promotion by staging his own ppv, *Survivor Series*, the same night. Further, McMahon informed cable companies that they would never be granted the rights to another WWF show if they offered another wrestling ppv on the same day as *Survivor Series*. Fearful of losing their lucrative relationship with McMahon, only five cable companies offered *Starrcade* to their subscribers. McMahon's machinations spelled doom for Crockett and his company.[20]

Crockett, however, continued to fight the WWF, but he found himself consistently outmaneuvered by McMahon. In January 1988, Crockett held another ppv, the *Bunkhouse Stampede*, with a lively eight-man battle royal in a steel cage as the main event. McMahon responded by staging his own card, the *Royal Rumble*, the same night. However, rather than make wrestling fans pay for the show on ppv, McMahon offered the card free on the USA Network. Not surprisingly, Crockett's ppv performed dismally against the WWF product. Crockett's promotion never recovered from this defeat. Crockett (and the NWA itself) staggered toward oblivion as 1988 continued. Faced with the complete annihilation of his family's business, Crockett found an out at the end of the year. With Jim Barnett, recently ousted from his WWF position, serving as the mediator, Crockett sold his promotion (which, by this point, effectively constituted the NWA) to Ted Turner for more than $9 million.[21]

McMahon's efforts also succeeded in driving out Verne Gagne's AWA. After losing many of his stars to the WWF, Gagne struggled to maintain his market share. The AWA did continue to possess a few top-flight performers such as Stan Hansen and Curt Hennig, and it maintained a strong tag-team division, anchored at various times during the decade by the Road Warriors, the Midnight Rockers, and the team of Hennig and Scott Hall. However, the roster proved to be too thin to sustain the organization. Gagne also continued to use the aging Nick Bockwinkel as his perennial champion, which did little to attract younger fans. Even worse, Gagne himself made sporadic main event comebacks during the decade. The scramble by cable networks to cash in on wrestling's popularity during the mid-1980s provided a glimmer of hope for the AWA as it earned a prime-time Tuesday slot on ESPN. The AWA also experimented with joint promotions with other federations and instituted its own annual pay-per-view event, *Superclash*.[22]

Although it failed to sustain the AWA, Gagne's *Superclash* offered a novel approach to ppv's. Gagne organized it as a showcase for the top performers from promotions unaligned with either the NWA or WWF. Along with AWA performers, the cards featured wrestlers from the Jerry Jarrett–Jerry Lawler Memphis promotion and Fritz Von Erich's World Class organization in Texas, which left the NWA midway through the decade. From this cooperative effort, the idea developed that a "unified" champion of independent promotions would emerge. As with the attempt to place all NWA promotions under the control of one individual, the creation of the "unified" championship stirred jealousies between the promoters, which doomed the plan to failure. This attempt to combat the WWF also suffered due to the inability of the promotions involved to offer a truly national challenge to McMahon's company. While Gagne continued to promote shows in a few Western cities, the united promotions only had strength in the Mississippi Valley and parts of Texas. They simply did not possess the necessary resources to create a legitimate threat to the WWF. By the end of the decade, the "unified" concept proved moribund. The final *Superclash*, in December 1988, attracted only sixteen hundred fans. Veteran ring announcer Gary Michael Cappetta called it the "worst pay-per-view event with which I have ever been associated."[23]

In fact, all of Gagne's moves to revitalize the promotion proved inadequate to stanch the AWA's decline. His ESPN show, *Tuesday Night Slams and Jams*, looked amateurish and low-budget compared to the WWF product, and the production values of the company's syndicated *Superstars of the AWA* rivaled those found on public access. *Superstars* featured announcer Larry Nelson on a set that consisted of nothing but a desk and a television set in front of an AWA banner. Gagne's attempts to attract the MTV crowd proved, if anything, even more inept. In 1986, Gagne staged *WrestleRock*, which featured the combination of a fifteen-match wrestling card and concert. After the matches, which culminated in a Gagne main event, country singer Waylon Jennings performed. Gagne then attempted a *WrestleRock* tour that featured Molly Hatchet. Completely out of touch with current popular culture, and wedded to outdated notions of the business, Gagne's AWA fell apart as soon as ESPN cancelled the Tuesday night program. In 1991 the promotion officially closed.[24]

McMahon's successes of the mid-1980s set the stage for excesses at the end of the decade. The WWF head, who proved so astute in the business of wrestling, attempted to expand his empire beyond the ring, with the same disastrous results he encountered in nonwrestling endeavors during the 1970s. In 1989, he sank $20 million into the WWF movie *No Holds Barred*. McMahon intended the film to serve both as a vehicle for Hogan and as a method of advancing WWF storylines. He planned to develop Hogan's protagonist in the film, the Mighty Zeus (Tiny Lister), into the WWF's leading heel. The film bombed at the box office, but McMahon, unwilling to admit his mistake, pressed ahead with the lackluster feud between Hogan and Zeus. McMahon also tried his hand at boxing promotion. He took charge of the bout between aging star "Sugar" Ray Leonard and journeyman Don Leland. As with *No*

Holds Barred, the match generated neither excitement nor profit. McMahon coupled these moves with a new lavish lifestyle that siphoned off much of the WWF's profits. McMahon built Titan Tower in Connecticut as the new home of his company, purchased a large house in exclusive Boca Raton, Florida, and began surrounding himself with expensive toys and trinkets. He even funded research into a, never-released, WWF perfume.[25]

While McMahon's moves in the 1980s threatened his own business, he also made a move than many in wrestling perceived as a threat to the entire business. Since the establishment of state athletic commissions in the early twentieth century, boxers, wrestlers, and their promoters found themselves required to pay state licensing fees as part of doing business. In 1989, McMahon decided that he would move to avoid paying these fees. In a meeting with the New Jersey Athletic Commission, WWF representatives admitted that their matches did not represent legitimate athletic contests because the victors were predetermined. McMahon announced that his product could not be considered a sport, and therefore should not be licensed, because the WWF merely offered "sports entertainment." McMahon's decision to break the kayfabe led to the abolition of licensing fees but also made him an archvillain to many in the industry.

Outside of wrestling McMahon also came to be viewed as suspect. McMahon's longtime fascination with bodybuilding threatened to destroy his empire even more rapidly than his profligate spending. In the summer of 1991, McMahon debuted his latest creation, the World Bodybuilding Federation (WBF). McMahon hoped to develop the bodybuilders into wrestling-like characters, then sell the public on them through a weekly television program and ppv's. At the same time, the federal trial of Dr. George Zahorian began. Zahorian's legal difficulties came from his violations of 1988's Omnibus Anti-Drug Abuse Act, which significantly stiffened the penalties for steroid trafficking. During Zahorian's trial evidence surfaced that linked his illegal activities to the WWF. During the late 1980s, Zahorian, a member of the Pennsylvania Athletic Commission, served as the WWF's house doctor for the syndicated TV show tapings in Allentown, Pennsylvania. Prosecutors found receipts in Zahorian's files that showed regular drug shipments to McMahon, Hogan, Roddy Piper, and a host of other wrestlers, as well as to Titan Tower.

For McMahon, his connections to Zahorian came at the worst possible time. His heavy new involvement in the steroid-larded bodybuilding industry served only to connect McMahon with performance-enhancing drugs. And in the WWF, McMahon had begun the process of building the Ultimate Warrior (Jim Hellwig) into his long-term replacement for Hogan. The Warrior became the WWF champion in 1990, and he continued to factor heavily in the organization into 1991. Within the wrestling industry, rumors floated freely that Hellwig's magnificent physique came from the use of steroids. To counter these difficulties, McMahon and Hogan both publicly admitted to experimenting with steroids, and the WWF chief announced a new drug-testing program in his company. The WBF, however, suffered irreparable harm and withered away. McMahon's contrition also did not save him from implication in the Zahorian matter. In 1993, McMahon faced three indictments for conspiring with Zahorian to distribute steroids to wrestlers. Although McMahon successfully defended himself against the charges, his reputation suffered significant damage. The drug scandals and mediocre storylines of the early 1990s led to a sharp decrease in WWF revenues.[26]

McMahon's woes opened the door for Turner and the WCW to become the preeminent force in the wrestling business. However, the mismanagement of the WCW allowed McMahon to survive this potential threat. Turner failed to recognize that experience with other forms of television programming did not qualify someone to manage a wrestling organization, regardless of how heavily that organization relied on television for survival. The TBS boss, therefore, stumbled badly in the first few years of his direct involvement with WCW by appointing veteran television executives from his company to run his new wrestling operation. Initially, Turner assigned Jim Herd to manage WCW, who, in turn, appointed Dusty Rhodes as his primary writer. Rhodes used his position to phase out longtime nemesis Ric Flair. In October 1991, the Nature Boy not only showed up on WWF television but appeared still wearing the NWA belt, which no one in the chaotic Turner organization had bothered to make him return. In a face-saving measure, the Turner organization began to distinguish its house WCW belt from the NWA title (and officially withdrew from the moribund NWA in September 1993). The title belt embarrassment also led Turner to replace Herd with another TV veteran, Bill Shaw, who brought in Bill Watts of the ill-fated UWF to serve as his chief lieutenant. Before being fired for racist comments in an interview with *Pro Wrestling Torch*, Watts managed to alienate much of the WCW talent. His refusal to accept criticisms of his management style eventually propelled Watts to fire many of the WCW's most recognizable performers, including Ole Anderson, Scott Steiner, and "Ravishing" Rick Rude.[27]

Watts's firing in 1993 opened the door for Eric Bischoff to move up in the WCW hierarchy. Bischoff began his career as a TV announcer for the collapsing AWA in 1989. He latched on in a low-level position with the WCW after Gagne shut down his promotion. Bischoff's energy and vision allowed him to leapfrog more established potential replacements for Watts. He recognized that, for the WCW to compete successfully with McMahon, the WCW needed to shed its regional image and improve the production values of the promotion's television and ppv programs. Although Bischoff more accurately surmised the landscape of pro wrestling than had Rhodes and Watts, his eventual success also stemmed from circumstances outside his control. First, he found Hulk Hogan willing to take a break from his acting career in 1994. By promising Hogan total artistic freedom, Bischoff convinced the biggest name in wrestling to work a short-term program with Ric Flair in the summer of 1994. Then, in September 1995, Turner gave the WCW a two-hour block on his Turner Network Television (TNT) cable channel. This gave Bischoff the opportunity to compete head-to-head with the WWF and its Monday night flagship program. On September 11, 1995, the first night the two promotions ran their shows in direct competition, Bischoff opened the WCW's *Monday Nitro* by announcing the result of the main event, taped two weeks earlier, on the WWF's *Monday Night Raw*. Bischoff's statement not only broke one of wrestling's unwritten rules—not to ever acknowledge your competitors on air—but also represented the opening salvo in wrestling's most significant storyline of the 1990s, the "Monday night war."[28]

Bischoff used Turner's deep pockets to transform WCW's product into a slick vehicle capable of challenging the WWF. He also adopted the talent-raiding strategy that McMahon used so effectively during the early 1980s. Bischoff hired WWF announcers Bobby "the Brain" Heenan and "Mean" Gene Okerlund, then began to pilfer disgruntled WWF wrestlers. In early 1996, Bischoff hired Scott Hall, "Razor Ramon" in the WWF, and Kevin Nash, a recent WWF world champion under the name "Diesel." These two became known as the "Outsiders," and Bischoff developed an angle that hinted they might be invaders still employed by the WWF. The storyline proved so effective that McMahon attempted to stop it with an ill-advised copyright infringement lawsuit against WCW. At the July 1996, *Bash at the Beach* ppv Hulk Hogan returned to the WCW as the third "Outsider." As part of a brilliantly conceived angle, Hogan became the heel "Hollywood" Hulk Hogan, with his trademark yellow and red costume replaced with black. Hogan's appearance signaled the conversion of the Outsiders into an anti-hero group known as the New World Order (nWo) bent on taking over the WCW. The nWo subsequently provided the WCW with the vehicle to combat the WWF's dominance in the business. In late 1996, *Nitro* slipped ahead of *Raw* in the Monday night ratings. For the first time in more than a decade, McMahon could not claim to head wrestling's most successful promotion.[29]

McMahon responded by dramatically altering the content of his television programs. WWF product became darker and more violent. Although the shift began earlier, McMahon codified his new approach in a December 1997 pronouncement that came to be known as his "new directions" speech. The WWF chief declared that wrestling needed a new, adult approach. An approach that acknowledged sexuality, profanity, and the violence of American society. McMahon declared that the WWF would no longer offer wrestling fans the intelligence-insulting good guy versus bad guy dichotomy at the heart of professional wrestling for more than half a century. Rather, WWF performers would be antiheroes, offered to fans not in stark black or white, but in various shades of gray. McMahon promised fans wrestling loaded with WWF "attitude." The edgy "attitude" promoted by McMahon ushered in a new era in wrestling. No longer based around simple morality plays and the promotion of law and order and role models, WWF wrestling became, if not exactly adult, at least adult-themed.

"Attitude"-era WWF product became a bonanza of puerile and juvenile behavior. McMahon's television shows reveled in profanity, misogyny, coarse racial stereotypes, and sexuality. For example, McMahon created the Nation of Domination, a racially stereotyped heel organization that promoted African-American nationalism. To counter the nWo, McMahon developed Degeneration X (DX), which featured wrestlers such as X-Pac and "Mr. Ass" Billy Gunn and promoted the catchphrase "suck it." McMahon also began to hire young women to serve as WWF "divas." These women invariably became enmeshed in hypersexualized and demeaning storylines that often involved swimsuit competitions, clothes ripping, or in-ring groveling. As Patrice Oppliger noted, "Vince McMahon has elevated the sexuality of female wrestlers to its own branch of the business." In one infamous 1997 angle, Brian Pillman defeated Dustin Runnels (son of Dusty Rhodes) and gained the "services" of Runnels's wife Terri for one month. These developments spurred a conservative backlash and clashes with USA Network but also helped McMahon successfully fend off the challenge posed by Bischoff and the WCW.[30]

McMahon's biggest new draw of the period proved to be Texan Steve Williams. Williams wrestled as Steve Austin in the WCW before coming to the WWF. Thoroughly wasted as one of the "Hollywood Blonds" in the WCW, McMahon allowed Austin, after a misguided stint as the "Ringmaster," to become the ultimate example of the WWF's new antiheroes. Austin developed a ring persona later characterized as representative of "a truck driver drinking bad scotch before dawn." He eschewed elaborate ring garb and wore only black trunks or jean shorts and a vest emblazoned with smoking skulls and "Austin 3:16" (code for the mock scriptural "Austin 3:16 says I'm going to kick your ass"). "Stone Cold" Steve Austin drove a monster truck, drank beer in the ring, flashed his middle fingers at everyone, and seemed perpetually angry. His unfocused rancor eventually became directed at Vince McMahon.

The WWF owner worked himself into a storyline with Austin, and he became "Mr." McMahon, the despicable boss. The angle immediately connected with working-class wrestling fans. For decades wrestling served as a catharsis for blue-collar Americans venting their frustrations with employers, politicians, and foreigners by jeering rule-breaking heels. McMahon's character in the late 1990s WWF simply eliminated the symbolic middleman. He became the embodiment of the mean-spirited, heartless boss WWF fans dealt with during their workdays. By allowing "Stone Cold" to verbally and physically abuse him, McMahon helped convert Austin into the "downtrodden hero of economic America's white, grimy underbelly." Austin's popularity led to a late 1990s revitalization of the WWF. After eighty-three weeks with *Nitro* on top, the

WWF's *Raw* regained the Monday night ratings lead on April 13, 1998.[31]

Austin's success also demonstrated another factor that led to the WWF's eventual victory over the WCW: McMahon's talent for character development. During the WWF-WCW war of the 1990s, the WCW relied heavily on recycling established WWF stars, such as Hogan, "Macho Man" Randy Savage, and Nash, and the long-term appeal of veteran WCW/NWA performers, such as Flair, Sting, and Big Van Vader. Bischoff proved very ineffective in developing new, homegrown stars for the WCW. McMahon, however, created a host of popular new characters during the 1990s. New wrestlers such as Dwayne "the Rock" Johnson, Hunter Hearst Helmsley (a.k.a., Triple H and "The Game"), and Justin Bradshaw developed into major draws for the WWF. McMahon, as he did with Austin, also successfully took wrestlers who failed to receive the proper push in the WCW and built them into main event attractions in the WWF. Along with Austin, McMahon managed to build fan interest in WCW castoffs the Undertaker (Mark Callous), Mick "Cactus Jack" Foley, and Nash (who wrestled as "Oz" in the WCW before his WWF run as Diesel).

Bill Goldberg served as Bischoff's only significant new performer. The first person ever cut by the National Football League's Carolina Panthers, Goldberg became Bischoff's counter to Steve Austin. Goldberg's shaved head and black wrestling trunks appearance exactly copied the WWF star. Bischoff also tried to develop a similar tough guy image for Goldberg by having the former University of Georgia football player yell, spit, and flex his muscles during interviews. Goldberg, however, ended up serving far more as a modern version of Gus Sonnenberg than as an Austin surrogate. Like Sonnenberg, Goldberg built his reputation on usage of the flying tackle as his finishing move, and WCW announcers constantly referred to Goldberg's athletic prowess and football background. Goldberg proved to be a successful draw in the early stages of his career, during which he ran off an impressive string of quick victories, but fizzled as a champion. He defeated Hogan for the WCW title in July 1998, only to lose the championship to Kevin Nash in December of that year. After his title run, Goldberg's popularity dwindled as the WCW fell apart.[32]

McMahon's development of WWF "attitude" stemmed partly from developments within the wrestling industry. The WWF boss always strove to be on the cutting edge of the wrestling business due to a belief that this policy lay at the heart of his success. Although the WCW served as his only truly national rival during the 1990s, an upstart, East Coast organization began attracting a significant cult following during the period., Tod Gordon's Eastern Championship Wrestling (ECW) from Philadelphia represented merely one of the hundreds of small independent wrestling organizations across the country. Initially established in 1992, ECW's usage of aged former national stars such as Jimmy Snuka and Don Muraco served as the federation's only real distinction. In August 1994, a reconstituted version of the NWA, which included the ECW, held a tournament in Philadelphia to declare a new world champion. ECW belt holder Shane "the Franchise" Douglas emerged as the victor but refused the NWA title. The ECW then declared itself to be a national organization, withdrew from the NWA, and changed its name to Extreme Championship Wrestling.[33]

ECW's subsequent ability to survive as a viable promotion with programming only on local and low-rated sports cable networks developed out of the company's willingness to embrace the notion of "hardcore" wrestling. While American wrestling organizations long relied on juicing (intentional cutting and bleeding), cage matches, and foreign objects to generate excitement, some elements within Japanese professional wrestling developed a style of wrestling built entirely on bloodletting and props such as barbed wire, thumbtacks, and mild explosives. This violent style, best exemplified by Atsushi Onita's Frontier Martial-Arts Wrestling (FMW), served as an influence for a number of American wrestlers who traveled to Japan. Wrestlers such as Terry Funk and Mick Foley brought the style to America as hardcore, and Tod Gordon and Paul Heyman made the style the heart of ECW. For example, they encouraged fans to bring weapons to ECW shows and to hand the props to the performers during the matches. A number of the most popular ECW wrestlers established themselves purely on their willingness to engage in bloody, weapon-wielding matches with little regard paid to actual wrestling moves. ECW wrestlers of this ilk, such as Foley, Funk, the Sandman, and New Jack, can be viewed as modern disciples of the Sheik. The other "extreme" aspect of ECW involved the high-risk aerial maneuvers wrestlers such as Sabu and Rob Van Dam adapted from the high-flier style of wrestling practiced by Mexican *luchadores*.[34]

ECW's cult popularity virtually ensured that McMahon, always cognizant of trends within wrestling, would co-opt their style. McMahon's decision to move toward an ECW-like "attitude" received a significant boost from Vince Russo, one of McMahon's top aides, who proved to be the ECW's biggest supporter within the WWF. With Russo's prompting, McMahon moved to increase the sex and violence quotient in the WWF. He instituted a new WWF hardcore title, encouraged ECW wrestlers to show up at some WWF cards, and raided the upstart federation for talent. Among the most significant WWF signees would be Austin (who moved to ECW after being fired by Bischoff), Foley, Van Dam, and Taz. While the WCW did not demonstrate an inclination toward adopting the ECW's violent style, the Atlanta-based federation did hire many ECW wrestlers as a way to bring fresh talent into the promotion. Among others, the WCW hired Chris Benoit, Dean Malenko, Eddy Guerrero, Raven, and the Public Enemy tag team.[35]

Despite the injection of new talent from ECW, Bischoff's WCW continued to rely on old stars and hackneyed storylines for its main events. *Nitro*, as a result, became stale and tired at the same time that McMahon undertook the WWF's "attitude" adjustment. In one notorious March 1999 example, *Nitro* features no actual wrestling matches during the entire first hour of its broadcast. Bischoff attempted to counter the WWF by announcing, in April 1999, that the WCW would eliminate all content deemed unsuitable for children. This effort to provide family-friendly wrestling entertainment, however, failed to stop WCW's slide. With the WCW hemorrhaging money, Turner fired Bischoff in late 1999. With the attempt to clean up the WCW deemed a failure, Vince Russo became the new head of the WCW. Russo's eleventh-hour endeavors to keep WCW afloat served only to accelerate the company's decline.[36]

Not only did the company continue to lose money, but Russo used the WCW as his own bully pulpit. In keeping with his notions of the death of kayfabe, Russo routinely discussed business matters and backstage politics on *Nitro*, moves which alienated many longtime WCW fans. He also hurt ppv buys by completely devaluating the WCW world title. Along with actor David Arquette, Russo himself spent a stint as WCW champion. From January 2000 to March 2001, the WCW world title changed hands an astonishing eighteen times. This rapid turnover made the establishment of long-term angles (and the building of excitement over ppv blow-off matches) nearly impossible. With the company spiraling out of control under Russo, Turner rehired the discredited Bischoff but to no avail. Ratings and buy rates continued to skitter downward, with WCW losing $62 million in 2000.[37]

In early 2000 Turner, the largest single stockholder in Time Warner—which his cable companies belonged to—agreed to a merger with America On-Line (AOL). The new media conglomerate not only pushed Turner out of the daily operations of his cable companies but also moved to unload the more unprofitable portions of the Time Warner empire. The WCW stood as the single most unprofitable arm of Time Warner and, after the promotion's abysmal performance in 2000, the new chief executive officer of Turner Broadcasting Systems, Jamie Kellner, canceled all WCW programming in early 2001. The end of the WCW's cable television deal spelled the end of the company. On March 23, 2001, AOL Time Warner then sold the WCW's assets for less than $3 million to Vince McMahon. On April 4, 2001, HHG Incorporated, the parent company of ECW, filed for bankruptcy. After a disastrous television deal with The National Network (TNN), ECW had slipped into a WCW-like insolvency. Within weeks McMahon hired Paul Heyman and began using the ECW name on WWF programs. After almost twenty years of struggle, Vince McMahon finally achieved his goal. He owned professional wrestling.[38]

EPILOGUE

Vince McMahon's 2001 ascension to undisputed king of professional wrestling gave the WWF boss the opportunity to personally direct the future of wrestling in the United States. McMahon proved to be thoroughly dedicated to the late 1990s notion of WWF "attitude," even without the threat of other wrestling organizations nipping at his market share. While McMahon continued to promote the WWF as an edgy, adult-entertainment form, the company's product did undergo changes in the new millennium. The WWF came to rely increasingly on storylines driven by both the McMahon family and by wrestlers with the sort of bodybuilder physique Vince McMahon hoped to introduce before the steroid scandals of the early 1990s. McMahon also faced renewed criticisms not only from conservative and women's groups but new attacks from wrestling fans. As the sole national provider of professional wrestling McMahon became the target of many within the wrestling community unhappy about developments within the industry.

Much of the criticism of McMahon stems from his continued promotion of hardcore-style wrestling despite the reduced need to rely on such matches as a means of competing with rival organizations. The high-risk maneuvers and weapons that define hardcore wrestling present fantastically dangerous working environments for professional wrestlers. Serious injuries and shortened careers often result from prolonged involvement in these matches. The need to continue performing (and earning) after being injured in high-risk matches propels many wrestlers to rely on painkillers and illegal drug use. Hardcore matches result in in-ring injuries, which can increase use of prescription pain medications so that wrestlers can continue to engage in high-risk matches; a vicious cycle of bodily deterioration that takes a shocking toll of the wrestling fraternity. McMahon's continued, unnecessary reliance on hardcore matches in the WWF means that wrestlers must participate in dangerous encounters or spend their careers relegated to the netherworld of small, independent federations.[1]

A frighteningly high percentage of wrestlers die before the age 40 because of hardcore matches and outrageous stunts and gimmicks. The most notorious example of a professional wrestler dying as part of an unnecessary gimmick involved Owen Hart. A member of the legendary Hart wrestling family of Calgary, Owen fell eighty feet to his death during a May 1999 WWF pay-per-view entitled *Over the Edge*. As part of the night's storyline, Hart was supposed to descend, via a harness, from the catwalk located at the top of Kansas City's Kemper Arena. However, the harness broke as he stepped off the catwalk, and he plunged downward, hit his head on a ring turnbuckle, and collapsed in a corner of the ring. Demonstrating the callousness for which many criticize him, McMahon continued the card even after receiving word that Hart died from his injuries. Hart's televised death made his passing the most visible tragedy in wrestling history, but his terrible accident represented merely one more example of the fearful toll of present-day wrestling.[2]

While wrestling deaths occur at all levels of the business, critics point out that McMahon's WWF, a multibillion dollar industry, represents the only organization in wrestling with the ability to combat the withering effects of drug use and ring injuries. That WWF performers such as Hart, Eddy Guerrero, Curt Hennig, Davey Boy Smith, and Brian Pillman all died while involved with McMahon's organization points to the pervasive lack of concern for the safety of performers found at even the highest level of wrestling. *Dragonking Press Newsletter* editor Karl Stern maintains statistics on the wrestling profession that demonstrate the dangerous nature of wrestling. Stern's figures show a marked increase in the number of wrestlers dying under age 40 during the period after the mid-1990s rise of hardcore wrestling. For the past half-decade, an average of approximately ten wrestlers under 40 die every year. Most wrestling deaths are either suicides or drug related.[3]

McMahon's lack of concern for the welfare of wrestlers can be best illustrated by how he uses his family in WWF storylines. His daughter Stephanie, wife of wrestler Hunter Hearst Helmsley (Triple H), routinely appears in the role of spoiled rich girl and often engages in a hypersexualized role characteristic of the women of the WWF. Her in-ring appearances typically result in crowd chants of "bitch," which, apparently, does not faze her bottom-line-driven father. McMahon's son Shane also took on an increasingly significant on-air role in the organization in the new millennium. Shane, or "Shane O'Mac," juices and engages in high-risk aerial moves regularly on WWF cards. In one particularly dangerous stunt, Shane fell fifty feet from a scaffolding. McMahon himself also continues to wrestle in his role as evil owner "Mr. McMahon." His angles often include storylines concerning McMahon's control of specific wrestlers or his sexual domination of WWF "divas."[4]

During the last stages of McMahon's battle with WCW he took his company public. In October 1999, the WWF acronym, as a symbol for World Wrestling Federation Entertainment Incorporated, appeared on the New York Stock Exchange. The initial public offering helped provide the funds for finishing the fight with WCW (and the subsequent purchase of WCW). In 2001, *Business Week* ranked the company as the third best small company in America. McMahon's revenues for that year totaled $456 million. The WWF also continues to maintain a significant television presence. It presents original programming on cable on Monday and Thursday nights, offers a welter of syndicated shows, and McMahon also profitably renewed the company's relationship with MTV. Moreover, McMahon's company stands as the world's leading pay-per-view provider, with twelve American events annually.[5]

The television presence and enormous revenues of McMahon's company, however, cannot mask signs of trouble for the organization. In 2001, McMahon once again attempted to expand outside of wrestling and, once again, failed miserably. He created the Extreme Football League (XFL) as a counter to the National Football League (NFL). Although McMahon succeeded in attracting significant sponsorship and lucrative television deals for his new league, the abysmal on-field product faltered immediately. The league did not even complete its inaugural season. Spiraling expenses and the XFL fiasco meant that McMahon only showed a profit of $16 million on 2001's $456 million revenue. In 2002, a court forced McMahon to change the name of his wrestling organization to World Wrestling Entertainment (WWE) because he had violated terms of an agreement signed in the 1990s with the World Wildlife Fund. After twenty years promoting the WWF, McMahon found himself forced to rebrand his product.

Stagnant storylines and booking only compounded McMahon's newfound difficulties. The increased reliance on the McMahon family, especially perennial champion Triple H, hurt the WWE's ratings. The acquisition of the WCW created an opportunity for McMahon to develop an invasion storyline, similar to that used by the WCW with the New World Order (nWo), to offset the McMahon family oversaturation, but he squandered this chance. The invasion angle faltered, in part, because McMahon refused to sign the highest-paid former WCW stars, which left the WCW invasion force led by mid-card performers such as Buff Bagwell and Booker T. McMahon also worked his family into the storyline, with Shane "owning" the WCW and Stephanie controlling the ECW. The botched invasion angle ended after the poor-drawing *Survivor Series* pay-per-view in late 2001. McMahon, however, continued to market two distinct brands of WWE product, with the company's wrestlers split into *Raw* and *Smackdown* factions. After a lifetime struggling against opponents in the wrestling business, McMahon seemingly cannot operate without at least the illusion of rivals.[6]

The two WWE brands, however, offer very similar product. Wrestlers regularly move from one group to the other, and it is impossible to distinguish between the two brands. This similarity stems, in large measure, from the type of wrestlers with which McMahon now stocks his company. The biggest WWF stars of the late twentieth century have either been slowed by injury (Steve Austin, Mick Foley) or age (Undertaker, Shawn Michaels). Dwayne "the Rock" Johnson successfully transitioned from wrestler to actor, which cost McMahon his most popular performer. McMahon subsequently attempted to build the company around the superb Kurt Angle, but that former Olympic champion also faced serious injuries. The WWE boss responded to these setbacks in two ways. First, he attempted to recapture the mid-1990s magic of the nWo by bringing Hulk Hogan, Scott Hall, and Kevin Nash back to reprise their roles in that group. This move failed miserably, as the aged

Outsiders could no longer be counted on as sustained draws. Second, McMahon decided on a long-term strategy of recruiting heavily muscled power wrestlers who could use their enormous size to awe crowds. This shift toward bodybuilder types slowed the pace of typical WWE matches dramatically. The influx of chiseled physiques also spawned renewed rumors of widespread steroid use in the company. With widely publicized Congressional investigations of performance-enhancing drug use in sports under way, McMahon acted to forestall scrutiny of the WWE by announcing a new drug-testing policy in November 2005.

Despite McMahon's difficulties, his product continues to dominate American professional wrestling. A Tennessee-based National Wrestling Alliance (NWA) promotion, Total Non-stop Action (TNA), represents the only other company with national television exposure. TNA, however, faces its own problems. Their ratings are minuscule, and the company's television presence appears, at best, tenuous. While TNA features smaller, quicker wrestlers than the WWE, Vince Russo's prominent role in the company has led to the adoption of tactics similar to WWE "attitude." TNA television programs include hardcore matches (the "X" division) along with scantily clad female dancers (the double-entendre "TNA girls"). Despite these attempts to slavishly imitate the WWE, it seems unlikely that the underfunded TNA will ever pose any legitimate threat to McMahon's WWE. As the entrenched provider of pro wrestling in this country, McMahon possesses a market position not easily overcome. He enjoys the unique position of having his brand name inexorably linked with wrestling product in this country. Unless a well-financed operation backed by a cable company emerges, McMahon will continue to control and shape professional wrestling in the United States for the foreseeable future.

NOTES

INTRODUCTION

1. For recent scholarly examinations of wrestling, see Nicholas Sammond, ed., *Steel Chair to the Head: The Pleasure and Pain of Professional Wrestling* (Durham, NC: Duke University Press, 2005); Michael R. Ball, *Professional Wrestling as Ritual Drama in American Popular Culture* (Lewiston, NY: Edwin Mellen Press, 1990); Sharon Mazer, *Professional Wrestling: Sport and Spectacle* (Jackson: University of Mississippi Press, 1998); Marc Leverette, *Professional Wrestling, the Myth, the Mat, and American Popular Culture* (Lewiston, NY: Edwin Mellen, 2003).

2. For example, Benjamin Rader's widely used sports history text mentions wrestling in a discussion of preprofessional folk pastimes, and again in reference to early television's reliance on arena sports, but includes no discussion of the late nineteenth–early twentieth century period when wrestling represented a popular, legitimate sporting pastime. Rader, *American Sports: From the Age of Folk Games to the Age of Televised Sports*, 4th ed. (Upper Saddle River, NJ: Prentice Hall, 1998), 3, 14, 233.

3. For the view that television corrupted sports, see Benjamin G. Rader, *In Its Own Image: How Television Has Transformed Sports* (New York: Free Press, 1984). For a more benign view on television's relationship to sports, see Joan M. Chandler, *Television and National Sport: The United States and Britain* (Urbana: University of Illinois Press, 1988).

4. Quoted in Jim Wilson and Weldon T. Johnson, *Chokehold: Pro Wrestling's Real Mayhem Outside the Ring* (Philadelphia: Xlibris, 2003), 431.

CHAPTER I: ORIGINS

1. H. A. Harris, *Greek Athletes and Athletics* (Bloomington: Indiana University Press, 1966), 127–128.

2. R. Brasch, *How Did Sports Begin? A Look into the Origins of Man at Play* (London: Longman, 1972), 253–254; Michael Poliakoff, "Jacob, Job, and Other Wrestlers: Reception of Greek Athletics by Jews and Christians in Antiquity," *Journal of Sport History* 11 (Summer 1984): 48–65.

3. Wolfgang Decker, *Sports and Games of Ancient Egypt* (New Haven, CT: Yale University Press, 1992), 71–82; Steve Craig, *Sports and Games of the Ancients* (Westport, CT: Greenwood Press, 2002), 8–9.

4. For Greek sports as a religious pursuit, see Harris, *Greek Athletes and Athletics*; Waldo E. Sweet, *Sport and Recreation in Ancient Greece: A Sourcebook with Translations* (New York: Oxford University Press, 1987). For the Greek sports as purely intrinsic activities view, see Thomas F. Scanlon, *Eros and Greek Athletes* (New York: Oxford University Press, 2002); Allen Guttmann, "Sports Spectators from Antiquity to the Renaissance," *Journal of Sport History* 8 (Summer 1981): 5–27. Mark Golden makes a persuasive case that Greek athletics initially possessed a religious dimension, which diminished over time and eventually came to be underpinned by the notion of "demarcated differences, in other words, [they] created hierarchies—of events, festivals, genders, nations, and individuals." Golden, *Sport and Society in Ancient Greece* (Cambridge: Cambridge University Press, 1998), 4, 13–19.

5. E. Norman Gardiner, *Greek Athletic Sports and Festivals* (London: Macmillan, 1910), 128, 372–373; Harris, *Greek Athletes and Athletics*, 30.

6. Craig, *Sports and Games of the Ancients*, 97; Harris, *Greek Athletes and Athletics*, 110–112; David Matz, *Greek and Roman Sport: A Dictionary of Athletes and Events from the Eighth Century B.C. to the Third Century A.D.* (Jefferson, NC: McFarland, 1991), 72–73.

7. Gardiner, *Greek Athletic Sports and Festivals*, 435–450; Harris, *Greek Athletes and Athletics*, 105–109.

8. H. A. Harris, *Sport in Greece and Rome* (Ithaca, NY: Cornell University Press, 1972), 50–51; Craig, *Sports and Games of the Ancients*, 55–60, 234–237; Guttmann, "Sports Spectators," 9–10; Roland Auguet, *Cruelty and Civilization: The Roman Games* (London: Routledge, 1994).

9. John Marshall Carter, *Medieval Games: Sports and Recreations in Feudal Society* (Westport, CT: Greenwood Press, 1992), 34, 85; Johan Huizinga, *Homo Ludens: A Study of the Play Element in Culture* (reprint, Boston: Beacon, 1955), 179–180.

10. Sally Wilkins, *Sports and Games of Medieval Cultures* (Westport, CT: Greenwood Press, 2002), 149; John Marshall Carter, *Sports and Pastimes of the Middle Ages* (Lanham, MD: University Press of America,

1988), 24; Gerald W. Morton and George M. O'Brien, *Wrestling to Rasslin: Ancient Sport to American Spectacle* (Bowling Green, OH: Bowling Green University Press, 1985), 16–19.

11. Charles Morrow Wilson, *The Magnificent Scufflers: Revealing the Great Days When America Wrestled the World* (Brattleboro, VT: Stephen Greene Press, 1959), 4–5; Donald Walker, *Defensive Exercises: Comprising Wrestling and Boxing* (London: Thomas Hurst, 1840), 9; John Ford, *Prizefighting: The Age of Regency Boximania* (New York: Great Albion Books, 1972), 42. On English styles, see John Lee, *Wrestling in the North Country* (Consett: Ramsden Williams, 1953); Walter Armstrong, *Wrestliana: or, the History of the Cumberland & Westmoreland Wrestling Society in London since the Year 1824* (London: Simpkin, Marshall & Co., 1870).

12. Dennis Brailsford, *Sport and Society: Elizabeth to Anne* (London: Routledge & Keegan Paul, 1969), 17–19; Andrew Leibs, *Sports and Games of the Renaissance* (Westport, CT: Greenwood Press, 2004), 61–63; Alison Weir, *Henry VIII: The King and His Court* (New York: Ballantine, 2001), 105; Richard D. Mandell, *Sport: A Cultural History* (New York: Columbia University Press, 1984), 120–121.

13. Robert Malcolmson, *Popular Recreations in English Society, 1700–1850* (New York: Cambridge University Press, 1973), 31–32, 43, 57; Ford, *Prizefighting*, 89, 168–169; Bob Mee, *Bare Fists: The History of Bare-Knuckle Prize-Fighting* (Woodstock, NY: Overlook Press, 2001), 21; Elliot J. Gorn, *The Manly Art: Bare-Knuckle Prize Fighting in America* (Ithaca, NY: Cornell University Press, 1986), 19–24; Gary Cross, *A Social History of Leisure Since 1600* (State College, PA: Venture Publishing, 1990), 25–39; Dennis Brailsford, "Sporting Days in Eighteenth Century England," *Journal of Sport History* 9 (Winter 1982): 41–54.

14. Stephen Hardy, "Organized Sport and the Search for Community: Boston, 1865–1915" (Ph.D. diss., University of Massachusetts, 1980), 61–63; Allen Guttmann, "Puritans at Play? Accusations and Replies," in David K. Wiggins, ed., *Sport in America: From Wicked Amusement to National Obsession* (Champaign, IL: Human Kinetics, 1994), 3–13; Nancy Struna, "Puritans and Sport: The Irretrievable Tide of Change," in Steven A. Riess, ed., *The American Sporting Experience: A Historical Anthology of Sport in America* (New York: Leisure Press, 1984), 15–35.

15. Elliott J. Gorn, "Sports through the Nineteenth Century," in S. W. Pope, ed., *The New American Sport History: Recent Approaches and Perspectives* (Urbana: University of Illinois Press, 1997), 36–39; Nancy Struna, *People of Prowess: Sport, Leisure, and Labor in Early Anglo-America* (Urbana: University of Illinois Press, 1996), 143–164.

16. Allen Guttmann, *From Ritual to Record: The Nature of Modern Sports* (New York: Columbia University Press, 1978), 30; T. H. Breen, "Horses and Gentlemen: The Cult of Gambling among the Gentry of

Virginia," *William and Mary Quarterly* 34 (April 1977): 239–257; Struna, *People of Prowess*, 79, 105. A collection of colonial wrestling accounts can be found in Thomas L. Altherr, ed., *Sports in North America: A Documentary History*, 8 vols. (Gulf Breeze, FL: Academic International Press, 1997), vol. 1, pt. 1, 99–104.

17. Rupert Hughes, *George Washington: The Human Being and the Hero, 1732–1763* (New York: William Morrow, 1920), 31; James Thomas Flexner, *George Washington: The Forge of Experience (1732–1775)* (Boston: Little, Brown, & Company, 1965), 23; Bonnie S. Ledbetter, "Sports and Games of the American Revolution," *Journal of Sports History* 6 (Winter 1979): 29–40.

18. Elliott J. Gorn, "Gouge and Bite, Pull Hair and Scratch: The Social Significance of Fighting in the Southern Backcountry," in Wiggins, *Sport in America*, 35–50. In *Life on the Mississippi*, Mark Twain wrote of a rough-and-tumble wrestler who seemed to possess all of the self-promotion and ballyhoo that characterized twentieth-century professional wrestlers. Styling himself "Sudden Death and General Desolation," this grappler struck fear in potential opponents with pronouncements such as "blood's my natural drink, and the wails of the dying is music to my ear." Twain, *Life on the Mississippi* (reprint, New York: Harper, 1899), 32–33.

19. John Dizikes, *Sportsmen and Gamesmen* (Columbia: University of Missouri Press, 2002), 3; Altherr, *Sports in North America*, vol. 1, pt. 2, 143–146.

20. Silas Bent McKinley and Silas Bent, *Old Rough and Ready: The Life and Times of Zachary Taylor* (New York: Vanguard Press, 1946), 32; Jennie Holliman, *American Sports, 1785–1835* (Durham, NC: Seeman Press, 1931), 138–139, 149.

21. Morton and O'Brien, *Wrestling to Rasslin*, 20; Mike Chapman, *The Sport of Lincoln* (Newton, IA: Culture House, 2003), 12–30.

22. John R. Betts, "Mind and Body in Early American Thought," *Journal of American History* 54 (March 1968): 787–805; Roberta J. Park, "Biological Thought, Athletics, and the Formation of a 'Man of Character': 1830–1900," in J. A. Mangan and James Whalen, eds., *Manliness and Morality: Middle-Class Masculinity in Britain and America, 1800–1940* (New York: St. Martin's Press, 1987), 7–34; Peter Levine, "The Promise of Sport in Antebellum America," *Journal of American Culture*, 2 (Winter 1980): 623–634; Steven A. Riess, "Sport and the Redefinition of Middle-Class Masculinity in Victorian America," in Pope, *New American Sport History*, 173–184; Dizikes, *Sportsmen and Gamesmen*, 47–66; Robert Knight Barney, "German Forty-Eighters and *Turnvereine* in the United States during the Ante-Bellum Period," *Canadian Journal of History of Sport* 13 (December 1982): 62–79; Rupert Wilkinson, *American Tough: The Tough-Guy Tradition and American Character* (Westport, CT: Greenwood Press, 1984), 89.

23. Dizikes, *Sportsmen and Gamesmen*, 132–136, 249; Mee, *Bare Fists*, 129–139; Joel Franks, "California and the Rise of Spectator Sports, 1850–1900," *Southern California Quarterly* 71 (Winter 1989): 291–293; Melvin L. Adelman, "The First Modern Sport in America: Harness Racing in New York City, 1825–1870," in Wiggins, *Sport in America*, 95–114; Harvey Green, *Fit for America: Health, Fitness, Sport, and American Society* (New York: Pantheon, 1986), 1–100; Steven A. Riess, *City Games: The Evolution of American Urban Society and the Rise of Sports* (Urbana: University of Illinois Press, 1989), 13–52.

24. Melvin L. Adelman, *A Sporting Time: New York City and the Rise of Modern Athletics, 1820–1870* (Urbana: University of Illinois Press, 1986), 261–262; Rowland Berthoff, *British Immigrants in Industrial America, 1790–1950* (Cambridge, MA: Harvard University Press, 1953), 152; Gerald Redmond, *The Caledonian Games in Nineteenth-Century America* (Rutherford, NJ: Fairleigh Dickenson University Press, 1971), 48.

25. Wilson, *Magnificent Scufflers*, 26–28; Morton and O'Brien, *Wrestling to Rasslin*, 20–21.

26. Wilson, *Magnificent Scufflers*, 29–31; Gorn, *Manly Art*, 46. This is also fragmentary evidence suggesting that matches in an upright style, quite possibly collar-and-elbow, led to heavy wagering in Boston and New York. References to these matches can be found in the New York *Clipper* during the 1850s, but given the paper's far more extensive coverage of prizefights, it is obvious that pugilism was a far more popular sport than wrestling in eastern cities. Kirsch, *Sports in North America: A Documentary History*, 8 vols. (Gulf Breeze: Academic International Press, 1992), 3:369–372.

27. George B. Kirsch, *Baseball in Blue and Gray: The National Pastime during the Civil War* (Princeton, NJ: Princeton University Press, 2003), 29–33.

28. Lawrence Fielding, "Sport on the Road to Appomattox: The Shadows of Army Life" (Ph.D. diss., University of Maryland, 1974), 89–90, 106, 109, 305, 334, 444; Wilson, *Magnificent Scufflers*, 40–41; Morton and O'Brien, *Wrestling to Rasslin*, 21–22.

29. Fielding, "Sport on the Road to Appomattox," 112–113, 129–132; Kirsch, *Baseball in Blue and Gray*, 34; John R. Betts, *America's Sporting Heritage: 1850–1950* (Reading, MA: Addison-Wesley, 1974), 88–92.

CHAPTER 2: BARNSTORMERS

1. Michael Oriand, "Dreaming of Heroes: American Sports Fiction from the Beginning to the Present" (Ph.D. diss., Stanford University, 1976), 3; Frederic L. Paxson, "The Rise of Sport," *Mississippi Valley*

Historical Review 4 (September 1917), 146, 154; Benjamin G. Rader, *American Sports: From the Age of Folk Games to the Age of Televised Sports* (Upper Saddle River, NJ: Prentice Hall, 1998), 19–33; Betts, *America's Sporting Heritage*, 88–111.

2. Riess, *City Games*, 53.

3. Riess, *City Games*, 60–61; David G. Pugh, *Sons of Liberty: The Masculine Mind in Nineteenth-Century America* (Westport: Greenwood Press, 1983), 103–104; Betts, *America's Sporting Heritage*, 172; Roberta J. Park, "Physiology and Anatomy Are Destiny!? Brains, Bodies and Exercise in Nineteenth Century American Thought," *Journal of Sport History* 18 (Spring 1991): 49–63.

4. Riess, *City Games*, 86; Gorn, *Manly Art*, 137; S. W. Pope, *Patriotic Games: Sporting Traditions in the American Imagination, 1876–1926* (New York: Oxford University Press, 1997), 4.

5. Michael T. Isenberg, *John L. Sullivan and His America* (Urbana: University of Illinois Press, 1988), 96–97; Gorn, *Manly Art*, 98–99; Hardy, "Organized Sport and the Search for Community," 12; Jon Kingsdale, "The 'Poor Man's Club': Social Functions of the Working-Class Saloon," *American Quarterly* 25 (October 1973): 472–489; Mark Dyreson, "Playing for a National Identity: Sport, Immigration, and the Quest for a National Culture in American Social Thought, 1880–1919," *Proteus* 11 (Fall 1994): 40.

6. Aaron Baker, "Contested Identities: Sports in American Film and Television" (Ph.D. diss., Indiana University, 1994), 11–12; John R. Betts, "The Technological Revolution and the Rise of Sport, 1850–1900" in Steven A. Riess, ed., *The American Sporting Experience: A Historical Anthology of Sport in America* (West Point: Leisure Press, 1984), 146–147; Gunther Barth, *City People: The Rise of Modern City Culture in Nineteenth-Century America* (New York: Oxford University Press, 1980), 151–152; Riess, *City Games*, 71–72; Dizikes, *Sportsmen and Gamesmen*, 47–66; John R. Betts, "Sporting Journalism in Nineteenth-Century America," *American Quarterly* 5 (Spring 1953): 42–43; Frank L. Mott, *A History of American Magazines* (Cambridge, MA: Belknap Press, 1967), 209–222; Norris W. Yates, *William T. Porter and the Spirit of the Times* (Baton Rouge: Louisiana State University Press, 1957), 3–35.

7. Isenberg, *John L. Sullivan*, 82–96; Riess, *City Games*, 72; Betts, "Sporting Journalism," 50–51; Mandell, *Sport: A Cultural History*, 184–185.

8. Gorn, *Manly Art*, 98–99; *National Police Gazette*, April 3, 1880, February 21, 1885.

9. Guttmann, *From Ritual to Record*, 16; Adelman, *A Sporting Time*, 6.

10. Wilson, *Magnificent Scufflers*, 30.

11. *National Police Gazette*, March 27, 1880, April 10, 1880; Wilson, *Magnificent Scufflers*, 37.

12. Richard M. Haynes, "James H. McLaughlin—The Colonel," *Historical Wrestling Society Bulletin*, no. 6:1–4; *National Police Gazette*, February 1, 1879, February 14, 1880, January 31, 1885.

13. Royal Duncan and Gary Will, *Wrestling Title Histories*, 4th ed. (Waterloo, ON: Archeus, 2000), 8; Brooklyn *Daily Eagle*, March 11, 1870.

14. *National Police Gazette*, December 20, 1884, May 21, 1887, May 24, 1890, March 25, 1893; Brooklyn *Daily Eagle*, May 25, 1890, August 22, 1892; Mark S. Hewitt, *Catch Wrestling* (Boulder, CO: Paladin Press, 2005), 23–26.

15. Wilson, *Magnificent Scufflers*, 78.

16. *National Police Gazette*, June 26, 1880, November 8, 1884, December 27, 1884, December 20, 1890, September 24, 1892, January 21, 1893; Brooklyn *Daily Eagle*, February 3, 1886.

17. Duncan and Will, *Wrestling Title Histories*, 8; *National Police Gazette*, December 16, 1879.

18. Rader, *American Sports*, 123–126; Donald J. Mrozek, *Sport and American Mentality, 1880–1910* (Knoxville: University of Tennessee Press, 1983), 189–202; Arthur Inkersley, "Greco-Roman Games in California," *Outing* 5 (February 1895): 409–416.

19. Dakin Burdick, "The American Way of Fighting: Unarmed Defense in the United States, 1845–1945," (Ph.D. diss., Indiana University, 1999), 34–37; Hardy, "Organized Sport and the Search for Community," 74–78; E. Anthony Rotundo, "Learning about Manhood: Gender Ideals and the Middle-Class Family in Nineteenth-Century America," in Mangan and Whalen, *Manliness and Morality*, 35–51; Cross, *A Social History of Leisure Since 1600*, 143–147; Mrozek, *Sport and American Mentality*, 202–208.

20. Clifford Putney, *Muscular Christianity: Manhood and Sports in Protestant America, 1880–1920* (Cambridge: Harvard University Press, 2001), 45–47; Pope, *Patriotic Games*, 5–6; *National Police Gazette*, January 1, 1888.

21. Mee, *Bare Fists*, 190; Edward Van Every, *Muldoon: The Solid Man of Sport* (New York: Frederick A. Stokes, 1929), 131–160; Isenberg, *John L. Sullivan*, 265–267.

22. Nat Fleischer, *From Milo to Londos: The Story of Wrestling From 2000 BC to 1936* (New York: C. J. O'Brien, 1936), 33–35.

23. *National Police Gazette*, November 29, 1884, January 12, 1885.

24. *National Police Gazette*, March 24, 1888, March 9, 1889, April 6, 1889, July 13, 1889.

25. Van Every, *Muldoon*, 337; *National Police Gazette*, February 28, 1885, April 5, 1885; Morton and O'Brien, *Wrestling to Rasslin*, 32–34; Fleischer, *From Milo to Londos*, 43–47. Many of these European opponents earned their living as professional strongmen and viewed wrestling as a

lucrative sideline of that profession. Some, such as Carl Abs, given their strength and limited knowledge of holds, refused to wrestle any style other than Greco-Roman. *National Police Gazette*, April 5, 1885.

26. Richard M. Haynes, "William Muldoon—The Solid Man," *Historical Wrestling Society Bulletin*, no. 3:3; Morton and O'Brien, *Wrestling to Rasslin*, 26; Joe Jares, *Whatever Happened to Gorgeous George?* (Englewood Cliffs: Prentice Hall, 1974), 155; Fleischer, *From Milo to Londos*, 36–39.

27. Isenberg, *John L. Sullivan*, 193–194; Van Every, *Muldoon*, 71–83; Mrozek, *Sport and American Mentality*, 210–225; David L. Chapman, *Sandow the Magnificent: Eugen Sandow and the Beginnings of Bodybuilding* (Urbana: University of Illinois Press, 1994), 74–75, 83–84; *National Police Gazette*, February 28, 1885, March 10, 1888, January 5, 1889; Brooklyn *Daily Eagle*, June 13, 1886, December 18, 1887, April 29, 1888, November 10, 1889.

28. Van Every, *Muldoon*, 97–98.

29. Dizikes, *Sportsmen and Gamesmen*, 132–136, 249; Paxson, "Rise of Sport," 147; Gorn, *Manly Art*, 172–173; *National Police Gazette*, March 20, 1880, March 27, 1880, April 1, 1880, July 7, 1887.

30. Gorn, *Manly Art*, 220–222.

31. Theodore Dreiser, *Twelve Men* (New York: Boni & Liveright, 1919), 137; Isenberg, *John L. Sullivan*, 330; Brooklyn *Daily Eagle*, October 30, 1901.

32. Jeffrey T. Sammons, *Beyond the Ring: The Role of Boxing in American Society* (Urbana: University of Illinois Press, 1990), 30–44; Isenberg, *John L. Sullivan*, 290–293; Gorn, *Manly Art*, 217–218.

33. Van Every, *Muldoon*, 339; Wilson, *Magnificent Scufflers*, 59–61.

34. *National Police Gazette*, December 6, 1884, May 21, 1887, July 7, 1887, November 19, 1887, February 2, 1889, March 9, 1889, August 31, 1889; Brooklyn *Daily Eagle*, January 20, 1884, March 16, 1884, August 8, 1884. Despite the racial difficulties Sorakichi encountered in the United States, he did not relinquish the discriminatory attitudes of his homeland. William Harding noted that "Sorakichi is a gentlemanly athlete, an expert wrestler and always in good humor when he is not compared to a Chinaman, a race he detests." *National Police Gazette*, June 1, 1889.

35. Green, *Fit for America*, 225–228; Donald J. Mrozek, "The 'Amazon' and the American 'Lady': Sexual Fears of Women as Athletes," in Pope, *The New American Sport History*, 198–204; Roberta J. Park, " 'Embodied Selves': The Rise and Development of Concern for Physical Education, Active Games and Recreation for American Women, 1776–1865," in Wiggins, *Sport in America*, 69–94.

36. *National Police Gazette*, December 27, 1884, January 18, 1890, October 11, 1890, October 10, 1891, September 3, 1892, November 26,

1892; Brooklyn *Daily Eagle*, February 10, 1880, January 5, 1890; Karl Stern, *The Pioneers of Wrestling* (Haleyville, AL: Dragonking Press, 2002), 10; Mrozek, *Sport and American Mentality*, 212; Allen Guttmann, *Women's Sports: A History* (New York: Columbia University Press, 1991), 99–101.

37. Brooklyn *Daily Eagle*, May 6, 1887; *National Police Gazette*, June 15, 1889.

38. Gorn, *Manly Art*, 166, 203–205, 222–224; Isenberg, *John L. Sullivan*, 68–70; Burdick, "American Way of Fighting," 176.

39. Richard Knott, "The Sport Hero as Portrayed in Popular Journalism," (Ph.D. diss., University of Tennessee, 1994), 108; Gorn, *Manly Art*, 205.

40. Isenberg, *John L. Sullivan*, 221–227, 279–280, 300–301, 322–323; Gorn, *Manly Art*, 222–227.

41. Brooklyn *Daily Eagle*, March 27, 1888, May 2, 189–.

42. *National Police Gazette*, March 10, 1888, February 23, 1889, February 16, 1889, June 1, 1889, February 22, 1890, September 20, 1890.

CHAPTER 3: CATCH-AS-CATCH-CAN

1. Brooklyn *Daily Eagle*, May 25, 1879, August 17, 1884, June 12, 1898; *National Police Gazette*, April 18, 1885, October 20, 1888, January 1, 1890, December 31, 1892, October 27, 1894, December 22, 1900.

2. Dizikes, *Sportsmen and Gamesmen*, 275–276; Burdick, "American Way of Fighting," 100–101; Robert Ernst, *Weakness Is a Crime: The Life of Bernarr MacFadden* (Syracuse, NY: Syracuse University Press, 1991), 11–13; Hewitt, *Catch Wrestling*, 46–68. Shortly before his 1894 retirement, MacFadden claimed the welterweight championship of the world. *National Police Gazette*, February 24, 1894.

3. Mrozek, *Sport and American Mentality*, 161–188; Pope, *Patriotic Games*, 71–78; Dyreson, "Playing for a National Identity," 39–43; Cross, *A Social History of Leisure Since 1600*, 152–157; *National Police Gazette*, April 20, 1895.

4. *National Police Gazette*, January 5, 1889, August 24, 1889, November 11, 1893, April 25, 1903.

5. Brooklyn *Daily Eagle*, March 23, 1898, May 1, 1898, February 5, 1901; *National Police Gazette*, February 2, 1895, November 18, 1899, April 7, 1900, October 6, 1900, October 13, 1900, February 9, 1901, March 2, 1901, May 25, 1901, June 8, 1901, February 4, 1905; Graeme Kent, *A Pictorial History of Wrestling* (Feltham, Middlesex, UK: Spring Books, 1968), 143–144; Fleischer, *From Milo to Londos*, 65–67.

6. Frank Gotch, *Wrestling and How to Train* (New York: Richard K. Fox, 1913), 35; Van Every, *Muldoon*, 71–83; *National Police Gazette*, February 16, 1889, June 1, 1889.

7. *National Police Gazette,* January 28, 1905, February 25, 1905.

8. Lou Thesz and Kit Bauman, *Hooker: An Authentic Wrestler's Adventures Inside the Bizarre World of Professional Wrestling,* rev. ed. (Seattle: TWC Press, 2000), 11–12; *National Police Gazette,* March 10, 1888, September 26, 1891, July 6, 1895, February 6, 1904.

9. Arthur H. Lewis, *Carnival* (New York: Trident Press, 1970), 34–36; Hewitt, *Catch Wrestling,* 203–208; Minneapolis *Tribune,* May 3, 1970.

10. Sarah Hautzinger, "American Carnival Speech: Making the Jump," *Journal of American Culture* 13 (Winter 1990): 29–33; Carol L. Russell, "The Life and Death of Carnie," *American Speech* 79 (Winter 2004): 400–416; *National Police Gazette,* August 5, 1903. In his glossary of wrestling terms, Dave Flood notes that *kayfabe* is "probably some sort of convoluted pig-Latin version of the word fake." Flood, *Kayfabe: The Secret World of Professional Wrestling* (Chicago: Gambit, 2000), 69–86.

11. Brooklyn *Daily Eagle,* November 6, 1898; *National Police Gazette,* May 1, 1880, December 17, 1892, February 25, 1899, December 28, 1901, August 1, 1903, September 1904, February 25, 1905, August 19, 1905, June 3, 1905, July 20, 1905.

12. Brooklyn *Daily Eagle,* December 23, 1902; *National Police Gazette,* March 17, 1900, September 29, 1900, October 16, 1900, June 1, 1901, January 11, 1902, January 3, 1903; Sammons, *Beyond the Ring,* 22.

13. *National Police Gazette,* January 26, 1901, July 6, 1901, July 13, 1901, August 3, 1901, March 7, 1903, April 4, 1903.

14. Hewitt, *Catch Wrestling,* 1–2; *National Police Gazette,* December 25, 1879, September 24, 1892; Gotch, *Wrestling and How to Train,* 58, 61; Burdick, "American Way of Fighting," 235–237; Carlos Gutierrez and Julian Espartero, "JuJutsu's Image in Spain's Wrestling Shows: A Historic Review," *Journal of Asian Martial Arts* 13 (Summer 2004): 8–31.

15. *National Police Gazette,* January 6, 1894, June 10, 1905, August 4, 1906. Particularly sadistic catch wrestlers used these scientific holds to restrain an opponent in order to inflict pain through more primitive techniques. For example, in a 1904 match, the mean-spirited Charley "Yankee" Rogers obtained a combination half nelson with a crotch hold on Emil Selva and then dragged Selva face first across the mat before bridging him. Ibid., April 30, 1904.

16. Duncan and Will, *Wrestling Title Histories,* 8; *National Police Gazette,* January 7, 1887, March 19, 1887, November 10, 1888, June 14, 1890, January 10, 1903; Hewitt, *Catch Wrestling,* 5–12.

17. *National Police Gazette,* December 21, 1892, January 21, 1893, March 18, 1893; New York *Times,* March 3, 1893.

18. Martin Burns, *The Life Work of "Farmer" Burns* (Omaha, NE: A. J. Kuhlman, 1911), 79–110; Hewitt, *Catch Wrestling,* 17. The "Farmer," who

continued to compete after his fiftieth birthday, may have wrestled more matches than anyone in American history. Burns estimated he faced more than six thousand opponents. He died in 1937. As with Roeber, Lewis finished his career by losing worked matches to lesser opponents seeking notoriety by defeating a former champion.

19. Mike Chapman, *Frank Gotch: World's Greatest Wrestler* (Buffalo, NY: William S. Hein, 1990), 19–24; Hewitt, *Catch Wrestling*, 13–34; Gotch, *Wrestling and How to Train*, 9.

20. *National Police Gazette*, May 27, 1899, September 16, 1899, September 2, 1902, December 6, 1902, January 17, 1903, January 9, 1904, October 21, 1905; Hewitt, *Catch Wrestling*, 43–48.

21. Chapman, *Frank Gotch*, 30–33; *National Police Gazette*, May 25, 1901, March 21, 1903, February 20, 1904, February 27, 1904, March 26, 1904, October 21, 1905, November 25, 1905. Jenkins entered semiretirement in 1905 to become the wrestling instructor at West Point, a position he maintained for more than thirty years.

22. Chapman, *Frank Gotch*, 47–53; *National Police Gazette*, February 18, 1905, May 27, 1905, October 21, 1905; Karl Stern, "The Story of Fred Beell," *Dragonking Press Newsletter*, no. 43 (February 2002): 1–2. The December 1906 Gotch Beell match in New Orleans remains the single most controversial bout in professional wrestling history. A debate continues to rage over whether this match represents a "work." Wrestling historians who support the notion that the match was fixed point out that Beell's backers wagered heavily on him, despite the Wisconsin wrestler's poor showing against Gotch in a June 1905 defeat and that Gotch handily disposed of Beell in the profitable rematch eighteen days later. Gotch frequently engaged in questionable matches while on tour, which buttressed this theory. He repeatedly faced cronies Burns, Jack Carkeek, John "Charles Hackenschmidt" Berg, and, under a variety of pseudonyms, Emil Klank, which demonstrates that Gotch did not always operate honestly. Also, later Gotch apologists explained the defeat by asserting that the champion became dazed after banging his head on a ring post—an occurrence not mentioned in contemporary newspaper accounts, which do, however, note that Gotch suffered a cut above his eye after landing off the mat. However, if Gotch laid down for Beell as a means to make money on the rematch and to establish a marketable rival, it is difficult to explain why Gotch neither allowed Beell to look good in the rematch by carrying him nor ever again attempted to create another rival by losing. Gotch never lost again, not even a single fall. Chapman, *Frank Gotch*, 52; George J. Buckwell, "Frank Gotch," *Baseball Magazine* 8 (November 1911): 100; Karl Stern, "The Myth and Magic of Frank A. Gotch," *Dragonking Press Newsletter*, no. 71 (April 2004): 6–8; *National Police Gazette*, December 15, 1906.

23. Kent, *Pictorial History of Wrestling*, 146–148, 151–152; *National Police Gazette*, November 20, 1901, August 22, 1903, February 12, 1904, March 19, 1904.

24. Chapman, *Frank Gotch*, 29; *National Police Gazette*, July 16, 1904, April 1, 1905, May 20, 1905, July 15, 1905, June 9, 1906, June 23, 1906, October 13, 1906.

25. Chapman, *Frank Gotch*, 62–63, 68–70; Chicago *Tribune*, April 3, 1908. For an account of a similar 1908 convergence of patriotism and sport, see Pope, *Patriotic Games*, 45–49.

26. Chapman, *Frank Gotch*, 65–67; Chicago *Tribune*, April 4, 1908. Gotch's rough tactics most likely unnerved Hackenschmidt, who found such behavior beneath his dignity. In a 1903 article, Irish wrestler Tom McInerney posited that the Russian lacked the aggressive temperament needed for a successful wrestler. He noted that, in their recent match, Hackenschmidt "had plenty of chances to disable me and put me out of the match for good, but would not do so and just made the hold firm enough to secure a fall." Hackenschmidt himself stated that he found American wrestlers "far too rough and ready." *National Police Gazette*, August 22, 1903, July 15, 1905. Hackenschmidt's claim that Gotch came to the ring covered in oil cannot be taken seriously. Given that, by all accounts, both men sweated profusely on the hot day, any oil present would have quickly covered both men, rendering neither capable of obtaining holds. Further, the presence of a foreign substance could not have been hidden from the referee or close bystanders. For example, in a 1904 match, a Massachusetts wrestler named "Gilligan" attempted this trick, which the referee immediately discovered. Ibid., January 2, 1904.

27. Sammons, *Beyond the Ring*, 34–47; Geoffrey C. Ward, *Unforgivable Blackness: The Rise and Fall of Jack Johnson* (New York: Alfred A. Knopf, 2004), 137–165.

28. Al-Tony Gilmore, *Bad Nigger! The National Impact of Jack Johnson* (Port Washington, NY: Kennikat Press, 1975), 33–43, 59–72, 75–90; Ward, *Unforgivable Blackness*, 166–221, 234; Chapman, *Frank Gotch*, 80–85; Seattle *Post-Intelligencer*, January 24, 1904. During this same period, English wrestling also suffered from racial issues, particularly regarding wrestlers of color from areas under English imperial control. For an excellent article on this subject, see Joseph S. Atler, "Gama the World Champion: Wrestling and Physical Culture in Colonial India," *Iron Game History* 4 (October 1995): 3–9.

29. Chapman, *Frank Gotch*, 71–78.

30. Mathew Lindaman, "Wrestling's Hold on the Western World before the Great War," *Historian* 62 (Summer 2000): 779–798; Chapman, *Frank Gotch*, 91–102; Chicago *Tribune*, February 14, 1911, September 2–6, 1911. As with his 1908 defeat at the hands of Gotch, Hackenschmidt later

declared that the American used underhanded tactics to defeat him. In the 1911 rematch, the Russian claimed that Gotch paid one of Hackenschmidt's training partners to injure his knee deliberately. No evidence exists to support Hackenschmidt's assertion.

31. New York *Times*, December 31, 1911. Gotch made sporadic returns to the ring after his "official" retirement. In 1916, he launched a full comeback that ended when he broke his leg during an exhibition. In May 1917, he returned to the ring for one last match and defeated Leo Pardello in Chicago. Gotch died of kidney failure (attributed to the pounding he received in the ring) in December of that year. He was just under 40 years old.

CHAPTER 4: THE ART OF DECEPTION

1. Robert B. Weaver, *Amusements and Sports in American Life* (reprint, Westport, CT: Greenwood Press, 1968), 150.

2. Chapman, *Frank Gotch*, 121; Fleischer, *From Milo to Londos*, 179–187; Evansville *Press*, October 21, 1915. The title lineage proved equally murky in the marginalized lower-weight classes. During the same period, Mike Yokel, Joe Turner, Paul Bowser, Elmer Brown, Henry Gehring, and George Willoughby all claimed the middleweight championship.

3. Richard Haynes, "Joe Stecher—The Scissors King," *Historical Wrestling Society Bulletin*, no. 23:7–8.

4. Curley's nonathletic promotional efforts included managing American tours for Annette Kellerman, Lydia Pankhurst, and the Vienna Boys' Choir. Much of the following discussion of Curley's early career is based on the excellent research—unpublished, but available from several online sources—of wrestling historian Steve Yohe.

5. Richard Haynes, "Earl Caddock," *Historical Wrestling Society Bulletin*, no. 17:9–10; Fleischer, *From Milo to Londos*, 191–200.

6. Dizikes, *Sportsmen and Gamesmen*, 275–276; Anonymous, "Frank Gotch, Champion of Champions," *Baseball Magazine* 20 (February 1918): 359.

7. Hewitt, Richard Haynes, "Ed 'Strangler' Lewis," *Historical Wrestling Society Bulletin*, no. 9:1–2; Chicago *Tribune*, November 13, 1913; Hartford *Daily Courant*, March 16, 1919.

8. New York *Times*, January 31, 1920; Marcus Griffin, *Fall Guys: The Barnums of Bounce* (Hendersonville, TN: Rasslin' Reprints, 1997), 17; Charles Samuels, *The Magnificent Rube: The Life and Gaudy Times of Tex Rickard* (New York: McGraw-Hill, 1957), 217. First published in 1937, Griffin's book represented the first in-depth, published study of wrestling's "worked" era. As such, the book includes much valuable

information. However, it appears sportswriter Griffin based much of the work on information fed to him by "Toots" Mondt, which gives the book a distinctly biased coloring.

9. New York *Herald*, May 22, 1923.

10. Kenneth R. Boness, *Pile Driver: The Life of Charles "Midget" Fischer* (Philadelphia: Xlibris, 2002), 65–66.

11. Samuels, *Magnificent Rube*, 199; Bruce J. Evensen, *When Dempsey Fought Tunney: Heroes, Hokum, and Storytelling in the Jazz Age* (Knoxville: University of Tennessee Press, 1996), 1, 15–16; Roger Kahn, *A Flame of Pure Fire: Jack Dempsey and the Roaring '20s* (New York: Harcourt Brace, 1999), 231–232.

12. Griffin, *Fall Guys*, 32–33.

13. Fleischer, *From Milo to Londos*, 227–231. As an illustration of the ludicrousness of the inept Munn's claim to be the world's wrestling champion, one should keep in mind that Zbyszko, who easily dominated the ex-footballer, engaged in a 1928 shoot with the Indian wrestler Gama and was pinned by the Punjab native in less than one minute. Munn also launched a disastrous professional boxing career in which he lost both of his bouts via knockout. Munn died of kidney problems in 1931.

14. Marin Plestina, "Confessions of a Wrestler" (undated document in International Wrestling Institute and Museum archives); Griffin, *Fall Guys*, 25–27.

15. Hewitt, *Catch Wrestling*, 151–170.

16. Evensen, *When Dempsey Fought Tunney*, 70–71, 89; Mark Dyreson, "The Emergence of Consumer Culture and the Transformation of Physical Culture: American Sport in the 1920s," *Journal of Sport History* 16 (Winter 1989): 261–281; Bruce J. Evensen, "Jazz Age Journalism's Battle Over Professionalism, Circulation, and the Sports Page," *Journal of Sport History* 20 (Winter 1993): 229–246; Rader, *American Sports*, 134–152; Betts, *America's Sporting Heritage*, 250–276. For an extended discussion of the role of sportswriters in the "golden age of sports," see Mark Inabinett, *Grantland Rice and His Heroes: The Sportswriter as Mythmaker in the 1920s* (Knoxville: University of Tennessee Press, 1994). A reflection of the popularity the media helped develop for Lewis can be seen in the 1933 motion picture *The Prizefighter and the Lady*. Before the film's pivotal boxing match, a group of luminaries are introduced that includes most of the leading exponents of the "sweet science." The only nonboxer in the group was "Strangler" Lewis.

17. Philadelphia *Evening Bulletin*, May 27, 1930.

18. Clarence Eklund, *Forty Years of Wrestling: Its History and Transition* (Buffalo, NY: Buffalo Bulletin, 1947), 8; John C. Meyers, *Wrestling from Antiquity to Date* (St. Louis: self-published, 1931), 48; Kent, *A Pictorial History of Wrestling*, 185; Milton MacKaye, "On the Hoof," *Saturday Evening Post*, 208 (December 14, 1933): 35; Atlanta *Constitution*,

April 29, 1931; Honolulu *Star-Bulletin*, September 11, 1931; Minneapolis *Star*, December 17, 1953.

19. Griffin, *Fall Guys*, 40–45, 61–63; Richard Haynes, "Jim Londos," *Historical Wrestling Society Bulletin*, no. 8:1–4; Fleischer, *From Milo to Londos*, 266–296; New York *Times*, March 26, 1928; Los Angeles *Examiner*, October 11, 1934; Robert L. Jones, "Wrestling Finds a King at Last," *The Arena* 2 (August 1930): 22–23, 38.

20. New York *World-Telegram*, December 8, 1931; Washington *Post*, June 24, 1932.

21. Evensen, *When Dempsey Fought Tunney*, 48–49, 83; MacKaye, "On the Hoof," 37.

22. Peter Levine, "Oy Such a Fighter! Boxing and the American Jewish Experience" in Pope, *The New American Sport History*, 251–284; Leverette, *Professional Wrestling*; Jares, *Whatever Happened to Gorgeous George?* (Englewood Cliffs, NJ: Prentice Hall, 1974), 98; A. J. Liebling, "From Sarah Bernhardt to Yukon Eric," *New Yorker* 30 (November 13, 1954): 137; Chicago *Tribune*, February 19, 1931; New York *Times*, July 12, 1932.

23. Joe Bonomo, *The Strongman* (New York: Bonomo Studios, 1968), 229–233.

24. Springfield *Union*, August 29, 1933; Karl Stern, "The Most Famous Wrestler You Never Heard of...Nat Pendleton," *Dragonking Press Newsletter*, no. 71 (June 2004): 1–4; John Dinan, *Sports in the Pulp Magazines* (Jefferson, NC: McFarland, 1998), 104–129.

25. Griffin, *Fall Guys*, 63–71; Chicago *Tribune*, March 19, 1931; Boston *Daily Globe*, July 29, 1935; "The Hippo Hippodrome," *Literary Digest* 112 (February 6, 1932): 41.

26. Seattle *Post-Intelligencer*, January 16, 1934; Thesz and Bauman, *Hooker*, 55.

27. Jack Miley, "Jake's Juggernauts," *Collier's* 102 (October 22, 1938): 56–59; Boston *Daily Globe*, February 12, 1938. The California Athletic Commission, deeply troubled by the actions of Los Angeles promoter "Carnation" Lou Daro, passed stringent regulation that banned kicking, biting, and tossing opponents from the ring. Additionally, the commission barred promoters from wrestling, ruled that wrestlers could not compete more than three times a week and made it illegal for wrestlers to meet the same opponent more than four times in one year except for rematches at the same facility. Los Angeles *Times*, July 9, 1933. The Illinois State Athletic Commission passed similar regulations the same year—and even banned wrestling in the state for a period.

28. Richard Haynes, "Dick Shikat," *Historical Wrestling Society Bulletin*, no. 4:1–3; Columbus *Dispatch*, March 25, 1936, April 19, 1936, April 24–28, 1936, May 12, 1936.

29. Griffin, *Fall Guys*, 80–91.

30. Weaver, *Amusements and Sports in American Life*, 151; Gary Dean Best, *The Nickel and Dime Decade: American Popular Culture During the 1930s* (Westport, CT: Praeger, 1993), 91–106; Boston *Daily Globe*, July 26, 1935.

31. Thesz and Bauman, *Hooker*, 19–80.

32. Honolulu *Star-Bulletin*, September 23, 1936.

CHAPTER 5: GIMMICKS AND TELEVISION

1. Roland Barthes, "The World of Professional Wrestling," in Nicholas Sammond, ed., *Steel Chair to the Head: The Pleasure and Pain of Professional Wrestling* (Durham, NC: Duke University Press, 2005), 23–32.

2. Ventura County *Star*, April 29, 1936; "Baba & Behemoths," *Time* 27 (May 18, 1936): 54–55, 58.

3. Miley, "Jake's Juggernauts," 56–59.

4. Los Angeles *Times*, September 20, 1934, October 20, 1934; Joseph R. Svinth, "Kaimon Kudo, Man Mountain Dean, and 1930s Show Wrestling," *Wrestling Then and Now*, no. 92 (September 1997): 13; MacKaye, "On the Hoof," 37; Los Angeles *Times*, September 20, 1934.

5. Jares, *Whatever Happened to Gorgeous George?*, 35–36; Steve Yohe, "Maurice 'French Angel' Tillet Biography," *Dragonking Press Newsletter*, no. 52 (October 2002): 1–3.

6. Jares, *Gorgeous George*, 26–33; Kevin Britz, "Of Football and Frontiers: The Meaning of Bronko Nagurski," *Journal of Sport History* 20 (Summer 1993): 117–118; Washington *Post*, September 11, 1937; Robert Sklar, ed., *The Plastic Age (1917–1930)* (New York: George Braziller, 1970), 23; Stockton *Daily Record*, April 8, 1936. Aaron Baker noted that boxing films of the period also played on this nostalgia. These films often promoted a "populist prizefighter," thereby "mythologizing the working-class fighter whose actions promoted traditional agrarian notions of the common good." Wrestling films of the 1930s followed a similar formula. Baker, "Contested Identities,", 100–118.

7. Spokane *Spokesman-Review*, February 27, 1935; Stockton *Daily Record*, July 24, 1936, August 11, 1936; Fresno *Bee*, January 14, 1945; Jares, *Gorgeous George*, 79–80.

8. Edythe Farrell, "The Lady Wrestlers," *American Mercury* 228 (December 1942): 679; Florida *Times-Union*, December 3, 1997.

9. Jares, *Gorgeous George*, 49–64; Farrell, "Lady Wrestlers," 678; Los Angeles *Times*, February 21, 1989.

10. Jares, *Gorgeous George*, 45–46; Sarah Fields, "Female Gladiators: Gender, Law, and Contact Sport in America" (Ph.D. diss., University of

Iowa, 2000), 151–153; Douglas Owen Baldwin, ed., *Sports In America: A Documentary History*, 8 vols. (Gulf Breeze, FL: Academic International Press, 2000), 8:13–16; Guttmann, *Women's Sports*, 189–192; William H. Beezley and Joseph P. Hobbs, "'Nice Girls Don't Sweat': Women in American Sport," *Journal of Popular Culture* 16 (Spring 1983): 42–53; Mrozek, "The 'Amazon' and the American 'Lady'," in Pope, *The New American Sport History*, 198–214; Patrice A. Oppliger, *Wrestling and Hypermasculinity* (Jefferson, NC: McFarland, 2004), 124–125; Lou Thesz, "Dempsey Thumbs Down on Women Referees," *Official Wrestling* 1 (August 1951): 3–4.

11. Portland *Oregonian*, September 25, 1949.

12. Guttmann, *From Ritual to Record*, 137–139.

13. San Bernardino *Sun*, February 5, 1944.

14. Fresno *Bee*, January 1, 1942; Thesz and Bauman, *Hooker*, 87–94.

15. Statesville *Daily Record*, January 17, 1945; Council Bluffs *Nonpareil*, August 23, 1944; Fresno *Bee*, January 22, 1944; Paul Boesch, *Hey, Boy! Where'd You Get Them Ears?* (Houston: Minuteman Press, 2001), 182–188; Boesch, *The Road to Huertgen* (Houston: Gulf Publishing, 1962). The five killed were Midwestern wrestlers George Mack, Jack Ross, Hal Sabath, Garius Young, and Ben Reuben.

16. Jeff Neal-Lunsford, "Sport in the Land of Television: The Use of Sport in Network Prime-Time Schedules, 1946–1950," *Journal of Sport History* 19 (Spring 1992): 59; Rader, *In Its Own Image*, 32–35; Ron Powers, *Supertube: The Rise of Television Sports* (New York: Coward-McCann, 1984), 23–44; James Von Schilling, *The Magic Window: American Television, 1939–1953* (New York: Haworth, 2003), 1–92; Christina S. Jarvis, *The Male Body At War: American Masculinity During World War II* (DeKalb: Northern Illinois University Press, 2004), 5.

17. Neal-Lunsford, "Sport in Land of Television," 63, 66–74; Rader, *In Its Own Image*, 39; Von Schilling, *Magic Window*, 128–129; Susan K. Wilbur, "The History of Television in Los Angeles, 1931–1952—Part I," *Southern California Quarterly* 60 (Spring 1978): 70.

18. Rader, *In Its Own Image*, 4; Richard O. Davis, *America's Obsession: Sports and Society Since 1945* (Fort Worth, TX: Harcourt Brace, 1994), 74–77; Robert W. McChesney, "Media Made Sport: A History of Sports Coverage in the United States," in Lawrence A. Wenner, ed., *Media, Sports and Society* (Beverly Hills, CA: Sage, 1989), 60–61; Aaron D. Feigenbaum, "Professional Wrestling, Sports Entertainment and the Liminal Experience in American Culture" (Ph.D. diss., University of Florida, 2000), 62.

19. Chad Dell, "Researching Historical Broadcast Audiences: Female Fandom of Professional Wrestling, 1945–1960" (Ph.D. diss., University of Wisconsin–Madison, 1997), 4, 17–27, 98–99.

20. Rader, *In Its Own Image*, 39; Dell, "Historical Broadcast Audiences," 116; "Dog Bones and Flying Mares," *New Yorker* 24 (September 18, 1948): 23–24.

21. Thesz and Bauman, *Hooker*, 111.

22. Ibid., 94–110.

23. San Francisco *Chronicle*, June 1, 1948.

24. Oppliger, *Wrestling and Hypermasculinity*, 113–115; Ted Shane, "Gorgeous George The Wrestler," *American Mercury* 71 (July 1950): 64–71; Terry McNeill Saunders, "Play, Performance and Professional Wrestling: An Examination of a Modern Day Spectacle of Absurdity" (Ph.D. diss., University of California, Los Angeles, 1998), 96–97; Mazer, *Professional Wrestling*, 93–94.

25. Portland *Oregonian*, February 15, 1948.

26. Jares, *Gorgeous George*, 11–23; "Stanley," "News of the Mat World," *Ring Magazine* 27 (August 1948): 30–31.

27. Shane, "Gorgeous George," 65; Thesz and Bauman, *Hooker*, 115. George won the AWA title from Don Eagle in a 1950 match. There is strong evidence to suggest that his victory was a double-cross perpetrated by Pfefer and Chicago promoter Fred Kohler to both weaken the AWA (which continued to be a challenge to the NWA in the early 1950s) and to hurt Ohio promoter Al Haft, who both controlled Eagle and was locked in a bitter feud with Pfeffer. Further supporting this theory, George lost a highly publicized match with NWA champion Thesz two months later. Bill McCormack, "Another Indian Bites the Dust," *Wrestling Then & Now*, no. 116 (September 1999): 6–7.

28. Miami *Herald*, February 4, 1947.

29. Thesz and Bauman, *Hooker*, 117–125; Guy Le Bow, *The Wrestling Scene* (New York: Homecrafts, 1950), 79; Justin Murphy, *Titans of Capitolism* (Lake Havasu City, AZ: Epstein, 2005), chap. 4.

30. Jack Laskin, *One of the Boys* (Philadelphia: Xlibris, 2002), 48–51, 74–78.

31. Jares, *Gorgeous George*, 71–76; J. Fred MacDonald, *Television and the Red Menace: The Video Road to Vietnam* (New York: Praeger, 1985), 72–82; Hewitt, *Catch Wrestling*, 209–211. For an excellent discussion of the effect of anti-Communism on 1950s television, see Thomas Doherty, *Cold War, Cool Medium: Television, McCarthyism, and American Culture* (New York: Columbia University Press, 2003).

32. Jeffrey J. Mondrak, "The Politics of Professional Wrestling," *Journal of Popular Culture* 23 (Fall 1989): 139–149. Although provocative, and successful in detailing the 1950s, Mondrak's theory that wrestling's cyclical prosperity directly corresponds to eras of nationalism and isolationism does not bear close scrutiny. Mondrak posits that the 1930s, 1950s, and 1980s became successful periods for wrestling because these

sentiments dominated American society. While both of these ideas are readily apparent in the 1930s, wrestling struggled, particularly late, in that decade. Mondrak completely ignores that nationalism, isolationism, and professional wrestling all proved far more popular in the 1920s, a decade he does not address, than during the Depression Decade. Also, professional wrestling's turn-of-the-twentieth-century peak, another period not examined by Mondrak, developed in an era of nationalism and interventionist, expansionist foreign policy. Nor is it particularly credible to connect the American foreign policy of the 1950s, a decade marked by the drive to build global alliances against the threat of Communism, with isolationism. Foreign menaces typically only won titles for short periods, which set them up as "legitimate" challengers for faces. Of the foreign menaces of the period Hans Schmidt's several-month run as NWA United States champion in late 1956 and early 1957 stands as the greatest success. Significantly, Schmidt acted as a Nazi, not as a Russian Communist.

33. William Boddy, *Fifties Television: The Industry and Its Critics* (Urbana: University of Illinois Press, 1990), 207; Herman Hickman, "Rasslin' Was My Act," *Saturday Evening Post* 226 (February 6, 1954): 20–21, 101–102.

CHAPTER 6: HOLDING THE LINE

1. Rader, *In Its Own Image*, 32–35.
2. Wilbur, "History of Television in Los Angeles," 265.
3. Jares, *Whatever Happened to Gorgeous George?*, v.
4. Boesch, *Hey, Boy!*, 231–232.
5. Dell, "Researching Historical Broadcast Audiences," 200–290.
6. Wilson and Johnson, *Chokehold*, 238–241.
7. Warren Freedman, *Professional Sports and Antitrust* (New York: Quorum Books, 1987), 45–46; Sammons, *Beyond the Ring*, 130–183; Wilson, *Chokehold*, 257–262, 511–512. A former professional wrestler himself, Wilson posited that the "human cost"—blacklisting—of NWA practices most angered the Department of Justice. While this practice certainly did not help the NWA's case, Wilson, not surprising given his own background, significantly overstated the government's concern over this practice. Numerous private businesses and industries, as well as all levels of government, blacklisted individuals during the 1950s. Although these firings typically resulted from questions over an employee's political views, not as an attempt to monopolize a particular industry, the situation in wrestling cannot be viewed as either particularly unique or particularly troubling to government investigators. Wilson and Johnson simply did not appear to have examined wrestling's businesses practices within the larger

context of American society in the 1950s. In fact, their single brief mention of Red Scare–related blacklists was thoroughly inaccurate. They posited that a blacklist of "at least 324 . . . writers and actors . . . was established by Wisconsin Senator Joe McCarthy's House Un-American Activities Committee (HUAC) in 1947." Wilson and Johnson, *Chokehold*, 505.

8. Stephen S. Zashin, "Bodyslam From the Top Rope: Unequal Bargaining Power and Professional Wrestling's Failure to Unionize," *Entertainment and Sports Law Review* 22 (Fall 1994/Spring 1995): 13–15, 56; Freedman, *Sports and Antitrust*, 120; Wilson, *Chokehold*, 262–277.

9. Dave Meltzer, *Tributes II: Remembering More of the World's Greatest Professional Wrestlers* (Champaign, IL: Sports Publishing, 2004), 14–27; Duncan and Will, *Wrestling Title Histories*, 294–295; Freddie Blassie and Keith Elliot Greenberg, *Legends of Wrestling: "Classy" Freddie Blassie* (New York: Pocket Books, 2003), 67–116.

10. Larry Matysik, *Wrestling at the Chase: The Inside Story of Sam Muchnick and the Legends of Professional Wrestling* (Toronto: ECW Press, 2005), 15–27.

11. Boesch, *Hey Boy*, 233–234; Winnipeg *Free Press*, May 21, 1981; Minneapolis *Tribune*, May 12, 1981.

12. Dave Meltzer, *Tributes: Remembering Some of the World's Greatest Wrestlers* (Etobicoke, ON: Winding Stair, 2001), 115–121; Shaun Assael and Mike Mooneyham, *Sex, Lies, and Headlocks: The Real Story of Vince McMahon and the World Wrestling Federation* (New York: Crown, 2002), 14–15; Saunders, "Play, Performance, and Professional Wrestling," 101–103.

13. Jares, *Gorgeous George*, 46–49; Lillian Ellison and Larry Platt, *The Fabulous Moolah: First Goddess of the Squared Circle* (New York: Regan, 2002), 53–156.

14. Assael and Mooneyham, *Sex, Lies, and Headlocks*, 21–31. New York *Times*, June 26, 1976. Inoki later fought Leon Spinks in another wrestler versus boxer encounter. His interest in staging matches with nonwrestlers even led the Japanese champion to negotiate with representatives of Idi Amin. However, Inoki's match with the Ugandan dictator never occurred. Boston *Herald American*, December 31, 1978.

15. Meltzer, *Tributes II*, 82–93; Dan Murphy, *Bodyslams in Buffalo: The Complete History of Pro Wrestling in Western New York* (Buffalo: Western New York Wares, 2002), 30–56. The Sheik can be seen in all his glory in Farhat's self-financed motion picture *I Like to Hurt People*.

16. Louis M. Kyriakoudes and Peter A. Coclanis, "The 'Tennessee Test of Manhood': Professional Wrestling and Southern Cultural Stereotypes," *Southern Cultures* 3 (Fall 1997): 9, 12–13; Jim Freedman, "Will the Sheik Use His Blinding Fireball? The Ideology of Professional Wrestling," in Frank E. Manning, ed., *The Celebration of Society: Perspectives on*

Contemporary Cultural Performance (Bowling Green, OH: Bowling Green State University Press, 1983), 70–73.

17. Jack Brisco and William Murdock, *Brisco: The Life and Times of National Collegiate and World Heavyweight Wrestling Champion Jack Brisco* (Newton, IA: Culture House, 2003), 110–203. Although he never again became NWA world champion, Thesz went on to hold a variety of "outlaw" titles in the United States and Japan. He gradually slid into semiretirement during the late 1970s, but his last match, a five-minute encounter with Masahiro Chono, did not occur until 1990. The remarkable Thesz was 74-years-old at the time.

18. Meltzer, *Tributes II*, 185–186; Brisco, *Brisco*, 281; Ole Anderson and Scott Teal, *Inside Out: How Corporate America Destroyed Professional Wrestling* (Hendersonville, TN: Crowbar Press, 2003), 96; Larry Matysik, "Rolling Around the Mats," *Wrestling*, June 10, 1978, 2.

19. Meltzer, *Tributes*, 39–52.

20. Kyriakoudes and Coclanis, "Tennessee Test," 16.

21. Brisco and Murdock, *Brisco*, 211–218; Anderson and Teal, *Inside Out*, 129–135, 146–151.

22. Meltzer, *Tributes II*, 187–188; ibid., *Tributes*, 118; Anderson and Teal, *Inside Out*, 152–155; Ric Flair and Keith Elliot Greenberg, *To Be the Man* (New York: Pocket Books, 2004), 35–83; Charlotte *Observer*, October 5, 1975.

23. Meltzer, *Tributes II*, 182–187; Anderson and Teal, *Inside Out*, 136–145; Assael and Mooneyham, *Sex, Lies, and Headlocks*, 40–44; Wilson, *Chokehold*, 152–158, 170–179, 186–221; Brisco and Murdock, *Brisco*, 125–127.

24. Wilson and Johnson, *Chokehold*, 196–198.

25. Assael and Mooneyham, *Sex, Lies, and Headlocks*, 38–40.

26. Rich Tate, "A Tribute to Jim Barnett," available from www .georgiawrestlinghistory.com/peachstatepandemonium/articles/0012. html; Powers, *Supertube*; Ken Auletta, *Media Man: Ted Turner's Improbable Empire* (New York: Atlas Books, 2004), 31–34.

27. Louisville *Courier-Journal*, December 18, 1999; Milwaukee *Journal*, January 25, 1979; Jimmy Hart, *The Mouth of the South: The Jimmy Hart Story* (Toronto: ECW Press, 2004), 97–112; "In Perspective: Bill Apter Part II," *Wrestling Perspective* 14, no. 106:2; Jerry Lawler and Doug Asheville, *It's Good To Be the King...Sometimes* (New York: Pocket Books, 2003), 217–253; Brisco and Murdock, *Brisco*, 99.

CHAPTER 7: THE RISE OF VINCE McMAHON

1. Wilson and Johnson, *Chokehold*, 307–309.
2. Ibid., 364–366.

3. Anderson and Teal, *Inside Out*, 227–228; James J. Dillon, with Scott Teal and Philip Varriale, *Wrestlers Are Like Seagulls: From McMahon to McMahon* (Hendersonville, TN: Crowbar Press, 2005), 149. Vince J. McMahon died of cancer on May 27, 1984.

4. Larry Nelson and James R. Jones, *Stranglehold: An Intriguing Behind the Scenes Glimpse Into the Private World of Professional Wrestling* (Denver: Chump Change, 1999), 28; Assael and Mooneyham, *Sex, Lies, and Headlocks*, 19–20.

5. Brisco and Murdock, *Brisco*, 262–265; Assael and Mooneyham, *Sex, Lies, and Headlocks*, 16–20; Wilson, *Chokehold*, 370–371.

6. "T.V. Wrestling Guide," *Ring Wrestling*, no. 96 (June 1983): 60; Gary Michael Cappetta, *Bodyslams! Memoirs of a Wrestling Pitchman* (Jackson, NJ: Little Bro', 2000), 94–96; Rader, *American Sports*, 238.

7. Anderson and Teal, *Inside Out*, 236–239; Cappetta, *Bodyslams!* 94–95, 102–103; Wilson and Johnson, *Chokehold*, 379–381; William Taaffe, "How Wrestling Got TV in Its Clutches," *Sports Illustrated* 62 (April 29, 1985): 38.

8. Assael and Mooneyham, *Sex, Lies, and Headlocks*, 44–46; Anderson and Teal, *Inside Out*, 247–254; Brisco and Murdock, *Brisco*, 267–271; Flair and Greenberg, *To Be the Man*, 132–133.

9. Assael and Mooneyham, *Sex, Lies, and Headlocks*, 61–67.

10. Flair and Greenberg, *To Be the Man*, 113–117; Assael and Mooneyham, *Sex, Lies, and Headlocks*, 73–74. Prior, minor, attempts at closed-circuit wrestling include a demonstration of closed-circuit technology shown in Schnectady, New York, in 1946 and the local transmission of a 1971 card from the Olympic Auditorium in Los Angeles.

11. Saunders, "Play, Performance, and Professional Wrestling," 84–86; Philadelphia *Journal*, June 16, 1978; Bruce Newman, "Who's Kidding Whom?" *Sports Illustrated* 62 (April 29, 1985): 34.

12. John W. Campbell, "Professional Wrestling: Why the Bad Guy Wins," *Journal of American Culture*, 19 (Summer 1996): 129; John Fiske, *Understanding Popular Culture* (Boston: Unwin Hyman, 1989), 81–90.

13. Dizikes, *Sportsmen and Gamesmen*, 126–127; Feigenbaum, "Professional Wrestling," 119–147.

14. Newman, "Who's Kidding Whom?" 66–67; Ellison and Platt, *The Fabulous Moolah*, 166–177. While McMahon developed connections between rock music and the WWF into a central aspect of his promotion during the mid-1980s, wrestling had possessed deep connections to rock since the 1960s. From The Novas' tribute song to Reggie "the Crusher" Lisoski in 1965 to the wrestling-devoted Dictators of the late 1970s, professional wrestling factored into elements of the rock community. Several wrestlers also became directly involved in the music business. Freddie Blassie famously cut a single entitled "Pencil-Neck Geek," and Portland

biker-cum-wrestler Beauregard recorded an entire album in 1970, which he used as his entrance music. Pre-McMahon, however, the most successful direct connection between rock and wrestling involved the Southern tag team the Fabulous Freebirds (originally Buddy Roberts, Terry Gordy, and Michael "Purely Sexy" Hayes). The Freebirds built their entire career around an obsession with Lynyrd Skynyrd, a move that profoundly resonated with NWA audiences of the late 1970s and early 1980s. Outside the realm of rock music, Sweet Daddy Siki and Antonino Rocca both made records in the mid-1960s.

15. Assael and Mooneyham, *Sex, Lies, and Headlocks*, 57–58.

16. Cappetta, *Bodyslams!* 97–98; Wilson and Johnson, *Chokehold*, 375–378; Mazer, *Professional Wrestling*, 114; Michael Sorkin, "Faking It," in Todd Gitlin, ed., *Watching Television: A Pantheon Guide* (New York: Pantheon, 1986), 165; Robert E. Rinehart, *Players All: Performance in Contemporary Sport* (Bloomington: Indiana University Press, 1998), 63–66.

17. David Skolnick, "Still Funky Like a Monkey after All These Years," *Wrestling Perspective* 5 (1994): 9–10; Flair and Greenberg, *To Be the Man*, 167–169; Dillon, *Seagulls*, 180.

18. Brisco and Murdock, *Brisco*, 271–274; Anderson and Teal, *Inside Out*, 265–269; Dillon, *Seagulls*, 177; Wilson, *Chokehold*, 384–385; R. D. Reynolds and Bryan Alvarez, *The Death of the WCW* (Toronto: ECW Press, 2004), 29–33.

19. Saunders, "Play, Performance, and Pro Wrestling," 129–143.

20. Flair and Greenberg, *To Be the Man*, 157–162; Assael and Mooneyham, *Sex, Lies, and Headlocks*, 74–75.

21. Assael and Mooneyham, *Sex, Lies, and Headlocks*, 73–88.

22. Cappetta, *Bodyslams!* 108–113.

23. Nelson, *Stranglehold*, 131–132; Cappetta, *Bodyslams!* 148–149. The final *Superclash* featured a main event between Lawler and the ill-fated Kerry Von Erich and matches with wrestlers from the crudely comedic and sexualized Gorgeous Ladies of Wrestling (GLOW). Of Fritz Von Erich's five wrestling sons, four, including Kerry, died before their thirty-fifth birthday. Oriented toward cornpone humor and displays of scantily clad "farmers' daughters," GLOW's syndicated television program served as wrestling's answer to *Hee Haw*. For more info, see Barry Putterman, *On Television and Comedy: Essays on Style, Theme, Performer and Writer* (Jefferson, NC: McFarland, 1995), 189–196.

24. Nelson, *Stranglehold*, 127–129.

25. Assael and Mooneyham, *Sex, Lies, and Headlocks*, 81–84; "Phantom of the Ring," "Toons of the Times," *Wrestling Perspective*, V (1994): 10–11.

26. Wilson and Johnson, *Chokehold*, 398–430; Assael and Mooneyham, *Sex, Lies, and Headlocks*, 84–94.

27. Flair and Greenberg, *To Be the Man*, 191–207; Assael and Mooneyham, *Sex, Lies, and Headlocks*, 98–110; Cappetta, *Bodyslams!* 244; Reynolds and Alvarez, *Death of WCW*, 33–52.

28. Assael and Mooneyham, *Sex, Lies, and Headlocks*, 131–143; Cappetta, *Bodyslams!* 244–247; Reynolds, *Death of WCW, 52–63.*

29. Paul MacArthur and David Skolnick, "What's in the Name?" *Wrestling Perspective* 7 (1996): 1–4; Reynolds and Alvarez, *Death of WCW*, 63–133.

30. Oppliger, *Wrestling and Hypermasculinity*, 129–132; Wilson, *Chokehold*, 440–444; Pat McNeill, *The Tables All Were Broken: McNeill's Take on the End of Professional Wrestling As We Know It* (San Jose, CA: Writers Club Press, 2002), 187–190; New York *Post*, August 13, 2000.

31. Assael and Mooneyham, *Sex, Lies, and Headlocks*, 162; Leverette, *Professional Wrestling*, 63; Don Atyeo, *Violence In Sports* (New York: Van Nostrand, 1981), 363–364.

32. Reynolds and Alvarez, *Death of WCW*, 131, 134, 141–144.

33. Michael Lano, "ECW Forever," *Wrestling Then & Now*, no. 132 (February–April 2001): 10–11; John Lister, *Turning the Tables: The Story of Extreme Championship Wrestling* (Three Rivers, UK: Diggory Press, 2005), 11–44; Assael and Mooneyham, *Sex, Lies, and Headlocks*, 199–200. The adoption of the word "extreme" put the Gordon organization in line with larger trends within a sporting subculture that decried the soft, safe, and sanitized nature of "corporate" sports. Rinehart, *Players All*, 98–110.

34. Henry Jenkins IV, "Afterword, Part II," in Sammond, *Steel Chair to the Head*, 334–337; Adam Kleinberg and Adam Nudelman, *Mysteries of Wrestling Solved* (Toronto: ECW Press, 2005), 101–128; Lister, *Turning the Tables*, 45–64.

35. Assael and Mooneyham, *Sex, Lies, and Headlocks*, 199–203; Lister, *Turning the Tables*, 80–81, 119–134; "Where Is the WWF Going?" *Global Pro Wrestling News*, no. 32 (October 20, 1996): 1–2; "Mr. Zaremba," "ECW Lite, It's Everywhere," *Wrestling Then and Now*, no. 110 (March 1999): 8.

36. Reynolds and Alvarez, *Death of WCW*, 183–185; McNeill, *Tables All Were Broken*, 89–92.

37. Karl Stern, "Ego 101: How You Go From the Top Promotion in the World to Out of Business in Ten Easy Steps," *Dragonking Press Newsletter*, no. 76 (October 2004): 3; Reynolds and Alvarez, *Death of WCW*, 213–293.

38. Lister, *Turning the Tables*, 145–163; Assael and Mooneyham, *Sex, Lies, and Headlocks*, 250–252.

EPILOGUE

1. Providence *Journal*, May 27, 1999; Hartford *Courant*, May 27, 1999; Calgary *Herald*, May 26, 1999.

2. Assael and Mooneyham, *Sex, Lies, and Headlocks*, 1–5; "Owen Hart, 34, Dies After PPV Accident," *Figure Four Weekly*, no. 205 (May 31, 1999): 1–3; New York *Post*, May 30, 1999; Philadelphia *Daily News*, May 27, 1999.

3. Karl Stern, "Eat the Horse," *Dragonking Press Newsletter*, no. 68 (January 2004): 1–7.

4. Assael and Mooneyham, *Sex, Lies, and Headlocks*, 253–255.

5. Leverette, *Professional Wrestling*, 189–199.

6. Scott Keith, *Wrestling's One-Ring Circus: The Death of the World Wrestling Federation* (New York: Citadel Press, 2004).

BIBLIOGRAPHY

Adelman, Melvin. *A Sporting Time: New York City and the Rise of Modern Athletics.* Urbana: University of Illinois Press, 1986.

Altherr, Thomas L., ed. *Sports in North America: A Documentary History.* 8 vols. Gulf Breeze, FL: Academic International Press, 1997.

Anderson, Ole, and Scott Teal. *Inside Out: How Corporate America Destroyed Professional Wrestling.* Hendersonville, TN: Crowbar Press, 2003.

Armstrong, Walter. *Wrestliana: or, the History of the Cumberland & Westmoreland Wrestling Society in London Since the Year 1824.* London: Simpkin, Marshall, 1870.

Assael, Shaun, and Mike Mooneyham. *Sex, Lies, and Headlocks: The Real Story of Vince McMahon and the World Wrestling Federation.* New York: Crown, 2002.

Atler, Joseph S. "Gama the World Champion: Wrestling and Physical Culture in Colonial India." *Iron Game History* 4 (October 1995): 3–9.

Atyeo, Don. *Violence In Sports.* New York: Van Nostrand, 1981.

Auguet, Roland. *Cruelty and Civilization: The Roman Games.* London: Routledge, 1994.

Auletta, Ken. *Media Man: Ted Turner's Improbable Empire.* New York: Atlas Books, 2004.

"Baba and Behemoths." *Time* 27 (May 18, 1936): 54–55, 58.

Baker, Aaron. "Contested Identities: Sports in American Film and Television." Ph.D. diss., Indiana University, 1994.

Baldwin, Douglas Owen, ed. *Sports In America: A Documentary History.* 8 vols. Gulf Breeze, FL: Academic International Press, 2000.

Ball, Michael R. *Professional Wrestling as Ritual Drama in American Popular Culture*. Lewiston, NY: Edwin Mellen Press, 1990.

Barney, Robert Knight. "German Forty-Eighters and *Turnvereine* in the United States during the Ante-Bellum Period." *Canadian Journal of History of Sport* 13 (December 1982): 62–79.

Barth, Gunther. *City People: The Rise of Modern City Culture in Nineteenth-Century America*. New York: Oxford University Press, 1980.

Beezley, William H., and Joseph P. Hobbs. "'Nice Girls Don't Sweat': Women in American Sport." *Journal of Popular Culture* 16 (Spring 1983): 42–53.

Berthoff, Rowland. *British Immigrants in Industrial America, 1790–1950*. Cambridge, MA: Harvard University Press, 1953.

Best, Gary Dean. *The Nickel and Dime Decade: American Popular Culture During the 1930s*. Westport, CT: Praeger, 1993.

Betts, John R. *America's Sporting Heritage: 1850–1950*. Reading, MA: Addison-Wesley, 1974.

———. "Mind and Body in Early American Thought." *Journal of American History* 54 (March 1968): 787–805.

———. "Sporting Journalism in Nineteenth-Century America." *American Quarterly* 5 (Spring 1953): 42–43.

Blassie, Freddie, and Keith Elliot Greenberg. *Legends of Wrestling: "Classy" Freddie Blassie*. New York: Pocket Books, 2003.

Boddy, William. *Fifties Television: The Industry and Its Critics*. Urbana: University of Illinois Press, 1990.

Boesch, Paul. *Hey, Boy! Where'd You Get Them Ears?* Houston: Minuteman Press, 2001.

———. *The Road to Huertgen*. Houston: Gulf Publishing, 1962.

Boness, Kenneth. *Pile Driver: The Life of Charles "Midget" Fischer*. Philadelphia: Xlibiris, 2002.

Bonomo, Joe. *The Strongman*. New York: Bonomo Studios, 1968.

Brailsford, Dennis. *Sport and Society: Elizabeth to Anne*. London: Routledge & Keegan Paul, 1969.

———. "Sporting Days in Eighteenth Century England." *Journal of Sport History* 9 (Winter 1982): 41–54.

Brasch, R. *How Did Sports Begin? A Look into the Origins of Man at Play*. London: Longman, 1972.

Breen, T. H. "Horses and Gentlemen: The Cult of Gambling Among the Gentry of Virginia." *William and Mary Quarterly* 34 (April 1977): 239–257.

Brisco, Jack, and William Murdock. *Brisco: The Life and Times of National Collegiate and World Heavyweight Wrestling Champion Jack Brisco*. Newton, IA: Culture House, 2003.

Britz, Kevin. "Of Football and Frontiers: The Meaning of Bronko Nagurski." *Journal of Sport History* 20 (Summer 1993): 101–126.

Brohm, Jean-Marie. *Sport—A Prison of Measured Time.* London: Ink Links, 1978.

Burdick, Dakin. "The American Way of Fighting: Unarmed Defense in the United States, 1845–1945." Ph.D. diss., Indiana University, 1999.

Burns, Martin. *The Life Work of "Farmer" Burns.* Omaha, NE: A. J. Kuhlman, 1911.

Burstyn, Verda. *The Rites of Man: Manhood, Politics, and the Culture of Sport.* Toronto: University of Toronto Press, 1999.

Campbell, John W. "Professional Wrestling: Why the Bad Guy Wins." *Journal of American Culture* 19 (Summer 1996): 127–133.

Cappetta, Gary Michael. *Bodyslams! Memoirs of a Wrestling Pitchman.* Jackson, NJ: Little Bro', 2000.

Carter, John Marshall. *Medieval Games: Sports and Recreations in Feudal Society.* (Westport, CT: Greenwood Press, 1992.

———. *Sports and Pastimes of the Middle Ages.* Lanham, MD: University Press of America, 1988.

Chandler, Joan M. *Television and National Sport: The United States and Britain.* Urbana: University of Illinois Press, 1988.

Chapman, David L. *Sandow the Magnificent: Eugen Sandow and the Beginnings of Bodybuilding.* Urbana: University of Illinois Press, 1994.

Chapman, Mike. *Frank Gotch: World's Greatest Wrestler.* Buffalo, NY: William S. Hein, 1990.

———. *The Sport of Lincoln.* Newton, IA: Culture House, 2003.

Craig, Steve. *Sports and Games of the Ancients.* Westport: Greenwood Press, 2002.

Crawford, Garry. *Consuming Sport: Fans, Sport, and Culture.* London: Routledge, 2004.

Cross, Gary. *A Social History of Leisure Since 1600.* State College, PA: Venture Publishing, 1990.

Davis, Richard O. *America's Obsession: Sports and Society Since 1945.* Fort Worth, TX: Harcourt Brace, 1994.

Decker, Wolfgang. *Sports and Games of Ancient Egypt.* New Haven, CT: Yale University Press, 1992.

Dell, Chad. "Researching Historical Broadcast Audiences: Female Fandom of Professional Wrestling, 1945–1960." Ph.D. diss., University of Wisconsin–Madison, 1997.

Dillon, James J., with Scott Teal and Philip Varriale. *Wrestlers Are Like Seagulls: From McMahon to McMahon.* Hendersonville, TN: Crowbar Press, 2005.

Dinan, John. *Sports in the Pulp Magazines.* Jefferson, NC: McFarland, 1998.

Dizikes, John. *Sportsmen and Gamesmen.* Columbia: University of Missouri Press, 2002.

"Dog Bones and Flying Mares." *New Yorker* 24 (September 18, 1948): 23–24.

Doherty, Thomas. *Cold War, Cool Medium: Television, McCarthyism, and American Culture*. New York: Columbia University Press, 2003.

Dreiser, Theodore. *Twelve Men*. New York: Boni & Liveright, 1919.

Duncan, Royal, and Gary Will. *Wrestling Title Histories*, 4th ed. Waterloo, ON: Archeus, 2000.

Dyreson, Mark. "The Emergence of Consumer Culture and the Transformation of Physical Culture: American Sport in the 1920s." *Journal of Sport History* 16 (Winter 1989): 261–281.

———. "Playing for a National Identity: Sport, Immigration, and the Quest for a National Culture in American Social Thought, 1880–1919." *Proteus* 11 (Fall 1994): 39–43.

Edwards, Richard H. *Popular Amusements*. New York: Association Press, 1915.

Eisen, George. *Ethnicity and Sport in North American History and Culture*. Westport, CT: Greenwood Press, 1994.

Eklund, Clarence. *Forty Years of Wrestling: Its History and Transition*. Buffalo, NY: Buffalo Bulletin, 1947.

Ellison, Lillian, and Larry Platt. *The Fabulous Moolah: First Goddess of the Squared Circle*. New York: Regan, 2002.

Erb, Marsha. *Stu Hart: Lord of the Ring*. Toronto: ECW Press, 2002.

Ernst, Robert. *Weakness Is a Crime: The Life of Bernarr MacFadden*. Syracuse, NY: Syracuse University Press, 1991.

Evensen, Bruce J. "Jazz Age Journalism's Battle Over Professionalism, Circulation, and the Sports Page." *Journal of Sport History* 20 (Winter 1993): 229–246.

———. *When Dempsey Fought Tunney: Heroes, Hokum, and Storytelling in the Jazz Age*. Knoxville: University of Tennessee Press, 1996.

Farrell, Edythe. "The Lady Wrestlers." *American Mercury* 228 (December 1942): 674–680.

Feigenbaum, Aaron D. "Professional Wrestling, Sports Entertainment and the Liminal Experience in American Culture." Ph.D. diss., University of Florida, 2000.

Fielding, Lawrence. "Sport on the Road to Appomattox: The Shadows of Army Life." Ph.D. diss., University of Maryland, 1974.

Fields, Sarah. "Female Gladiators: Gender, Law, and Contact Sport in America." Ph.D. diss., University of Iowa, 2000.

Fiske, John. *Understanding Popular Culture*. Boston: Unwin Hyman, 1989.

Flair, Ric, and Keith Elliot Greenberg. *To Be the Man*. New York: Pocket Books, 2002.

Fleischer, Nat. *From Milo to Londos: The Story of Wrestling From 2000 BC to 1936*. New York: C. J. O'Brien, 1936.

Flexner, James Thomas. *George Washington: The Forge of Experience (1732–1775).* Boston: Little, Brown, 1965.

Flood, Dave. *Kayfabe: The Secret World of Professional Wrestling.* Chicago: Gambit, 2000.

Ford, John. *Prizefighting: The Age of Regency Boximania.* New York: Great Albion Books, 1972.

Franks, Joel. "California and the Rise of Spectator Sports, 1850–1900." *Southern California Quarterly* 71 (Winter 1989): 291–293.

Freedman, Warren. *Professional Sports and Antitrust.* New York: Quorum Books, 1987.

Gardiner, E. Norman. *Greek Athletic Sports and Festivals.* London: Macmillan, 1910.

Gilmore, Al-Tony. *Bad Nigger! The National Impact of Jack Johnson.* Port Washington, NY: Kennikat Press, 1975.

Gitlin, Todd, ed. *Watching Television: A Pantheon Guide.* New York: Pantheon, 1986.

Golden, Mark. *Sport and Society in Ancient Greece.* Cambridge: Cambridge University Press, 1998.

Gorn, Elliot J. *The Manly Art: Bare-Knuckle Prize-Fighting.* Ithaca, NY: Cornell University Press, 1986.

Gotch, Frank. *Wrestling and How to Train.* New York: Richard K. Fox, 1913.

Green, Harvey. *Fit for America: Health, Fitness, Sport, and American Society.* New York: Pantheon, 1986.

Griffin, Marcus. *Fall Guys: The Barnums of Bounce.* Hendersonville, TN: Rasslin' Reprints, 1997.

Gutierrez, Carlos, and Julian Espartero. "JuJutsu's Image in Spain's Wrestling Shows: A Historic Review." *Journal of Asian Martial Arts* 13 (Summer 2004): 8–31.

Guttmann, Allen. *From Ritual to Record: The Nature of Modern Sports.* New York: Columbia University Press, 1978.

———. "Sports Spectators from Antiquity to the Renaissance" *Journal of Sport History* 8 (Summer 1981): 5–27.

———. *Women's Sports: A History.* New York: Columbia University Press, 1991.

Hardy, Stephen. "Organized Sport and the Search for Community: Boston, 1865–1915." Ph.D. diss., University of Massachusetts, 1980.

Harris, H. A. *Greek Athletes and Athletics.* Bloomington: Indiana University Press, 1966.

———. *Sport in Greece and Rome.* Ithaca, NY: Cornell University Press, 1972.

Hart, Jimmy. *The Mouth of the South: The Jimmy Hart Story.* Toronto: ECW Press, 2004.

Hautzinger, Sarah. "American Carnival Speech: Making the Jump." *Journal of American Culture* 13 (Winter 1990): 29–33.

Haynes, Richard M. "James H. McLaughlin—The Colonel," *Historical Wrestling Society Bulletin*, no. 6:1–4.

Hewitt, Mark S. *Catch Wrestling: A Wild and Wooly Look at the Early Days of Pro Wrestling in America.* Boulder, CO: Paladin Press, 2005.

Hickman, Herman. "Rasslin' Was My Act." *Saturday Evening Post* 226 (February 6, 1954): 20–21, 101–102.

"Hippo Hippodrome." *Literary Digest* 112 (February 6, 1932): 41.

Holliman, Jennie. *American Sports, 1785–1835.* Durham, NC: Seeman Press, 1931.

Hughes, Rupert. *George Washington: The Human Being and the Hero, 1732–1763.* New York: William Morrow, 1920.

Huizinga, Johan. *Homo Ludens: A Study of the Play Element in Culture.* Reprint, Boston: Beacon, 1955.

Inabinett, Mark. *Grantland Rice and His Heroes: The Sportswriter as Mythmaker in the 1920s.* Knoxville: University of Tennessee Press, 1994.

Inkersley, Arthur. "Greco-Roman Games in California." *Outing* 5 (February 1895): 409–416.

Isenberg, Michael T. *John L. Sullivan and His America.* Urbana: University of Illinois Press, 1988.

Jares, Joe. *Whatever Happened to Gorgeous George?* Englewood Cliffs, NJ: Prentice Hall, 1974.

Jarvis, Christina S. *The Male Body at War: American Masculinity during World War II.* De Kalb: Northern Illinois University Press, 2004.

Jones, Robert L. "Wrestling Finds a King at Last." *The Arena* 2 (August 1930): 22–23, 38.

Kahn, Roger. *A Flame of Pure Fire: Jack Dempsey and the Roaring '20s.* New York: Harcourt, Brace, 1999.

Keith, Scott. *Wrestling's One-Ring Circus: The Death of the World Wrestling Federation.* New York: Citadel Press, 2004.

Kent, Graeme. *A Pictorial History of Wrestling.* Feltham, Middlesex, UK: Spring Books, 1968.

Kingsdale, Jon. "The 'Poor Man's Club': Social Functions of the Working-Class Saloon." *American Quarterly* 25 (October 1973): 472–489.

Kirsch, George B. *Baseball in Blue and Gray: The National Pastime during the Civil War.* Princeton, NJ: Princeton University Press, 2003.

Kleinberg, Adam, and Adam Nudelman. *Mysteries of Wrestling Solved.* Toronto: ECW Press, 2005.

Knott, Richard. "The Sport Hero as Portrayed in Popular Journalism." Ph.D. diss., University of Tennessee, 1994.

Kyriakoudes, Louis M., and Peter A. Coclanis. "The 'Tennessee Test of Manhood': Professional Wrestling and Southern Cultural Stereotypes." *Southern Cultures* 3 (Fall 1997): 8–27.

Lano, Michael. "ECW Forever," *Wrestling Then and Now*, no. 132 (Feb.–April 2001): 10–11.

Laskin, Jack. *One of the Boys*. Philadelphia: Xlibris, 2002.

Lawler, Jerry, and Doug Asheville. *It's Good To Be the King . . . Sometimes*. New York: Pocket Books, 2003.

Le Bow, Guy. *The Wrestling Scene*. New York: Homecrafts, 1950.

Ledbetter, Bonnie S. "Sports and Games of the American Revolution." *Journal of Sports History* 6 (Winter 1979): 29–40.

Lee, John. *Wrestling in the North Country*. Consett: Ramsden Williams, 1953.

Leibs, Andrew. *Sports and Games of the Renaissance*. Westport, CT: Greenwood Press, 2004.

Leverette, Marc. *Professional Wrestling, the Myth, the Mat, and American Popular Culture* Lewiston, NY: Edwin Mellen, 2003.

Levine, Peter. "The Promise of Sport in Antebellum America," *Journal of American Culture* 2 (Winter 1980): 623–634.

Lewin, Ted. *I Was a Teenage Professional Wrestler*. New York: Orchard Books, 1993.

Lewis, Arthur H. *Carnival*. New York: Trident Press, 1970.

Liebling, A. J. "From Sarah Bernhardt to Yukon Eric." *New Yorker* 30 (November 13, 1954): 132–149.

Lindaman, Mathew. "Wrestling's Hold on the Western World Before the Great War." *Historian* 62 (Summer 2000): 779–798.

Lister, John. *Turning the Tables: The Story of Extreme Championship Wrestling*. Three Rivers, UK: Diggory Press, 2005.

Lundin, Hjalmar. *On the Mat and Off: Memoirs of a Wrestler*. New York: Albert Bonnier, 1937.

MacArthur, Paul, and David Skolnick. "What's in the Name?" *Wrestling Perspective* 7 (1996): 1–4.

MacDonald, J. Fred, *Television and the Red Menace: The Video Road to Vietnam*. New York: Praeger, 1985.

MacKaye, Milton. "On the Hoof." *Saturday Evening Post* 208 (December 14, 1933): 8–9, 35–37, 40.

Malcolmson, Robert. *Popular Recreations in English Society, 1700–1850*. New York: Cambridge University Press, 1973.

Mandell, Richard D. *Sport: A Cultural History*. New York: Columbia University Press, 1984.

Mangan, J. A., and James Whalen, eds. *Manliness and Morality: Middle-Class Masculinity in Britain and America, 1800–1940*. New York: St. Martin's Press, 1987.

Manning, Frank E., ed. *The Celebration of Society: Perspectives on Contemporary Cultural Performance.* Bowling Green, OH: Bowling Green State University Press, 1983.

Matysik, Larry. *Wrestling at the Chase: The Inside Story of Sam Muchnick and the Legends of Professional Wrestling.* Toronto: ECW Press, 2005.

Matz, David. *Greek and Roman Sport: A Dictionary of Athletes and Events from the Eighth Century B.C. to the Third Century.* Jefferson, NC: McFarland, 1991.

Mazer, Sharon. *Professional Wrestling: Sport and Spectacle.* Jackson: University Press of Mississippi, 1998.

McCormack, Bill. "Another Indian Bites the Dust." *Wrestling Then and Now,* no. 116 (September 1999): 6–7.

McKinley, Silas Bent, and Silas Bent. *Old Rough and Ready: The Life and Times of Zachary Taylor.* New York: Vanguard Press, 1946.

McNeill, Pat. *The Tables All Were Broken: McNeill's Take on the End of Professional Wrestling As We Know It.* San Jose, CA: Writers Club Press, 2002.

Mee, Bob. *Bare Fists: The History of Bare-Knuckle Prize-Fighting.* Woodstock, NY: Overlook Press, 2001.

Meltzer, Dave. *Tributes: Remembering Some of the World's Greatest Wrestlers.* Etobicoke, ON: Winding Stair, 2001.

———. *Tributes II: Remembering More of the World's Greatest Professional Wrestlers.* Champaign, IL: Sports Publishing, 2004.

Meyers, John C. *Wrestling from Antiquity to Date.* St. Louis: self-published, 1931.

Miley, Jack. "Jake's Juggernauts." *Collier's* 102 (October 22, 1938): 56–59.

Mondrak, Jeffrey J. "The Politics of Professional Wrestling." *Journal of Popular Culture* 23 (Fall 1989): 139–149.

Morton, Gerald W., and George M. O'Brien. *Wrestling to Rasslin: Ancient Sport to American Spectacle.* Bowling Green, OH: Bowling Green University Press, 1985.

Mott, Frank L. *A History of American Magazines.* Cambridge, MA: Belknap Press, 1967.

Mrozek, Donald J. *Sport and American Mentality, 1880–1910.* Knoxville: University of Tennessee Press, 1983.

Murphy, Dan. *Bodyslams in Buffalo: The Complete History of Pro Wrestling in Western New York.* Buffalo: Western New York Wares, 2002.

Murphy, Justin. *Titans of Capitolism.* Lake Havasu City, AZ: Epstein, 2005.

Neal-Lunsford, Jeff. "Sport in the Land of Television: The Use of Sport in Network Prime-Time Schedules, 1946–1950." *Journal of Sport History* 19 (Spring 1992): 56–76.

Nelson, Larry, and James R. Jones. *Stranglehold: An Intriguing Behind the Scenes Glimpse Into the Private World of Professional Wrestling.* Denver: Chump Change, 1999.

Newman, Bruce. "Who's Kidding Whom?" *Sports Illustrated* 62 (April 29, 1985): 28–70.

Oppliger, Patrice A. *Wrestling and Hypermasculinity.* Jefferson, NC: McFarland, 2004.

Oriand, Michael. "Dreaming of Heroes: American Sports Fiction from the Beginning to the Present." Ph.D. diss., Stanford University, 1976.

"Owen Hart, 34, Dies After PPV Accident." *Figure Four Weekly*, no. 205 (May 31, 1999): 1–3.

Park, Roberta J. "Physiology and Anatomy are Destiny!? Brains, Bodies and Exercise in Nineteenth Century American Thought." *Journal of Sport History* 18 (Spring 1991): 49–63.

Patrick, Lucille Nichols. *The Candy Kid: James Calvin "Kid" Nichols, 1883–1962.* Cheyenne, WY: Flintlock, 1969.

Paxson, Frederic L. "The Rise of Sport." *Mississippi Valley Historical Review* 4 (September 1917): 143–168.

Poliakoff, Michael. "Jacob, Job, and Other Wrestlers: Reception of Greek Athletics by Jews and Christians in Antiquity." *Journal of Sport History* 11 (Summer 1984): 48–65.

Pope, S. W., ed. *The New American Sport History: Recent Approaches and Perspectives.* Urbana: University of Illinois Press, 1997.

———. *Patriotic Games: Sporting Traditions in the American Imagination, 1876–1926.* New York: Oxford University Press, 1997.

Powers, Ron. *Supertube: The Rise of Television Sports.* New York: Coward-McCann, 1984.

Pugh, David G. *Sons of Liberty: The Masculine Mind in Nineteenth-Century America.* Westport, CT: Greenwood Press, 1983.

Putney, Clifford. *Muscular Christianity: Manhood and Sports in Protestant America, 1880–1920.* Cambridge, MA: Harvard University Press, 2001.

Putterman, Barry. *On Television and Comedy: Essays on Style, Theme, Performer and Writer.* Jefferson, NC: McFarland, 1995.

Rader, Benjamin G. *American Sports: From the Age of Folk Games to the Age of Televised Sports.* Upper Saddle River, NJ: Prentice Hall, 1998.

———. *In Its Own Image: How Television Has Transformed Sport.* New York: Free Press, 1984.

Redmond, Gerald. *The Caledonian Games in Nineteenth-Century America.* Rutherford, NJ: Farleigh Dickenson University Press, 1971.

Reynolds, R. D., and Bryan Alvarez. *The Death of the WCW.* Toronto: ECW Press, 2004.

Rickard, John. "The Spectacle of Excess: The Emergence of Pro Wrestling in the United States and Australia." *Journal of Popular Culture* 33 (Summer 1999): 129–137.

Riess, Steven A. *City Games: The Evolution of American Urban Society and the Rise of Sports.* Urbana: University of Illinois Press, 1989.

———., ed. *The American Sporting Experience: A Historical Anthology of Sport in America.* New York: Leisure Press, 1984.

Rinehart, Robert E. *Players All: Performance in Contemporary Sport.* Bloomington: Indiana University Press, 1998.

Russell, Carol L. "The Life and Death of Carnie." *American Speech* 78 (Winter 2004): 400–416.

Sammond, Nicholas, ed. *Steel Chair to the Head: The Pleasure and Pain of Professional Wrestling.* Durham, NC: Duke University Press, 2005.

Sammons, Jeffrey T. *Beyond the Ring: The Role of Boxing in American Society.* Urbana: University of Illinois Press, 1990.

Samuels, Charles. *The Magnificent Rube: The Life and Gaudy Times of Tex Rickard.* New York: McGraw-Hill, 1957.

Saunders, Terry McNeill, "Play, Performance and Professional Wrestling: An Examination of a Modern Day Spectacle of Absurdity." Ph.D. diss., University of California, Los Angeles, 1998.

Scanlon, Thomas F. *Eros and Greek Athletics.* New York: Oxford University Press, 2002.

Shane, Ted. "Gorgeous George the Wrestler." *American Mercury* 71 (July 1950): 64–71.

Sklar, Robert. *The Plastic Age (1917–1930).* New York: George Braziller, 1970.

Skolnick, David, "Still Funky Like a Monkey After All These Years." *Wrestling Perspective* 5 (1994): 9–10.

"Stanley," "News of the Mat World," *Ring Magazine* 27 (August 1948): 30–31.

Stern, Karl. "Eat the Horse." *Dragonking Wrestling Newsletter*, no. 68 (January 2004): 1–7.

———. "Ego 101: How You Go From the Top Promotion in the World to Out of Business in Ten Easy Steps." *Dragonking Wrestling Newsletter*, no. 76 (October 2004): 1–3.

———. "The Most Famous Wrestler You Never Heard of ... Nat Pendleton." *Dragonking Press Newsletter*, no. 71 (June 2004): 1–4.

———. "The Myth and Magic of Frank A. Gotch." *Dragonking Press Newsletter*, no. 71 (April 2004): 6–8.

———. *The Pioneers of Wrestling.* Haleyville, NC: Dragonking Press, 2002.

———. "The Story of Fred Beell." *Dragonking Press Newsletter*, no. 43 (February 2002): 1–2.

Struna, Nancy. *People of Prowess: Sport, Leisure, and Labor in Early Anglo-America*. Urbana: University of Illinois Press, 1996.

Svinth, Joseph R. "Kaimon Kudo, Man Mountain Dean, and 1930s Show Wrestling." *Wrestling Then and Now*, no. 92 (September 1997): 13.

Sweet, Waldo E. *Sport and Recreation in Ancient Greece: A Sourcebook with Translations*. New York: Oxford University Press, 1987.

Taaffe, William. "How Wrestling Got TV in Its Clutches." *Sports Illustrated* 62 (April 29, 1985): 38.

Thesz, Lou. "Dempsey Thumbs Down on Women Referees." *Official Wrestling* 1 (August 1951): 3–4.

Thesz, Lou, and Kit Bauman. *Hooker: An Authentic Wrestler's Adventures Inside the Bizarre World of Professional Wrestling*, rev. ed. Seattle: TWC Press, 2000.

"T.V. Wrestling Guide." *Ring Wrestling*, no. 96 (June 1983): 60.

Van Every, Edward. *Muldoon: The Solid Man of Sport*. New York: Frederick A. Stokes, 1929.

Von Schilling, James. *The Magic Window: American Television, 1939–1953*. New York: Haworth, 2003.

Walker, Donald. *Defensive Exercises: Comprising Wrestling and Boxing*. London: Thomas Hurst, 1840.

Walker, Tommy Lee, Jr. "Turned Upside Down: Carnivalesque Inversions in Professional Wrestling." M.A. thesis, Bowling Green State University, 2001.

Ward, Geoffrey C. *Unforgivable Blackness: The Rise and Fall of Jack Johnson*. New York: Alfred A. Knopf, 2004.

Weaver, Robert B. *Amusements and Sports in American Life*. Reprint, Westport, CT: Greenwood Press, 1968.

Weir, Alison. *Henry VIII: The King and His Court*. New York: Ballantine, 2001.

Wenner, Lawrence A. ed. *Media, Sports and Society*. Beverly Hills, CA: Sage, 1989.

Wiggins, David K., ed. *Sport in America: From Wicked Amusement to National Obsession*. Champaign, IL: Human Kinetics, 1994.

Wilkins, Sally. *Sports and Games of Medieval Cultures*. Westport, CT: Greenwood Press, 2002.

Wilkinson, Rupert. *American Tough: The Tough-Guy Tradition and American Character*. Westport: Greenwood Press, 1984.

Wilson, Charles Morrow. *The Magnificent Scufflers: Revealing the Great Days When America Wrestled the World*. Brattleboro, VT: Stephen Greene Press, 1959.

Wilson, Jim, and Weldon T. Johnson. *Chokehold: Pro Wrestling's Real Mayhem Outside the Ring*. (Philadelphia: Xlibris, 2003).

Workman, Mark. "The Differential Perception of Popular Dramatic Events." *Keystone Folklore* 23 (Fall 1979): 1–10.

Yates, Norris W. *William T. Porter and the Spirit of the Times.* Baton Rouge: Louisiana State University Press, 1957.

Yohe, Steve. "Maurice 'French Angel' Tillet Biography." *Dragonking Press Newsletter*, no. 52 (October 2002): 1–3.

Zashin, Stephen S. "Bodyslam From the Top Rope: Unequal Bargaining Power and Professional Wrestling's Failure to Unionize." *Entertainment and Sports Law Review* 22 (Fall 1994/Spring 1995): 1–56.

Zeigler, Earle F. *A History of Sport and Physical Education to 1900.* Champaign, IL: Stipes, 1973.

INDEX

About the Author

SCOTT M. BEEKMAN is Visiting Assistant Professor of History at Ohio University. He is the author of *William Dudley Pelley: A Life in Right-Wing Extremism and the Occult* (2005).